Goodbye
Christ?

PETER KERRY POWERS

GOODBYE CHRIST?

CHRISTIANITY, MASCULINITY,
AND THE NEW NEGRO RENAISSANCE

THE UNIVERSITY OF TENNESSEE PRESS
Knoxville

Permission is gratefully acknowledged for the following sources:

Cane by Jean Toomer. Copyright © 1923 by Boni & Liveright, renewed © 1951 by Jean Toomer.
Used by permission of Liveright Publishing Corporation.

Color and Culture: Black Writers and the Making of the Modern Intellectual by Ross Posnock, Cambridge, Mass.:
Harvard University Press, Copyright © 1998 by the President and Fellows of Harvard College.

Dust Tracks on a Road by Zora Neal Hurston. Copyright © 1942 by Zora Neale Hurston;
renewed © 1970 by John C. Hurston. Reprinted by permission of HarperCollins Publishers.

God's Trombones by James Weldon Johnson, copyright © 1927 by Penguin Random House LLC;
copyright renewed © 1955 by Grace Nail Johnson. Used by permission of Viking Books, an imprint
of Penguin Publishing Group, a division of Penguin Random House LLC. All rights reserved.

"Goodbye Christ," "A Christian Country," and "To Certain 'Brothers'" from *The Collected Poems of Langston
Hughes* by Langston Hughes, edited by Arnold Rampersad with David Roessel, Associate Editor,
copyright © 1994 by the Estate of Langston Hughes. Used by permission of Alfred A. Knopf, an imprint of the
Knopf Doubleday Publishing Group, a division of Penguin Random House LLC. All rights reserved.

LIBRARY OF CONGRESS CATALOGING-IN-PUBLICATION DATA

Names: Powers, Peter Kerry, 1959- author,
Title: Goodbye Christ?: Christianity, masculinity, and the new Negro renaissance / Peter Kerry Powers.
Other titles: Christianity, masculinity, and the new Negro renaissance
Description: First edition. | Knoxville: The University of Tennessee Press, 2018. |
Includes bibliographical references and index. |
Identifiers: LCCN 2017004064 (print) | LCCN 2017025887 (ebook) | ISBN 9781621903741 (pdf) |
ISBN 9781621903734 (printed case)
Subjects: LCSH: American fiction–African American authors–History and criticism. | Harlem Renaissance. |
Christianity in literature. | Religion in literature. | Masculinity in literature. | Race relations in literature. |
African Americans–Religion. | American fiction–20th century–History and criticism. |
Christianity and literature–United States–History–20th century. |
Religion and literature–United States–History–20th century.
Classification: LCC PS153.N5 (ebook) | LCC PS153.N5 P69 2018 (print) | DDC
810.9/89607307471–dc23
LC record available at https://lccn.loc.gov/2017004064

*To the memory of Joseph Skerrett—teacher, mentor, and friend;
and to the love and patience of my wife, Shannon, and my children,
Colin and Devon, who all put up with a father and husband
whose mind has been in the 1920s this past decade or more.*

CONTENTS

ACKNOWLEDGMENTS

Goodbye Christ? was written in bits and pieces and went through many revisions over a good many years. So it will be impossible to mention everyone by name who contributed to or supported the thinking and writing of this book. To the many people who contributed to my life and learning related to this book in ways great and small, I am truly thankful. This book could not have been written without the substantial material support of Messiah College over several years, and the intellectual and moral support of many colleagues. To represent all of them I will especially thank President Kim Phipps and Provost Randy Basinger, as well as the wonderful colleagues I have had in the English Department and in the School of Humanities since I became Dean. Innumerable students contributed in the classroom to this book as their lively imaginations and sharp intellects made my mind better than it could have been on its own. To represent all of them I especially thank student assistants Janel Atlas, Vic Sensenig, and Kerry Hasler-Brooks, the last of whom I am now pleased to call a colleague in the English Department and School of the Humanities at Messiah College. Carmen McCain at Westmont University was and remains an inspiration. I am indebted to Charlotte McCash and Alicia Fleming for helping me with the final preparation of the manuscript.

Additionally, colleagues and institutions across the country have contributed to my thinking through their responses and engagement on many different occasions and in many different venues. The research librarians in the Schomburg Center for Research in Black Culture in New York, the Moorland-Spingarn Research Center at Howard University, the Amistad

Center at Tulane, the Beinecke at Yale, and many other librarians provided support in many different ways. While I'm sure they would not remember, I was lucky enough to attend a summer conference at Penn State University in 1998 on the Harlem Renaissance where I got to learn from Bernard Bell, Billy Joe Harris, Nellie McKay, and others, a context in which I first had an inkling there might be a book on this subject. Important parts of this manuscript were conceived of and written early on through the support of a Fellowship in Arts Commentary from the Pennsylvania Council for the Arts and of a Coolidge Fellowship from the Association for Religion and Intellectual Life. I'm grateful to *Religion and American Culture* for originally publishing my thinking about Zora Neale Hurston in "Gods of Physical Violence, Stopping at Nothing: Masculinity, Religion, and Art in the Work of Zora Neale Hurston." *Religion and American Culture,* vol. 12, no. 2, 2002, pp. 229–47; and to *African American Review* for originally publishing my work on Countee Cullen in "'The Singing Man Who Must Be Reckoned With': Private Desire and Public Responsibility in the Poetry of Countee Cullen." *African American Review,* vol. 34, no. 4, 2000, pp. 661–78. I am grateful for the hard work of the University of Tennessee Press and the good people there, including the readers of the text who helped me arrive at important revisions that improved the final product. Special thanks to Thomas Wells for seeing the possibility in this book and helping me see it through to completion, and to Annalisa Zox-Weaver, whose careful editing sharpened my prose, and Jon Boggs for his help in the final run.

Finally, I would especially mention the great people who are a part of MELUS, the Society for the Study of Multi-Ethnic Literature of the United States. This book would not be possible without the collective vision for this literature that MELUS nurtures and sustains. Though I see them much less often since I went into administration, I'm especially thankful for colleagues Amritjit Singh, John Lowe, Thomas Ferraro, Bonnie TuSmith, and particularly Joseph Skerrett, to whose memory this book is dedicated. My only sorrow associated with this book is that I worked too slowly to be able to present Joe with a personal copy. His support and friendship and what I think could only be called wisdom made this book possible.

GOODBYE
CHRIST?

INTIMATE DISTANCE
Faith and Doubts of the Cultural Fathers

> Then God sat down—
> On the side of a hill where he could think;
> By a deep, wide river he sat down;
> With his head in his hands,
> God thought and thought,
> Till he thought: I'll make me a man!
>
> —James Weldon Johnson, "The Creation"

> Goodbye Christ
> Jesus Lord God Jehova
> Beat it on away from here now.
> Make way for a new guy with no religion at all—
>
> —Langston Hughes, "Goodbye Christ"

> Young man—
> Young man—
> Your arm's too short to box with God.
>
> —James Weldon Johnson, "The Prodigal Son"

The Harlem Renaissance grew up in the shadows of churches. And more than shadows. It grew up in the churches, in the sanctuaries that provided platforms for performances, in the people who were primary readers and inspiring sources of theme and character, in the church-owned or related colleges that educated many of the writers and artists and the broadest swath of their audience, in the history of churches that first framed what it might mean to envision a new black nation with New Negro men and women, and in the language and music that provided a matrix for the artistry and intellectual discourse that developed between 1900 and 1940. This sense of imbricated proximity is illustrated by a quick search of buildings and institutions on the website "Digital Harlem," or by brief surveys of maps associated with the study of Harlem during the period. Large Christian institutions sat on the same block as popular nightclubs. Glittering hot spots on street corners balanced on a fulcrum of massive religious institutions situated in the middle of a block.[1] Innumerable fly-by-night speakeasies stood cheek-by-jowl with equally uncountable and ephemeral storefront and spiritualist churches. And, in some respects, the worlds they created mirrored one another when they did not interpenetrate, a fact that artists like Langston Hughes, Zora Neale Hurston, and Aaron Douglas recognized and represented. The nightclubs gave birth to urban jazz, and urban churches gave birth to gospel blues. The literati and the jazz performer alike tried to make their words and music preach. Churchmen and public intellectuals together felt as if they were birthing a new race and, in their own spheres and in their own ways, making plain the pathway of its coming.

An exhaustive explication of the spirituality of Harlem or, more broadly, of African America in the early twentieth century is not the focus of this study. However, *Goodbye Christ?* demonstrates that it is imperative to trace a metaphorical map of Christian belief and practice in order to grapple with the nature of the New Negro Renaissance in general; that movement—or, perhaps more properly, those movements, since this study builds on the current scholarly consensus that there are many competing versions of the New Negro—understood and felt itself in relationship to, and often in fundamental competition with, the vitality of Christian faith and the churches that were its institutional embodiment. Thus, *Goodbye Christ?* posits at the outset that Ann Douglas's assertion that "The spirit uptown [in Harlem], as downtown, was militantly secular" is simply false (*Terrible Honesty* 83). Or at least false for anyone who bothered to turn right or left off of Lenox Avenue, or who walked through Harlem on a Sunday morning instead of a Friday night. Christianity, and religious practice more broadly, was both a subject and a matrix for the cultural production of the New Negro Renaissance, and consequently of the twentieth-century African American literature that was to follow.

Saying this at the outset also requires a set of caveats and apophatic declarations about what *Goodbye Christ?* is not saying or setting out to say. We are so riven by religious contention that our academic discourse is not facile in talking about the power of religion or its influence on our shared culture; scholars who attempt such speech run the risk of being mistaken for either scoffers in the temple or proselytizers in the streets. To say that Harlem was not a haven of secularity is not to say simultaneously that the New Negro Renaissance was actually a religious movement; though, one must say that religious institutions and movements bore with them a compelling rhetoric of both newness and blackness that overlapped with other versions of the New Negro that were more explicitly political or cultural in orientation. Nor is it to say that New Negro intellectuals and artists were really crypto-Christians; though some, like Countee Cullen, were overtly Christians, others, like Claude McKay, reaffirmed an abandoned faith late in life, and others, like Du Bois, remained so closely guarded as to declarations of personal faith that an industry can and has been devoted to parsing personal beliefs. Still others, like James Weldon Johnson, were resolutely and publically agnostic while writing hymns, speaking and singing in churches, and producing literature so thoroughly "Christian" in form and content that the work is used in public worship and devotion to the present day. Finally, invoking the religious context of the New Negro Renaissance risks falling into an alluring bog that posits the religiosity and spiritual fervor of African Americans as a naturally occurring phenomenon, a racialized pit shared or flirted with by writers as different as Harriet Beecher Stowe and W. E. B. Du Bois. *Goodbye Christ?* is not saying or trying to say that genuine African Americans were Christians, that Christianity was the last best means of unifying the race, that African Americans were better Christians than white Americans, or that African Americans are somehow naturally religious or Christian. Many have stated such things. This book does not.[2] As a context, the pervasiveness of Christian belief and practice among African Americans in the early decades of the twentieth century says nothing of the specific beliefs and practices of the literati and other cultural artists and intellectuals in the Renaissance. As this book will suggest, many individual writers and artists were themselves ambiguous about or openly hostile to the religious practices around them. If Christianity was pervasive in African America, it is very true that large numbers of African Americans were also not Christians. Moreover, insofar as African American intellectuals were connected to explicitly secular intellectuals in the white establishment, the tone of intellectual work itself was often explicitly "secular" in a simplistic sense of that word. Nevertheless, as a context, religious African America cannot be ignored. The pervasive and pressing religious context of African America had the character of a cultural, political, and existential concern for a group of men and women eager to define themselves as the leaders of

4

INTRODUCTION

a race of people. *Goodbye Christ?* seeks to delineate the under-told story of how African American intellectuals sought to negotiate their entanglement with black religion, particularly black Christianity.

My use of the term "negotiate" suggests that relationships with and within African American Christianity were hardly straightforward, and were often fraught with tensions, rivalries, and unresolved desire. Unlike earlier generations of intellectuals who were embedded in the church—Frederick Douglass, for instance, was a minister, a fact often forgotten or unremarked—the early twentieth century saw the first fruition of a new generation of independent thinkers who may or may not have been Christians, but who clearly understood their intellectual and artistic vocations as independent from the authority and practice of the church. Nevertheless, this intellectual independence came at a price as the intellectual "Talented Tenth" considered its relationship to the masses of black Christians filling pews on Sunday mornings. Anna Pochmara, describing the tensions surrounding racial representation, notes the following:

> The perennial dilemma faced by representatives of the underprivileged stems from the fact that privilege entailed in the leading position distances them from the community they represent. They are forced to strategically balance between an assertion of agency through disidentification from the masses, on the one hand, and legitimization of racial identity, on the other, whose authenticity is frequently established through identification with the folk or with the working class. (11)

Here, Pochmara focuses her thinking on the question of class and economic privilege, a factor that is imbricated in various ways with questions of religious belief. Indeed, as with many other things, the intelligentsia was divided about religious practice, with the older generation much preferring or quietly indulging the high church forms of mainline churches and the younger generation celebrating—if not believing in—the ecstatic forms of worship identified with the underclass. For my own purposes, I will simply point out that differences of religious belief independently raised difficult questions of representativeness for the newly developing intelligentsia in the early twentieth century. A driving question of the period for artists and intellectuals was how they were to represent and lead a race so broadly Christianized when they themselves were not Christians, or at least when they did not see their intellectual efforts as embedded in or beholden to the leadership and the strictures of church authority and dogma. African American intellectuals and artists of the period felt both intimate with and distant from the race they represented in part because of differences of religious belief and practice. The effort to negotiate this sense of intimacy and distance is at once one of the most powerful and enduring, and one of the most complicated and contradictory elements of African American cultural production of the first decades of the twentieth century. The ultimate claim of *Goodbye Christ?* is that the manner in which New Negro intellectuals approached this question of cultural entanglement with Christianity set the terms for subsequent intellectual negotiations with the religious practices of the African American rank and file through the rest of the twentieth century. The modes of this engagement and negotiation are various, depending on differences of class, belief, aesthetic and intellectual practice, and many other factors. Some artists, such as Oscar Micheaux, Zora Neale Hurston, and, at times, Langston Hughes, chose direct confrontation with Christian beliefs and practices. Others such as Du Bois and James Weldon Johnson attempted to appropriate Christian worship as an aesthetic form in order to establish a secularized art that was continuous with but did not depend upon the specifics of Christian belief. Still others, like Countee Cullen, were themselves Christians, but attempted to imagine different forms of Christian faith that fit more comfortably with their intellectual frameworks or personal identities. The ensuing chapters of *Goodbye Christ?* examine these approaches and others, looking first at the problem of belief and unbelief in African American writers, continuing on to how African American intellectuals confronted anti-intellectualism in the churches, and concluding with an examination of how discourses of the body and sexual desire were deployed to imagine forms of blackness that were in tension with those forms of life officially promulgated by the Christian churches. In pursuing these investigations, *Goodbye Christ?* seeks the following: to give a more comprehensive picture of the importance of religion to our understanding of African American culture production; to suggest that, far from an epiphenomenon of race, class, or "folk culture," religious practices and traditions are relatively independent forces that affected the development of African American letters; and, finally, to suggest that the ways in which Harlem Renaissance writers strove to negotiate the terms of their relationship to African American Christianity has had an enduring consequence for the nature of African American cultural production to the present.

Scholarship on African American culture between *The Souls of Black Folk* and the demise of the Harlem Renaissance is both deep and diverse. Nevertheless, critical conversation concerning the New Negro Renaissance from

Langston Hughes to David Levering Lewis to the present has not taken full
account of the Christian context of African America in the period between
1900 and 1940. Criticism up to Lewis, and in the immediately ensuing
response to his definitive work, was dominated by concern with the relationship of black writers to white patrons. For writers like Hughes, Richard
Wright, Nathan Huggins, and Lewis, the dominant question of the Renaissance was its attempt to meet the aesthetic and cultural terms set by white
America, an attempt that has almost universally been regarded as a failure.
Lewis's arguments were complicated in ensuing years by critics such as
George Hutchinson and Ann Douglas, who ably showed the complex interactions of black and white writers such that it was really impossible to delineate a Manichaean division between white and black aesthetic enterprises.
Manhattan really was mongrel, whatever my disagreements with Douglas
about its religious character uptown. In a more political vein, scholars such
as William Maxwell, Barbara Foley, and Gary Holcomb show the persistent
importance of socialism and communism among black thinkers and writers
such as Hubert Harrison, Hughes, and McKay—a connection that created
a tremendous amount of fluidity between not only black and white radical
writers and movements within the United States, but also across borders in
ways that suggest the internationalist flavor of New Negro experience even
when manifest content may have focused on the local culture of the folk.
Most recently, gender and sexuality studies have opened up a new sense of
complexity, division, multiplicity, and contest within the African American
community itself that can otherwise be obscured by a singular focus on the
realities of racialized division. Feminist studies have pointed out the internal divisions maintained by patriarchal privilege within the Renaissance,
and gender and sexuality studies have indicated the degree to which ideas
about sexuality, masculinity, and femininity were deeply contested within
the race. Viewed in such a light, the New Negro Renaissance was a deeply
fissured and multifaceted cultural moment, best understood as not having
essential features but as a highly energized network of competing ideas,
ideologies, social circumstances, personal preferences, and cultural needs.
As Paul Gilroy suggests in *Against Race*, racializing logic can obscure the
multiplicity of so-called black experience and marginalize the experience
of gender, class, education, national origin, and other forms of identity in a
hasty homogenization. Scholarship on the New Negro since Levering Lewis
has clearly been seeking to break through that homogenizing racial logic
to get at the multiplicities and the inconsistent logic of human social and
cultural life during this tumultuous period.

My own work is indebted to all this previous scholarship in various ways.
What I hope to add to the discussion about the New Negro is the degree to

which religious discourse and practice was a significant, sometimes dominating, presence in this tumult. As Joseph Sorett has recently pointed out,
almost all literary and cultural studies of African America in this period
assume, with Douglas, that cultural secularization had been realized with the
publication of Toomer's *Cane*, and religion, or at least formal religion, had
been relegated to the dustbin (6). While more recent scholarship has included
some commentary on the religious contexts and contests of the period—
certainly more than existed up to and including *Mongrel Manhattan*—it has
not been the focus of any extant monograph on the period.

Thus we have missed the complexity of African American intellectual
engagement with religion, a complexity generated both by personal contexts
and by the pervasiveness of Christianity in everyday life. For instance,
Countee Cullen's tortured struggle to integrate masculine, sexual, racial,
and religious identities is well known to scholars of African American literature. The temptation is to take Cullen as a special case: He was gay or
bisexual in a world more homophobic than our own; he was a Christian
beset by intellectual doubts and anxieties; he was the child of a preacher,
adopted; he was insecure. Nevertheless, I would argue that Cullen's doubts
and uncertainties were, in many respects, those of the intelligentsia as a
whole. Most African American writers, like Cullen, had familial and other
personal ties to Christian churches and told a familiar modern story of
the long journey away from and very rarely back toward the faith of their
fathers and mothers. Cullen's stepfather was a minister, but so was Hurston's
father. Cullen was a fairly pious Sunday School attendant in his youth, but
so was Du Bois. Hughes struggled so valiantly to please his devout aunt
that he faked a Christian conversion, an experience that he describes as
one of the signature traumas of his life. Even writers whose connections to
dominant strains of Protestantism were more tenuous, such as Toomer and
Thurman, were aware of and worked out of a sense of Protestant dominance.
Little wonder, then, that literary and intellectual attention to the church
was often colored with tones of Bloom's anxiety of influence. Like Cullen,
every African American writer of the time struggled to reconcile a Christian
inheritance—literal or cultural—with secular desires.

Indeed, despite Douglas's contentions, perhaps the only class uptown
for whom Christian practice was not a regular feature of everyday life was
the intellectual class. Although many writers characterized the devotion of
African Americans as the primitive residue of an embarrassing racial past,
evidence suggests the Christian churches were the racial present. Collectively,
Christian churches represented the single most financially, politically, and
culturally powerful social institution through which African Americans
attempted to work out racial destiny and personal identity. Such churches

were also the only substantial African American institutions relatively free of white patronage and cultural interference. Thus what I have called the secular desires of the artists and intellectuals at the time must be understood within the context of the material power and the broad-based appeal of Christianity among the African American masses. Writers often felt trapped between a longing for a secular race that did not exist—or at least for acceptance by a religious readership that sometimes viewed their impieties with suspicion—and the ineluctable fact of an African-American Christian faith that they did not share.

In the face of such cultural tensions, African American writers deployed a sometimes-divided rhetoric that attempted to both assert the superiority of the secular intelligentsia to Christianity and portray the work of artists and intellectuals as the inheritors of the best spiritual impulses of black culture. This rhetoric has many dimensions, but often hinges on a discourse of gender. Marlon Ross points out that quests for racial empowerment and racial leadership have often entailed a rhetoric of manliness and, just as importantly, unmanliness. Speaking of early twentieth-century intellectuals, Ross notes the degree to which race leaders were positioned, and positioned themselves, in terms of acceptable levels of virility. According to Ross,

> Public accusations of unmanliness have been thrown sporadically at the most highly visible black male writers—including Washington, Du Bois, Trotter, Pickens, White, and Locke—even though these men took care to delineate radically different approaches to the role of manhood reform in race uplift. . . . [The] task of reforming the race necessarily involves a question of individual black men's capacity for manly leadership, a question that quickly leads to suspicion, innuendo, and accusation concerning the virility of rival men. (175)

Anna Pochmara has built on Ross's insights by noting that understanding the literary positioning of black male writers needs in some sense both a Bloomian paradigm and a paradigm drawn from Gilbert and Gubar. For Pochmara,

> The black male writer is caught in a double bind between the need to engage in 'heroic warfare' with his strong predecessors and the need to establish a legitimate patrilineal lineage, which will both validate black male authorship and set off the specters of social illegitimacy resulting from white men's symbolic and biological fathering of black children. These two conflicting endeavors are differently entangled in the politics of masculinity. (9–10)

The insights of Ross and Pochmara focus almost exclusively on the intramural contests between secular black intellectuals and literary figures. However, this discourse was also deployed in intraracial contests between secular and religious leaders as they vied with one another for modern forms of leadership. Christian ministers regularly declared the manly virtues of the Christian religion while openly doubting the fainting masculinity of a life devoted to letters. Harlem writers regularly imagined the masculine insufficiency of the Christian religion generally and of its male leadership specifically. While no single vision of manhood is possible to delineate, establishing the manly virtues of one's own discourse and doubting the manliness of another was a central preoccupation in the effort to determine whether the racial future would have a religious or secular cast.

For New Negro writers—especially but not exclusively male writers—imagining Christianity as a religion of women, children, and doddering old men cleared a rhetorical space for the secular intellectuals who yearned for and expected a new racial future. They typified Christian religiosity by employing the stereotype of the black Christian man as an Old Negro Uncle Tom, submissive to the point of death, accepting suffering and the loss of his manhood in preference for the greater rewards of a white heaven. For the New Negro, the Old Negro was plainly a Christian, and, if a man at all, a suspect man at best.

In some respects, this rhetoric is deeply familiar. Nietzsche was not the first to believe Christianity was servile and unmanly, and in the United States couching a critique of organized religion in the rhetoric of a failed manliness would have stretched back at least to Emerson, if not before. Nevertheless, this stereotype obscures the strong historical traditions of what has been described as a virile or muscular Christianity, one that declared among European and African Americans alike that the surest route to a fully realized manhood was though a militant Christian faith. Indeed, one reason Harlem writers were compelled to critique the manliness of the church and assert the manliness of their own intellectual enterprise lay in the fact that one of the most obvious and important ways of establishing one's masculine credentials in African American culture had always been and continued to be through the Christian church. In the late nineteenth century, Bishop Daniel Payne argued that the A.M.E. church provided more than a refuge for free blacks. They found "freedom for the development of a true Christian manhood," which allowed them to "suffer hardships as good soldiers of the cross" (Fulop and Raboteau 94). In 1891, Payne justified the existence of the A.M.E. Zion church because it provided for the realization of a "heaven-created manhood" (Becker 183), and in 1888 Payne argued, "The glorious manhood of Jesus Christ is the only true type of real manhood . . . Study him, study him as your model; study the perfect model of manhood until he shall be conformed in you" (192). Similarly, Episcopal Bishop Alexander Crummell proclaimed the deep intimacy of Christianity and manhood as a motive force in the quest for freedom: "But do not forget that manhood has been reached under great civil deprivations. Even in the times of the Caesars, St. Paul could exhort men in 'the city of God'— 'Quit you like men, be strong!' And the first Christians, under greater civil disabilities than ours, were the grandest of their kind" (Crummell 120–121).

This rhetoric was hardly a relic of the nineteenth century; throughout the early decades of the twentieth century, the idea that the Christian church was an engine of manhood formation remained a centrally important trope of the internal rhetoric of the church and of the race as a whole. For instance, in 1922, church historian Charles Spencer Smith exhorted the race onward through the masculine example of antebellum missionary William P. Quinn, describing him as having "the faith and daring of Paul, the intrepidity of Francis Asbury, and the blood and iron of Bismarck. He was matchless in heroism, superb in courage, and relentless in his attacks on the foes of his people. He was a militant soldier of the cross. He was a giant in his day" (17).

Even in the midst of New Negro theorizing, some church leaders saw this newness best embodied in the church. Reverdy Ransom, a strong proponent of the social gospel, defended Christianity as the only resource for peace between the races: "The Negro, who is 'the poor, blind Samson in our land,' is growing new locks; not to destroy, but to build better and stronger temples of freedom and goodwill whose doors swing wide to welcome all mankind to enter and dwell together in absolute equality in the bonds of brotherhood and peace. This faith is as strong as the right hand of God" (*Writings* 170). Ransom also saw in the New Negro not the antithesis of Christ but his latter day avatar, as his poem "The New Negro" makes clear:

HE KNOWS HIS PLACE, to keep it
As a sacred trust and heritage for all,
To wear God's image in the ranks of men
And walk as princes of the royal blood divine,
ON EQUAL FOOTING everywhere with all mankind.
With ever-fading color on these shores,
The Oriental sunshine in his blood
Shall give the warming touch of brotherhood
And love, to all the fused races in our land.
He is the last reserve of God on earth,
Who, in the goodly fellowship of love,
Will rule the world with peace.

Ransom saw Christian manhood embodied not in the weak men that popu-
lated so much of the Renaissance literature but in the heavyweight world
champion Jack Johnson, who made a national tour, speaking in African
American churches on the virtues of Christian manhood.[3] Such rhetoric
reinforced the sense of social power that attached to the church as the only
well-developed and independent institution among African Americans.

This analysis suggests that New Negro literary renderings of both gender
and religion were strategic and constructed within a pre-existing discourse
rather than being transparent renderings of the nature of religion and gender among African Americans. Depictions of Christianity and gender were
rhetorical, not simply realistic. Such strategic positioning was necessary
because the institutional, cultural, and imaginative power of the church at
the time threatened rather than shrank from the vision of a secular African American future. Although constructions of Christian manhood were
thoroughly rhetorical as well, they were not simply a product of oratori-
cal flourish on the part of a few sermonizers. The discourse reflected the
real institutional power of the Christian churches throughout this period
as well as their broad social dominance.[4] Indeed, in 1920 African American men regularly established their masculine credentials not by writing a
book of verse or a novel but by becoming leaders within the flourishing
churches and religious movements that dominated the Harlem scene. The
years of the Great Migration through at least 1926 saw African American
church attendance and membership actually grow in both raw numbers and
percentages of the African American population. Northern churches grew
exponentially, as struggling congregations became juggernauts seemingly
overnight. Salem Methodist Episcopal, led by Countee Cullen's foster father,
Frederick Asbury Cullen, grew from a small storefront mission church with
three members to a three-thousand-member congregation between 1902
and 1919. In 1926, at the putative height of the Harlem Renaissance, the
circulation of The Crisis had already begun dropping precipitously from
its all-time high of 100,000 in 1919, reaching a low of 10,000 in 1932
(Moon 385). During the same period 60 percent of African Americans were
regularly involved in church at some significant level, a number that had
not fallen since Du Bois's study of the Negro Church in 1903. According to
the Negro Year Book of 1937, total black church membership grew from
39.1 percent of adult males and 64.4 percent of adult females in 1906 to
45.5 percent of adult males and 73.1 percent of adult females in 1926,
for a total church membership of approximately 60 percent at the height
of the Harlem Renaissance, slightly more than their white counterparts.
By comparison, the church membership of white males remained stable,

and that of white females dropped slightly. These statistics do not account for church attendance by persons who never became church members ("Percent of Negro and White Men and Women"). Collectively, the churches and their ministers signified far more cultural authority than any group of intellectuals could hope to achieve. Crowded pews meant swelling coffers, and churches benefited from soaring property values as well. Following the immigrants to upper Manhattan, Abyssinian Baptist sold its 59th street building and built one of the most imposing religious edifices in Manhattan to house its burgeoning congregation.[5] Soon, more wealth and property, and therefore power, were concentrated in the religious institutions of Harlem than in any other sector of African American society, so much so that how the churches used their money vexed other institutional leaders like Du Bois and James Weldon Johnson.

The social influence was felt not simply in pews and prayer meetings but in boardrooms, civic clubs, and political parties. And, indeed, in literary salons. In many respects, African American Christianity evinced not the dying fall of a premodern sensibility but rather a form of religious modernization. One manifestation of this religious modernity was new, elaborate, and complex forms of institutional life within which men established a sense of both cultural leadership and personal purpose. Father Divine is remembered less for his theological innovations than for the seemingly miraculous feasts that he provided for his followers, becoming in some metaphorical sense an institutional patriarch feeding his children. Many ministers in the traditional churches tended toward a version of the social gospel and sought to use their churches to serve the people of God on earth. Bishop Reverdy Ransom of the African Methodist Episcopal Church and Adam Clayton Powell, Sr. of Abyssinian Baptist both instituted a variety of ministries to the urban poor and advocated for public policies on their behalf. Even a theological conservative such as Frederick Asbury Cullen, who claimed to never preach politics from the pulpit, became president of the local chapter of the NAACP, helped organize the Silent Parade of 1919, visited President Wilson in the aftermath of the Brownsville, Texas, riots, and promoted various social ministries through his church and through the YMCA (F. A. Cullen 49–58).[6]

Although writers as different as Hurston and Du Bois dismissed the official churches as quasi-white organizations and the storefront churches as the home of manipulative charlatans, such arguments tended to gloss over the many ways in which traditional and new religious movements met real social and psychic needs in Harlem. Thus religious life was not divorced from a sense of masculine or feminine self-respect but was the matrix within which male or female power could be exercised. As Benjamin Mays describes the typical congregant in an urban church of the 1920s, "Frequently their souls are crushed and their personalities disregarded. Often they do not feel 'at home' in the more sophisticated Negro group. But in the church on X street, she is Mrs. Johnson, the Church clerk; and he is Mr. Jones, the chairman of the Deacon Board" (Mays and Nicholson 426). Though restricted in some respects, religious organizations provided a genuine space of freedom for the exercise of leadership, responsibility, and initiative that could make a substantial difference in the lives of others. In this way, religious organizations provided the necessary context out of which individual identity grew and individual power was implemented.

The cultural power of the church was not exercised exclusively within the pews or the walls of the Sunday school assembly. Indeed, many intellectuals worried or puzzled over the fact that the inescapable presence of Christianity in Negro life reinforced prevailing cultural stereotypes about African Americans. Scholars of African American life at the time took seriously the notion that African Americans were uniquely religious. Adopting the racialist categories of his time like Du Bois before him, Melville Herskovits wondered whether religiosity was not an indelible feature of Negro life as such: "The tenability of this position is apparent when it is considered how, in an age marked by skepticism, the Negro has held fast to belief. Religion is vital, meaningful, and understandable to the Negro of this country because . . . it is not removed from life, but has been deeply integrated into the daily round" (*The Myth of the Negro Past* 207, quoted in Fauset 4).

Concerned about the stereotyping such a view could entail, Arthur Fauset rightly argued that blacks were no more religious than whites when measured by church membership (97), but this does not belie religion's pervasive institutional and cultural importance. To some degree, the centrality of the church to African American cultural life meant that nearly every social organization in Harlem included some kind of religious flavoring. Fraternal orders such as the Masons explicitly drew on scripture in their organizational rituals, and members were often openly recognized as upstanding and important members of mainstream churches. Similarly, the black church in Harlem was sometimes referred to as the "NAACP on its knees" (Lincoln and Mamiya 209). This could not have been strictly true since central figures of the NAACP such as James Weldon Johnson and Du Bois had traveled some intellectual distance from the faith of their childhoods, and both chafed at the overwhelming influence of the church. Nevertheless, the aphorism does suggest the degree to which the religious and the secular interpenetrated one another in much of Harlem's social and political life. Philip Randolph, though an avowed atheist, conceived of the Brotherhood of Sleeping Car Porters in quasi-religious terms, depended upon good relations with the church for the development of the union, and employed a frankly religious rhetoric in promoting the union's political ambitions (Taylor 11–20). Finally, perhaps the most popular organization for racial uplift, Marcus Garvey's Universal Negro Improvement Association, presented itself organizationally and rhetorically in quasi-religious terms. Children of members were baptized into both the Christian religion and association membership. Mass meetings were shaped around liturgies reminiscent of the high churches of the Christian faith, and the organization maintained a hierarchy of chaplains intended to minister to the spiritual needs of the membership. Garvey called upon Africans to create a black God to replace the white God they had inherited from slave masters in order to secure the manhood of the race (Blum and Harvey 161–62).

This is not to say that churches were completely unaware—or unwary—of the growing and vocal strength of the secular intelligentsia. Indeed, sometimes the church was actively antagonistic to a perceived threat to its cultural hegemony. Christian ministers sometimes fretted about the atheism of the intellectuals. They more often decried the moral degradation of popular and literary culture in Harlem and elsewhere. The established churches welcomed poets to the degree that they represented African American achievement, but Langston Hughes had preachers prevent him from reading his blues poetry from the pulpit (De Jongh 24). Wallace Thurman was accosted and prayed over by a group of Christian women dismayed by his degrading and sinful portrayal of the race in his fiction. Preachers regularly railed against the bohemianism that Hughes and some others embraced, and preachers of every type spoke against the overtly erotic sound of jazz and the morally degrading effect of clubs wherein it could be heard. With white counterparts, black ministers protested the work of Oscar Micheaux on moral grounds and succeeded in having him censored. The church, then, surely could display the philistine moralism of which it was regularly accused.

Nevertheless, for the most part Christian attitudes toward artists and writers were typified by benign if not dismissive neglect. This was primarily because the churches had an intellectual and cultural life sufficient to their needs. The storefront churches by and large had no interest in "high" culture of the kind represented by Countee Cullen. Their preaching and singing were a poetry and drama of their own, as Langston Hughes recognized. The mainline denominations supported institutions of higher education, educated their ministers as best they could, and expressed themselves aesthetically in choirs and rituals of their own. For the mainline churches, theology and preaching were intellectual work of the highest order, regardless of their reputation in academe. Of course, some of the churches of the black bourgeoisie provided an official religiosity for the cultural aspirations of the Harlem Renaissance. Abyssinian Baptist Church was the site of the most famous wedding of the period—that of Countee Cullen and Yolanda Du Bois. Poets and writers of the period sometimes read to large crowds in the sanctuaries of tony churches or to students at church-sponsored colleges.

Still, influence on the church was scant and the welcome of the church for cultural innovations was uneven. In comparison to the cosmic claims made by churches and their preachers, the claims of a sonnet or a portrait or a play could seem wispy indeed. In comparison to the bulwark of the church, the promises of books and music and paintings rested on the insecure foundation of white approval and seemed to have little to do with bread for the table or bread for the soul. As early as 1885, Alexander Crummell wrote against the idea that aesthetics could take the place of the traditional virtues in winning blacks full citizenship and manhood rights. "Style and beauty," he writes, "are secondary to duty and moral responsibility. Men cannot live on flowers. Society cannot be built up upon the strength which comes from rose-water" ("New Ideas" 120–21). It's a critique worthy of Levering Lewis. It's certainly an attitude that had changed but little when Jean Toomer published *Cane* in 1923.

The lukewarm attitude of the churches may be the best evidence for Langston Hughes's suggestion in 1940 that almost no one in Harlem seemed to notice or care that a renaissance had taken place (*Big Sea* 178). On the whole, the churches didn't really seem to need or want what the intelligentsia had to offer. By contrast, writers and artists could hardly ignore the church. Any artist taking up the experience of African Americans in the twenties could not escape noticing that the crowded churches on Sunday morning matched—when they did not exceed—the crowded clubs and speakeasies on Saturday night. Every major writer of the period addressed African American religious life generally and Christianity in particular in some significant way. Even so vigorous an opponent of Christianity as Zora Neale Hurston drew consistently on Christian themes and imagery in her work and found in other religious practices a form of artistic creativity. Whether the rural south as in Toomer's *Cane* or Hurston's *Jonah's Gourd Vine*, the storefront churches of Hughes's poetry, or the mainline sophisticates of Cullen's neglected novel *One Way to Heaven*, Christian religious practices provide the backdrop, characters, imagery, and theme of most of the important work of the Renaissance, even when they are deployed to resist the religious traditions that they reference.

Moreover, engagement with religion hardly seems to have been simply a begrudging necessity born of an inevitable cultural ground. Whatever the specific distance between the metaphysical convictions of individual Harlem intellectuals and the black masses, many writers and artists sought various forms of compromise and negotiation with the cultural reality of the Christian religion. How else to explain the achievement of agnostic James Weldon Johnson in *God's Trombones,* perhaps the single work of the height of the Harlem Renaissance that continues to be read regularly outside of college classrooms because it is read as a part of Christian worship and devotion. Similarly, Hughes wrote not only poems that were blues but also poems that were sermons. Du Bois wrote explicitly about not only his doubts concerning religious belief but also what appear to be heartfelt and moving prayers throughout his life. These prayers were often explicitly designed to encourage other African Americans. However, reading them, one can't help but feel they must have been for Du Bois's personal encouragement as well, enough so that debates about the precise character of Du Bois's religious beliefs continue to the present. Finally, the relatively stalwart anti-Christian Zora Neale Hurston saw in the black preacher the purest form of African American poetry, a model to be emulated.

Sorett has rightly noted that intellectuals and artists of the period were in some respects devoted to developing a racial aesthetic that relied on or at least regularly referenced the idea of a racialized spirituality, and that this spirituality was in various ways continuous with at least the language of Afro-Protestantism in the official churches (19–54). My own reading focuses much more specifically on the agonistic relationship between the churches and the newly formed secular intelligentsia, seeing the aestheticization of traditional Christian forms of life and the development of a generalized racial spirituality as part and parcel of the processes of the development of that intelligentsia and of secularization itself as it was to be found among African Americans. Nevertheless, it is surely the case that these forms of aesthetic negotiation were necessary, both as a practical matter of cultural power and because many artists genuinely viewed the church as a site of racial origins and racial creativity. Although entering into debates about the nature of secularization is not a primary purpose of this book, it is important to say that those debates have been renewed in the past fifteen years, ranging from vigorous advocacy for a new secularism to a debunking of the notion of the secular altogether. Among other things what these debates have surely pointed out is that the idea of the secular is not unitary or universal. They have also pointed out that the secular and the religious have had, and continue to have, an uneasy relationship. Criticism of New

Negro cultural production has tended to use a fairly simple binary form of that argument—assuming that "the secular" is simply the opposite of anything that can be characterized as religious—primarily because many New Negro artists themselves equated certain forms of secularity with the idea of the New Negro's entry into the modern world. However, I agree with Calhoun et al. when they note that the "secular" is not simply the absence of religion, or what is left over as religion dies off and the human race reaches a more rationalized apotheosis. As they put it, "although secularism is often defined negatively—as what is left after religion fades—it is not in itself neutral. Secularism should be seen as a presence. It is something. . . ."(5).

That is, like religion, the secular is constructed through practices, norms, traditions, institutions, power relations, and ways of speaking. As Talal Asad points out, these come into being, are reproduced, and are sustained in a wide variety of ways, often very unevenly depending on time, circumstance, economy, and culture. The secular can and does coexist with various forms of spirituality and religion and isn't to be equated with atheism. Indeed, I am in broad agreement with Van der Veer that "the spiritual and the secular are produced simultaneously as two connected alternatives to institutionalized religion in Euro-American modernity" (1097). Or at least they can be. Similarly, the process of aestheticizing received Christian cultural forms can become a means of loosing the artist or intellectual from the controlling power of religious forms and institutions, even while allowing for a more generalized sense of connection to an inherited Christian language through the figures of art or spirituality. What is crucial is the relative sense of freedom from a primary identity in or responsibility to the church, freedom pursued in the name of a broader and supposedly more public and rational racial consciousness. In a Bloomian paradigm, this kind of creativity is both an act of homage and an act of destruction. It brings the New Negro into imaginative being and also into a new form of social being that is in a peculiarly ambiguous and even tension-filled relationship with his or her Christian forbearers.

What this overview should make clear is that the quest to establish a tradition of modern African American arts and letters addressed not simply a powerful and encompassing white cultural reality but also a culturally powerful and encompassing black religious reality. Almost every interpreter of the Harlem Renaissance from Langston Hughes to the present has pointed out that artists and intellectuals sought to secure racial justice through a politics of recognition based on visible achievement in the arts. However, a similar politics of recognition drove these same cultural workers to secure their status within the race, and this quest was made necessary by the prestige and power of Christianity among African Americans. If the tone of literary and intellectual life uptown was sometimes aggressively secular, this may have been so because the tone uptown was so broadly Christian. Rhetorical aggression in this instance signifies not so much intellectual security as the need to clear a space for the secular work they hoped to pursue.

Thus, the work of the Harlem Renaissance is marked as much by argument and collaboration, by conflict and compromise, by negotiation and confrontation concerning religion within African American communities as it is by the collaborations and tensions across the color line. Harlem writers may have often imagined the Old Negro as a doddering and pious Uncle Tom, but they could not have helped but know that when Reverdy Ransom and Adam Clayton Powell and their many brethren spoke, people listened, every week, and by the millions. This suggests that African American religious contexts and interlocutors were easily as important and as much a source of creative tension as the encompassing white context. In seeking to establish a form of literary and cultural patrimony, African American intellectuals contended not only with dominant white cultural force but also with Christian forefathers whom Du Bois rightly called men at the center of a group of men, speaking with a religious voice to a culture with religious ears. A secular intelligentsia was a cultural tradition to be born, but not without struggle and not without attention to the religious grounds out of which it was springing.

To the degree that this was a question of leadership, and given that leadership was itself in practice and in imagination overwhelmingly male, anxieties over religion were often articulated explicitly or implicitly through a discourse of masculinity, and anxieties about masculinity were articulated explicitly or implicitly through a discourse of religious faith. The task of *Goodbye Christ?* is to analyze this particular discursive framework to see how New Negro writers in the early decades of the twentieth century sought to loosen the grip of Christianity on the racial imagination such that a space might be cleared for their own cultural work and for the development of a secular African American intelligentsia in general. Contrary to approaches to the New Negro Renaissance that have emphasized the overwhelming secularity of the movement and the moment, *Goodbye Christ?* attends to the massive and in fact growing popularity of large and powerful churches during this period, taking seriously the notion that preachers were men at the center of cultural discourse in part because Christianity remained central to black self-conception during the period. If this is so, then understanding the power of those churches and the tensions that were sometimes evident in relationships with the newly developing intelligentsia is essential to understanding the work that New Negro Renaissance writers undertook.

The structure and scope of *Goodbye Christ?* reflects this overall goal. The next two chapters of this book look at two seminal figures, W. E. B. Du Bois and Langston Hughes, in works written nearly four decades apart that chart an autobiographical unease with their own status vis-à-vis Christian faith, an unease that needed to be addressed and, where possible, reconciled. This pairing is used to suggest both the diversity of discourses surrounding Christianity and masculinity, and the surprising range of similarity between writers occupying different ideological and historical spaces. Moreover, the pairing of a text from 1903 with a text from 1940 suggests that when I use the terms "Harlem Renaissance" or "New Negro Renaissance"—terms I tend to use interchangeably—I am interested in a historical continuum much broader than the truncated periodization that relegates the movement from 1923 and the publication of *Cane* to 1929 and the Great Depression. My choice of texts suggests that I am in agreement with those who see the New Negro Renaissance and its concerns stretching back into the late nineteenth century and continuing at least to the period of WWII. The middle section of this book overlaps to some degree with the first but focuses primarily on the figure of the educated man as an ambivalent culture hero in the fictions of the period. On the one hand, fictional men of education were avatars of the male New Negro writers themselves, but they existed in a strangely isolated and isolating space in relationship to the religious communities they sought to lead and serve. The championing of education as a form of liberation drew deeply on historical developments in African American culture and on the growing role of education in American culture as a whole. At the same time, the discourses of education as a mode of liberation or empowerment ran full-steam into African American forms of anti-intellectualism that were driven, at least in part, by religious conviction. Artists as diverse as Hughes and Du Bois—whom I examine again in detail—Toomer, Larsen, and Micheaux wrestled with the contradiction that education promised to save the educated but also created distance and alienation from what might otherwise be assumed, naively, to represent a cultural homeland. The inability of education itself to resolve this conflict, as well as the ways in which education continued to serve the broader purposes of a patriarchal social order, are tensions that motivate the development of these fictions. The final section of this book moves from mind to body, looking at the ways in which African American writers engaged the newly developing discourses of the primacy of the body and physicality, especially as sex and sexuality came to be seen as driving factors in the creation of art and culture. Such work inevitably grappled with traditional proscriptions regarding sex and sexuality that have been at the center of African American forms of Christian faith as much as other cultural forms of Christian faith. In very different ways writers and artists like Countee Cullen, Richard Bruce Nugent, and Zora Neale Hurston sought to reconcile conflicts between the burgeoning discourse of the body and its sex with the traditional morality of Christian faith itself.

In deciding to write about the religious contexts of the cultural work associated with the Harlem Renaissance, I have sometimes felt as if I'd entered a vast and finely appointed house that is too sparsely occupied. To some degree, Christianity in twentieth-century African American cultural studies, and especially literary studies, remains the elephant in the room about which intellectuals have only just begun to speak. In his important investigation of the relationship of African literary production to religion, Josef Sorett opens with a discussion of Benjamin Mays's monograph on African American literature from 1938, *The Negro's God as Reflected in His Literature*. This beginning is telling, since in many respects there have been almost no other extended efforts to account for the centrality of religion in general, and Christianity in particular, to African American literary work in the twentieth century. Certainly none focused on the period associated with what has been called the New Negro Renaissance.

Goodbye Christ? does not pretend to be an exhaustive account. There are more books to be written about the relationship of Christianity to African American literary and cultural life in the twentieth and now twenty-first centuries, ones that could account for the many changes and continuities between the years of the Harlem Renaissance and Ta-Nehisi Coates's publication of *Between the World and Me*. The conclusion of this book outlines what some of those future scholarly endeavors might have to consider. Among other things, I think this book suggests that the Harlem Renaissance was very far from a hothouse invention that failed. All forms of modernism, after all, imagined themselves fantastically as curatives for the world's ills. Falling short of such inflated goals is surely not the best measure by which to judge a literary or intellectual movement. What most literary movements manage is to change the world of literature and intellectual life in some measure.

This is no small feat. The writing associated with the Renaissance set the discursive terms through which a newly secularizing African American intelligentsia engaged the Christian churches of the race. Those discursive terms continued to shape African American intellectual and creative work throughout the twentieth century and, arguably, have continued to do so to our own day. Whatever one's view of the consequences of that discourse, this is a legacy with which to reckon.

"OLD AS RELIGION, AS DELPHI AND ENDOR"

Secular Patrimony in *The Souls of Black Folk*

Perhaps no intellectual leader of the twentieth century grappled more insistently with the dynamics of being both intimate with and distant from the people he hoped to lead and for whom he hoped to speak than did W. E. B. Du Bois. His signature concept regarding racial leadership—the talented tenth—embodied and sought to resolve the problem of being both a part of and apart from the less talented (or less lucky) nine-tenths of the race. The concept of the Veil and the metaphysical view of race that Du Bois sometimes embraced occluded the tensions he felt as the scion of free Northern blacks living at a very great cultural and historical remove from the waves of southern migrants who were the primary shapers of African American culture in the early decades of the century. His fervent advocacy for education united the idealism of the educated classes with the hopes and strivings of uneducated laborers, even while underscoring the uniqueness of his own autobiography and authenticating his right to speak on behalf of those who could not speak for themselves. All of these issues are central to Du Bois's signature text, *The Souls of Black Folk*, and their threads can be traced through the later work of Du Bois's differentiating and seemingly inexhaustible career. Moreover, to the degree that *Souls* framed the intellectual urgencies of the Harlem Renaissance even among those who resisted its specifics, the text can be understood as a manifesto, defining the essential nature of black culture and mapping its appropriate response to systemic racism in the United States. It is, as well, an autobiographical argument for a form of secular leadership and for Du Bois as its most authentic representative.

I use the terms "secular" and "autobiography" in a guarded sense, not least because there has been a great deal of ink spilled trying to define the precise nature of Du Bois's religious beliefs. As I suggested in my introduction, the term "secular" does not presume any specific thing about the nature of the cosmos but is more properly conceived as a means of organizing and reproducing social, institutional, and personal practices. Advocates for various forms of the secular may or may not themselves have religious beliefs. Indeed, it is a point of some contention within and without Christian political thinking as to whether the notion of an explicitly secular or religiously neutral domain springs directly from Christian thinking about divine and natural law.[1] One may work confidently at one's secular vocation in city hall or in the science lab while praying to one's God in the privacy of one's office or attending mass on Sunday morning. A separate realm of the secular city is sustained and valued precisely so that religious devotion will not be polluted by the corruption of politics or other forms of secular endeavor. This chapter argues, in something of the opposite direction, that Du Bois believed that the intellectual, cultural, and political life of African Americans was hampered by its captivity to the dominant forms of church life in the early twentieth century. When Du Bois imagines his secular intellectual heaven, he imagines himself walking arm in arm with Aristotle, not alone in the garden with Jesus. The talented tenth in Du Bois's thought is a fundamentally secular notion not because it is focused on political, intellectual, educational, and artistic achievement, but rather because the full achievement of these human goods is understood to be separate from the interests, theological framework, and control of the church.

However, to say Du Bois advocated for a secular understanding of leadership, and for a secular version of the black nation, is not to say anything specific about Du Bois's personal religious convictions. Scholars of Du Bois's life and work dispute the nature of those convictions. Some see him as a thoroughgoing atheist; others find in him an enthusiastic believer. Manning Marable declares a middle ground by defining what he describes as Du Bois's "spiritual identification with . . . black faith" ("Black Faith" 31). The most recent and thorough investigation of DuBois's engagement with religion

from Gary Dorrien finds that Du Bois self-consciously engaged with, was
an advocate for, and was a primary influencer of the Black Social Gospel
movement. Dorrien at the same time indicates that it is impossible to define
precisely what Du Bois himself actually believed. Dorrien suggests that such
a stance was not atypical. Others, such as Carter Woodson, advocated for
an activist church and continued their involvement in such churches while
being ambiguous about affirming any particular dogma of the church. In
this sense, engagement with the church was a pragmatic necessity for men
like Woodson and Du Bois rather than a matter of personal conviction
(Dorrien 30–31). I am comfortable using the generic and ill-defined term
"agnostic" to capture these uncertainties, but even that term does not seem
adequate to the man who could pen the kinds of agonized wrestling with
the God of his imagination found in "Litany of Atlanta," in "Credo," or in
"The Prayers of God" from *Darkwater*:

> Awake me, God! I sleep!
> What was that awful word Thou saidst?
> That black and riven thing—was it Thee?
> That gasp—was it Thine?
> That pain—is it Thine?
> Are, then, these bullets piercing Thee?
> Have all the wars of all the world,
> Down all dim time, drawn blood from Thee?
> Have all the lies and thefts and hates—
> Is this Thy Crucifixion, God,
> And not that funny, little cross,
> With vinegar and thorns?
> Is this thy kingdom here, not there,
> This stone and stucco drift of dreams? (123)

Such passages are agnosticism of a sort, more questioning than affirming,
but one that is as much an agonized jousting with the possibilities of a God
who seems indifferent as it is the passivity of intellectual irresolution.

In the final instance, I think it is impossible to say what Du Bois believed
at any particular moment of a very long and stupendously productive life.
However, what does seem very clear is that Du Bois's construction of what
Marable calls "black faith" in *The Souls of Black Folk* reveals a conflicted
relationship to the churches that institutionalized, the men who led, and the
dogmas that codified "black faith" in the American experience through the
nineteenth and early twentieth centuries. In part, this ambiguity turned on
personal predilections. Du Bois grew up in mainline Protestant churches at

some distance from the low-church evangelicalism and spiritual fervor of the largest number of African Americans. As he was beginning his scholarly career, Du Bois's agnosticism brought him into conflict with administrations at Wilberforce and Atlanta University. While Marable is clearly right that Du Bois reserved his most vehement denunciations for the hypocrisy of white churches, as early as 1891, he said of the black churches, "A religion that won't stand the application of reason and common sense is not fit for an intelligent dog" ("Black Faith" 21).[2] And stories of white Christian hypocrisy are often accompanied by tales of black Christian complicity, as in "The Second Coming" in *Darkwater*. As late as 1933, he comments on the need to find some rapprochement between the growing unchurched population—with whom he apparently identifies—and the religious convictions of the black masses (*Crisis* 333). Dorrien notes that in 1940, many years after he first refused to lead prayers for the faculty, Du Bois returned to Wilberforce to deliver the commencement address and used the occasion to ridicule the school's Christian legacy as a "childish belief in fairy tales, a word-of-mouth adherence to dogma, and a certain sectarian exclusiveness" (22).

These matters of personal belief and practice are interesting in and of themselves, but they also point to the difficulty that Du Bois faced as he contemplated the Christian churches and their role in African American culture at the turn of the century. If it were true that the preacher embodied the one real image of African American leadership, how then could Du Bois convincingly assert his own vision of a secular leadership class, a talented tenth? Given the dominance of the Christian church, it is unsurprising that Du Bois saw in the religious men around him the first form of his desire for racial leadership. Nevertheless, such men were often antithetical to his vision of black progressivism and cultural idealism. As Gary Dorrien points out, although our contemporary picture of the black church assumes a church that is socially and politically engaged, the black church has always been as diverse and complicated as the rest of the Christian church. Indeed, Dorrien suggests that the explicit political activism associated with Reverdy Ransom—and in a different way even with Adam Clayton Powell—was a distinctly minority position among African American churchmen of the 1920s. We may assume this was even more the case in 1903. Thus, Du Bois, the Northern agnostic, was in an acutely delicate position. How, in his "high silk hat, gloves and walking cane, and his dapper Vandyke beard" (Marable, *W.E.B. Du Bois* 22), could he measure up to or displace the black preacher with Bible uplifted? What had black religion, the "one expression of [the Negro's] higher life," to do with the higher life of opera, literature, and philosophy? And certainly what had it to do with explicit political and racial activism?

Du Bois articulates and seeks to resolve this problem through a complicated discourse of masculinity. It is not unusual to note that contests for leadership have most often been defined culturally and institutionally as contests between men, and I am largely in agreement with Hazel Carby's analysis that Du Bois could not imagine that women were meaningful candidates for intellectual and political leadership; rather, talented tenth women played the important but subordinate roles of helpmeets, mothers, and assistants (10). Ironically, there were certain senses in which segments of religious life provided more effective avenues for female leadership than did Du Bois's imaginative framework. While dominant mainline churches reflected the church's historical patriarchal bias, holiness and other spiritualist movement depended more on the charism of the Spirit for defining leadership and cultural authority, and women were often led by the Spirit into preaching and other leadership roles. By the 1920s, female bishops and ministers in such churches were not uncommon, and in some instances they came to play an important role in the life of cultural luminaries, James Baldwin being only one instance. More broadly, the church was clearly the domain of women in the pew if not the pulpit, and it could not have persisted without the attendance, congregational leadership, and financial support of women.

Nevertheless, female leadership was still a minority and, if anything, the dominance of women in the pew played well to Du Bois's rhetorical strategy of overcoming the preacher and winning over his followers by asserting the superiority of his own version of masculinity. The church was a feminine space, its men failing or flailing. To insist the "spirit of the LORD" had metaphorically left the church and its leaders was to simultaneously insist that a manlier response to the spirit of the new age might be found in the leadership provided by a secular intelligentsia, and that intelligentsia was most perfectly embodied in Du Bois himself.

Du Bois waged this rhetorical battle for leadership by asserting a superior form of manliness based on the ability to speak and write well. This ability is on the one hand aesthetic: eloquence is the hallmark of the accomplished man and necessary to modern leadership. It is also cognitive: effective and coherent expression is the hallmark of knowledge necessary for effective leadership. At first blush, attaching masculinity to reading and writing seems like an odd choice given the physicality attached to many popular forms of masculinity in European and in African American cultures alike. Paragons of masculinity have often been popularly imagined as doers not thinkers, as fighters not speakers, as brawn not brains. Indeed, in later chapters of this book, I will detail how even within the black church excessive education and cultured refinement could cast doubt on both one's masculinity and one's spiritual fervor. Nevertheless, for Du Bois, in a context where preachers were best known for their ability to move the people through their language and through their ability to read the scriptures when others could not, establishing a ground for his own leadership focused on the subtle but definite superiority of the modern intellectual as an interpreter, a man of words who could better address the needs of a modern racial people. In Du Bois's rhetoric, the men of the churches might be good and even gifted people, but their gifts were inadequate for effective leadership in the twentieth century. The true inheritors, the real men who spoke—and wrote—with tongues of flame, were the modernizing leaders of the diversifying urban scene in Harlem, Chicago, Atlanta, and elsewhere.[3]

THE SOULS OF BLACK FOLK AND THE ARGUMENT AGAINST CHRISTENDOM

Du Bois begins his investigation into the souls of black folk with a personal meditation: "Between me and the other world there is ever an unasked question. . . . How does it feel to be a problem? . . . At these I smile, or am interested, or reduce the boiling to a simmer, as the occasion may require. To the real question, how does it feel to be a problem? I answer seldom a word" (9). The passage is well known and, for my purposes, requires only the observation that it heads a chapter titled "Of Our Spiritual Strivings." The words "soul" and "spirit" of course have generic and nonreligious usages in academic and in popular culture, and did so in 1903. Nonetheless, even today these terms retain a penumbra of their traditional meanings in defining a metaphysical anthropology. In 1903 in the United States, the terms would have been most resolutely and readily identified with Christian anthropology. Indeed, justifications for slavery in the United States developed in part through arguments and doubts about whether African Americans had souls at all. In the colonial era churches and politicians argued as to whether a Christian could enslave another Christian, with sentiment leaning against the idea. Consequently, arguments in favor of slavery turned on the question of whether Africans could become Christians at all, a question that fundamentally doubted their humanity. Until slave-owners came to believe that Christianization provided a means of ideological control, slavery depended on doubts that Africans could be saved, this because they lacked the singularly defining human feature of Christian anthropology, the soul itself. African writers in the early Republic like Phyllis Wheatley and Olaudah Equiano asserted their rights to be understood as human beings with human dignity through a discourse of salvation; they did indeed have souls that needed saving and had, in fact, been saved. The discourse of the soul for African Americans was also a discourse about human and political equality. Du Bois is clearly drawing on this tradition of the soul as signifier of humanity in the title and arguments of his signature book. Black souls matter, one might say.

Nevertheless, for Du Bois, both "the souls" and "the spiritual striving" of black folk were largely removed from the specifics of Christian anthropology, and he understands them as fundamentally secular entities. African American individuals and communities will realize and develop their souls not through the disciplines of Christian spirituality but by overcoming barriers to racial achievement. It is not quite right to say that Du Bois abandons or rejects traditions of African American "soul talk"; this would create a chasm between himself and the spiritual sensibilities of the religious rank and file. But if Du Bois does not completely abandon the common religious rhetoric of the people, he does empty it of its specific contents and contexts to make room for other, more secular sensibilities.

This transposition of religious rhetoric and sensibilities to secular alternatives is a central device in Du Bois's investigation of black religion in "Of the Faith of the Fathers." Even the title of this chapter is interesting. Du Bois's choice of the definite article "the" instead of the possessive pronoun "our" commonly associated with the hymn "Faith of Our Fathers" creates an objectifying distance. Robert Stepto points out that Du Bois went to some length to revise the chapter titles of what were once disparate essays. "Strivings of the Negro People" became "Of Our Spiritual Strivings." "Faith of the Fathers" came from an essay entitled "The Religion of the American Negro" (Stepto 53–54). To be sure, the revised language is less distant and academic than the original, a signal of Du Bois's desire for more than just academic success. But, at the same time, the care that Du Bois took in revision makes the differences striking. Unlike his present tense identification with racial striving, signaled in the introduction titled "Our spiritual striving," this faith is an artifact of the past, a faith of the fathers rather than the present of the American Negro.

Commentators have rightly noted that "Of the Faith of the Fathers" begins as a narrative of return wherein the Northern intellectual locates himself within the wellsprings of the lives of the Southern black folk. This became a central narrative form of the Harlem Renaissance as Northern intellectuals and artists sought to authenticate their academic and artistic ambitions in relationship to the unlettered masses. Discussing the specific case of Jean Toomer's *Cane*, Mark Whalan points out that this narrative of return is rooted in a historical phenomenon in which Northern African Americans, motivated by the missionary zeal of the racial uplift movement, journeyed to the South in order to staff schools and other social service projects, a journey that had other permutations as Southern African Americans travelled to college in either Northern or Southern cities before returning to their hometowns and villages to provide education and racial leadership (*Manhood and Modernism* 150). This story shaped the biographies of not only Du Bois and Toomer but also intellectual luminaries such as James Weldon Johnson and many others. By the period of the Harlem Renaissance proper this specific narrative had been attenuated to some degree by the rising tide of the Great Migration north. Nevertheless, many narratives of the period emphasize the journey south as a journey into the heart of black experience. The narrative form authenticated one's own voice through a baptism in blackness that certified one's authority to speak for the people who were not there to speak for themselves. This narrative countered the authenticating narratives used by some Southern black leaders like Booker T. Washington, who established authority by reminding his readers that he had been born in the heart of Southern blackness. This strategy was used by writers like Zora Neale Hurston, who emphasized her nativity in the South as a source of authority for her intellectual and artistic work. Retman notes that for Hurston, it was as important to establish distance since she presumed the authority of intimacy in her Southern heritage (164). In *Mules and Men*, Hurston insists that her Southernness gave her a natural authority, while her education gave her an earned authority to speak in ways that other intellectuals could not:

> When I pitched headforemost into the world I landed in the crib of negroism. From the earliest rocking of my cradle, I had known about the capers Brer Rabbit is apt to cut and what the Squinch Owl says from the house top. But it was fitting me like a tight chemise. I couldn't see it for wearing it. It was only when I was off in college, away from my native surroundings, that I could see myself like somebody else and stand off and look at my garment. Then I had to have the spy-glass of Anthropology to look through at. (1)

Among the next generation of writers, Richard Wright posited his vision of the nightmare of the South over and against the inauthentic and whitened voices of the Harlem Renaissance. The South, then, became a contested terrain in the imagination of intellectuals in the first decades of the twentieth century—who could speak authentically for the Southern black, and why? It also became a spiritual geography through which some African American intellectuals could assert the essential unity of the racial experience and, as a corollary, could assert their essential connection with the people.

For Du Bois, the pilgrimage into the backwoods and hamlets of Tennessee is one means of demonstrating that he is—despite the differences of education, class, familial history, and geography—bone of the bone and flesh of the flesh with the people he seeks to lead. Du Bois's pilgrimage narrative is one of the most powerful in establishing the trope of Southern immersion as essential to the black experience. Nevertheless, his is also a journey that demonstrates both carefully calibrated intimacy and clearly defined distance. While Du Bois is immersed in the South throughout the scene, he is clearly not buried in or absorbed by it, and the most significant and obvious wall of separation is that of religious experience and practice. Du Bois is in the midst of black worship but also remains firmly outside the absorbing ecstatic frenzy of the masses. While his rhetoric early in the chapter is eloquent and literary rather than the cool and objectifying analysis of academic sociology, he maintains a posture of distance and observation rather than participation.

> It was out in the country, far from home, far from my foster home, on a dark Sunday night. The road wandered from our rambling log-house up the stony bed of a creek, past wheat and corn, until we could hear dimly across the fields a rhythmic cadence of song—soft thrilling, powerful, that swelled and died sorrowfully in our ears. I was a country school-teacher then, fresh from the East, and had never seen a Southern Negro revival. To be sure, we in Berkshire were not perhaps as stiff and formal as they in Suffolk of olden time; yet we were very quiet and subdued, and I know not what would have happened those clear Sabbath mornings had someone punctuated the sermon with a wild scream, or interrupted the long prayer with a loud Amen! And so most striking to me, as I approached the village and the little plain church perched aloft, was the air of intense excitement that possessed that mass of black folk. A sort of suppressed terror hung in the air and seemed to seize us—a pythian madness, a demoniac possession, that lent terrible reality to song and word. The black and massive form of the preacher swayed and quivered as the words crowded to his lips and flew at us in singular eloquence. The people moaned and fluttered, and then the gaunt-cheeked brown woman beside me suddenly leaped straight into the air and shrieked like a lost soul, while round about came wail and groan and outcry, and a scene of human passion such as I had never conceived before. (119–20)

Du Bois's narrative negotiates the distance between his own experience and history and that of this paradigmatic, even stereotypical, scene of black life. He is in the country, "far from home." At the same time, the autobiographical narrative itself establishes a form of familiarity and intimacy, one that lends him authority to speak about the scene even without complete identification. Du Bois qualifies the fact that he is far from home by saying he is far from his "foster home." The substitution obscures Du Bois's point of origin, even, metaphorically, his parentage. Du Bois may be referring either to the home where he lived while at Fisk or to his home in the East, but either home would be inadequate or inauthentic. The journey to the plain church in the wilderness becomes a journey toward mythic origins, toward an authentic home.

However, if Du Bois is on a pilgrimage toward origins, his representation of both himself and the home he finds continues to establish both intimacy and distance. If he questions the authenticity of his foster home, he also doesn't abandon it to the ecstasies of Southern black worship. While he says that the group had been seized by terror, by a pythian madness, Du Bois himself is never seized by this madness. The narrative presents Du Bois as the master of the moment rather than a participant in it. The scene is remarkable for being inarticulate, characterized by music, groans, shrieking, and outcries, all of which are narrated in prose that is cool and calibrated without being academic, an aesthetic choice that establishes Du Bois's connection to the scene while sustaining distance from it.

To some degree, this problem with narrative choices, tone, and approach reflects common tensions within the newly developing social sciences such as sociology—a still new field of which Du Bois was a leading light—and especially modern anthropology as practiced by Franz Boas and others. Just how much of an observer and how much of a participant should one be in developing valid intellectual knowledge about a people? The difficulties of this question and its impact on the development of modernism has been analyzed comprehensively in different ways by Susan Hegemen and by Marc Manganaro, and the issue is widely discussed in the scholarship on Zora Neale Hurston especially. This dynamic is effectively summarized by Daphne Lamothe in her analysis of the ways in which black social scientists took on the complicated and sometimes unmanageable mantle of being both insiders and outsiders to the communities they investigated. For Lamothe,

> Ethnographic discourse may have had its rhetorical place, but it also had its pitfalls because it emphasized the Black intellectual's position of superiority and detachment in relation to people who suffered the same political disenfranchisement as they and to whom they thus felt politically and culturally allied. African American documenters of Black culture were in the position to demonstrate both detachment from the culture and an authentic identification with it. (15)

Although I have reservations about Lamothe's tendency to envision African American social scientists of the period as postmodernists before their time, as well as her tendency to assume racial solidarity as a given rather than a constructed artifact in the work of people like Du Bois and Hurston, her description of the fundamental problem of being both insider and outsider, both intimate with and distant from an envisioned nation of followers, is spot on.

In *The Souls of Black Folk*, the screws of this dilemma are turned tighter yet by the complicated nature and multiple purposes of the book. *The Souls of Black Folk*, and especially the chapter "Faith of the Fathers," is not a straightforwardly sociological or even ethnographic study seeking to establish valid intellectual discourse about African American culture—although part of the power of the book is that it does that and sets a frame for many further contributions of such work. It is also an autobiographical narrative seeking to establish certain truths about Du Bois himself in the public mind. This autobiographical element gives the book a doubled nature that is part of its productive tension. By way of a brief comparison, one could look at a book published in the same year as *Souls*, Du Bois's nearly forgotten sociological study of black religion, *The Negro Church*. That work is, in every respect, a straightforward, largely empirical, sociological study of similar themes and issues as those taken up in *The Souls of Black Folk*. Du Bois evinces no concerns with his positioning vis-à-vis the subject of his inquiry and occupies the typical role of objective observer surveying data from on high. The Negro Church—its social structure and status—is the object of study and concern. By comparison, in *The Souls of Black Folk*, the status of W. E. B. Du Bois and the validity of his connection to black religion is one of many motivating objects of study and concern. If a Northern black intellectual sought to establish an authentic voice of leadership by speaking of his intimate knowledge of the South, and if religious ecstasy was a singularly defining feature of black life in the South, how to negotiate this gap in spiritual sensibilities?

Du Bois attacks this problem in different ways, but chief among them is a focus on the sounds rather than the words or ideologies or beliefs of black Christianity, as well as on his own status as an interpreter of the meaning of the sounds of culture. Music, as opposed to the language of the preacher or the church more generally, enables Du Bois to negotiate the distance between his own intellectual predilections and religious fervor. When Du Bois suggests that the three fundamental expressions of black religious spirit are "the Preacher, the Music and the Frenzy" (120), the parallel syntax suggests equality among the three. However, Music is clearly preeminent. By

comparison, the Frenzy and the Preacher are treated at best only ambiva-
lently and often seem to be targeted in ways that Booker T. Washington and
others are challenged in other parts of *The Souls of Black Folk*. The long
passage I quoted above is riven with the tension of attraction and repul-
sion, divided between music, which attracts, and other oral expressions that
repel: the haunting melodies of the sorrow songs at a distance set against
the shrieking and preaching of all-too-embodied black country folk. The
music draws the narrator "home" to the site of racial authenticity. While
music attracts and thrills him, it is the gaunt-cheeked woman beside him
who leaps suddenly to her feet and shrieks; it is the people round about him
who "wail and groan and outcry" in a way that he fears may be humorous
or embarrassing. At a distance from the actual embodiment of black worship, black music is the carrier of spirit that is thrilling and powerful. But
when actually felt and experienced within the social context of the worship
itself, the scene becomes awful, characterized by the shrieking of a woman
whose ecstasies are akin to the madness of the Delphic Oracle. Du Bois goes
so far as to say that his own representations appear grotesque and funny.
Yet only two things appear grotesque or funny, the Preacher and the Frenzy,
whereas the Music is the "one true expression of a people's sorrow, despair,
and hope" (120).

Troubling over how to understand "The Frenzy," Du Bois interprets black
worship as a latter-day manifestation of Greek mystery religions—or at least
in the same spirit as those religions. This interpretive move both universal-
izes black religious experience and locates it within a narrative of historical
progress. On the one hand, understanding black religion through Greek
categories lends this Frenzy cultural prestige; at the same time, atavistic
frenzy is superseded by the reflective intellect of the modern man. Of deep
concern to Du Bois and other intellectuals of the period was whether the
irrationality they found inherent in religion retarded racial development,
whatever positive role it may have played in the survival of white oppression. Du Bois's association of black worship with Delphi both honors and
displaces black faith, placing it within a universalizing human history while
transcending it through a narrative of enlightenment by which that very
history leaves the frenzy of Delphi for greater things.[4] The ravings of the
Delphic Oracle are hardly the image of rational and scientific inquiry that
Du Bois spent his early career pursuing and which he continued to pursue
by simultaneously writing treatises like *The Negro Church*. Nor was the
Delphic Oracle the image of the educated talented tenth that he was promoting. However, just as the oracle required recorders and interpreters, so
too did the ecstasies of black faith represented in that log church require a
translator and spokesperson, a role Du Bois was prepared to fulfill.

It is worth a brief excursus at this point to note that in Du Bois's rendering the Frenzy is specifically associated with women—the woman who rises shrieking beside him, the raving Delphic oracle, the witch of Endor. Despite Du Bois's depiction of the preacher as a man at the "centre of a group men" (120), in some respects it seems much more clearly the case that the preacher is a man at the center of a group of women. Moreover, the references cast religious experience in a specifically gendered mode by which the irrationality of the Frenzy—however powerful it may be—is associated with and dominated by women whose presence may diminish the men who rely upon them.

To some degree, this depiction could merely be rendering a sociological reality in that multiple studies documented the predominance of women in the pew, contributing to the general concern at the turn of the twentieth century that religion had been "feminized."[5] This depiction of the Frenzy as feminine, or at least woman-centered, became a trope of Harlem Renaissance writing in years to come. In *Along This Way*, James Weldon Johnson recalls the ring shouts of his childhood as the particular obsession of his Aunt Venie and his great-grandmother Sarah (22). Kabnis's unsettled reaction to the ecstatic worship of women is a sign of his alienation from Southern black experience in Jean Toomer's *Cane*. And, in perhaps the most startling depiction of religious ecstasy to come out of the Renaissance, Nella Larsen depicts the false conversion of Helga Crane as compelled and accompanied by the overwhelming ecstasies of women:

> For a single moment she remained there in silent stillness, because she was afraid she was going to be sick. And in that moment she was lost—or saved. The yelling figures about her pressed forward, closing her in on all sides. Maddened, she grasped at the railing, and with no previous intention began to yell like one insane, drowning every other clamor, while torrents of tears streamed down her face. She was unconscious of the words she uttered, or their meaning: "Oh God, mercy, mercy. Have mercy on me!" but she repeated them over and over.
>
> From those about her came a thunder-clap of joy. Arms were stretched toward her with savage frenzy. The women dragged themselves upon their knees or crawled over the floor like reptiles, sobbing and pulling their hair and tearing off their clothing. Those who succeeded in getting near to her leaned forward to encourage the unfortunate sister, dropping hot tears and beads of sweat upon her bare arms and neck. (113–14)

The meaning of such moments of Frenzy in African American literature of this period varies from text to text and author to author. For Larsen, it becomes a signature of the psychological abuse women suffer under patriarchy. For both Johnson and Toomer, the Frenzy signifies an uncanny otherness that is passing away but nevertheless registers a palpable cultural loss. For Du Bois, the association of the traditional black religion with feminine frenzy is a sign of its instability or at least a sign of the weakness of the preachers in the church who do so little to channel it to positive good. Du Bois's association of black worship with the story of Endor points toward this failure. In the biblical story of the witch of Endor, King Saul of Israel has been abandoned by God and cut off from his prophets. While fighting against both the Philistines and God's anointed successor, David, Saul must seek wisdom from "a woman that hath a familiar spirit at Endor" (I Samuel 28.7). This signifies his failed leadership; the LORD has departed and now rests upon David as the true leader of the people.

There is, then, a strong if subtle critique of both the Frenzy and the Preacher rather than a straightforward ethnographic analysis of their role in African American culture. Just as the spiritualism of Endor or the frenzy of Delphi decentered Hebrew and Greek men and even exposed their failed leadership, the presence of the preacher in the midst of this African American Christian frenzy diminishes his authority, particularly among the cultural elite to whom Du Bois's work is mostly addressed. In Du Bois's rendering, distinguishing the preacher from the shrieking woman at Du Bois's side is difficult. The preacher is said to have a "singular eloquence" even while we cannot actually hear the preacher's words. Indeed, Du Bois's particular interest in the role of effective communication underscores the silence to which the preacher is relegated. Rather than eloquence, what we primarily experience is the preacher's physicality. He is a "black and massive form" that sways and quivers and whose words seem less eloquent than spewing as they "crowded onto his lips and flew at us" (120). He is more like the Delphic oracle or the shrieking woman beside Du Bois than the effective communicator of that life. The preacher stands out only a bit from the moaning and crying of the people around him, his preaching a variation on the general pythian madness. Indeed, the preacher maintains his preeminence not by being a true expression of the people—as the music is—but by having "a certain adroitness with deep-seated earnestness, of tact with consummate ability" (120). While the preacher is not depicted as a charlatan, he is situated where he is because of his political maneuvering and his rhetorical skills, not because he incarnates the spirit of the people.

Thus, despite Du Bois's general tone of respect for and even identification with the people he is observing, his rhetoric and imagery create both distancing and displacement. He certainly does not aspire to be the man at the center of *this* particular group of women, and he remains strategically aloof from the Frenzy itself: he does not represent himself as frenzied like the preacher of his story but as observing the frenzy of others. This displacement is reemphasized as Du Bois develops a historical narrative in which the preacher is cast as a leader, but a leader whose time is surely past. Du Bois suggests that the preachers have abandoned the strong forefathers of ages past, a virile ancestry in which Du Bois locates racial authenticity. The truest spirit of the souls of black folk is located in the leaders of slave revolts prior to the Civil War, indeed, even further back, to the earliest moments of African experience on the shores of the Americas. By contrast, the black preacher is complicit in the continued suffering of African peoples:

> In spite, however, of the success as that of the fierce Maroons, the Danish blacks, and others, the spirit of revolt gradually died away under the untiring energy and superior strength of the slave masters. . . . Nothing suited his condition then better than the doctrines of passive submission embodied in the newly learned Christianity. Slave masters early realized this, and cheerfully aided religious propaganda within certain bounds. The long system of repression and degradation of the Negro tended to emphasize the elements in his character which made him a valuable chattel: courtesy became humility, moral strength degenerated into submission, and the exquisite native appreciation of the beautiful became and infinite capacity for dumb suffering. The Negro, losing the joy of this world, eagerly seized upon the offered conceptions of the next; the avenging Spirit of the Lord enjoining patience in this world under sorrow and tribulation until the Great Day when He should lead His dark children home, —this became his comforting dream. His preacher repeated the prophecy, and his bards sang, — "Children, we all shall be free / When the Lord shall appear!" (125)

Christianity reinforces the superiority of the slave masters and diminishes the masculinity of the enslaved. The true manifestation of Negro spirit died away and Christian leaders merely repeat tired phrases that anticipate an otherworldly freedom. The quietism of the Invisible Institution and the Negro church that Du Bois narrates here has long been a subject of hot debate, though most scholars would now agree with Hans Baer and Merill Singer that the history of black religions in America has been a continuous combination of both accommodation and protest and that it has been characterized by a stunning degree of diversity not easily captured in the singular phrase "The Black Church." Even while Du Bois did not have the benefit of studies by Genovese, Raboteau, or Wilmore, he was surely cognizant of the long history of protest in black Christianity, both among the slaves and in the free Negro churches. Indeed, Dorrien's study makes clear that in the late nineteenth and early twentieth centuries, Du Bois was intimately involved with the pioneers of the black social gospel that linked Christian faith to the quest for social and political progress. All of these factors point to Du Bois constructing a narrative of leadership rather than giving a straightforward historical or sociological account of the relationship of Christian faith to social progress.

Central to his narrative is the effort to decenter the abstract figure of Christianity itself, embodied in the narrative by the male preacher and the shrieking woman. Du Bois, by contrast, calls the people back to an original purity characterized by strong and resisting men and by civilized women. Du Bois concludes his narrative by giving the preacher the only words he is allowed to speak throughout the essay, words from a spiritual that encourage quietism and otherworldliness. These "virtues" suggest impotence: "fatalism," a "lax moral life," and "laziness" (125). Indeed, the words of quietism are the last words that we hear from the preacher at all. The "dumb suffering" of the people calls for a voice of protest, but no such voice is forthcoming. As the passage continues, Du Bois recognizes a brief upsurge of activism during the abolitionist movement. These words of rebellion are not spoken by the preacher and the bards, as in the earlier formulation, but by the bards alone, poets like himself who encourage the people to rebellion:

> "O Freedom, O Freedom, O Freedom over me!
> Before I'll be a slave
> I'll be buried in my grave,
> And go home to my Lord
> And be free." (126)

While this sentiment retains the flavor of otherworldliness common to many of the spirituals, it is an otherworldliness attained through resistance and a refusal to be dominated rather than by the passive resignation of the preachers. In bringing his narrative up to the present, Du Bois makes clear that the churches and their preaching embody admirable characteristics, but these characteristics must themselves be transcended in the souls of black folk; indeed, in some respects they lie very far from the truest foundations of the people's spirit and their spiritual strivings:

> Between the two extreme types of ethical attitude which I have thus sought to make clear wavers the mass of the millions of Negroes, North and South; and their religious life and activity partake of this social conflict within their ranks. Their churches are differentiating, —now into groups of cold, fashionable devotees, in no way distinguishable from similar white groups save in color of skin; now into large social and business institutions catering to the desire for information and amusement of their members, warily avoiding unpleasant questions both within and without the black world, and preaching in effect if not in word: *Dum vivimus, vivamus.* (129)

By the end of this essay, Du Bois has enacted not simply a historical analysis or survey of black faith or even a history of the faith of the fathers but also an increasingly straightforward critique of black religion. At the end of the passage quoted above, Du Bois invokes a preacher who speaks not in his own words or the words of his religion. His mouth utters Du Bois's Latin substitution: While we live, let us live. According to Du Bois, despite their massive popular appeal, the churches and their preachers are self-indulgent, encourage the worst vices of the people, and have strayed far from the deepest spirit of the people they are supposedly leading.

SONG AND HYMNS AND SECULAR PSALMS:
MUSIC AND THE PROMISE OF RACIAL UNITY

Du Bois's distance from both The Frenzy and The Preacher ironically positions him as the true inheritor and articulator of the spirits of the people, a rhetorical move he achieves throughout *Souls of Black Folk* by allegiance to the third element of his trinity: The Music. By turning to music, Du Bois embraces black religious spirit as an essentially aesthetic object, a work of art that transports the people into unity beyond the specific differences of creed and practice. This effort to separate the spiritual vitality of music from the primitive crust of religious frenzy characterized much of Du Bois's later consideration of African American culture and religion. Paul Allen Anderson notes that this kind of division is central to Du Bois's arguments about the role of orchestrated versions of the "sorrow songs" performed by singing groups from Hampton or Fisk. Anderson notes that in a conflict in 1933 with the *New York Times* critic Olin Downes, Du Bois argued forcefully against Downes's assumption that hymns and spirituals as sung in a traditional revival setting were more authentic and powerful than the artistic renderings by the Fisk University Choir:

> Insulted by Downes's comments, du Bois wrote in the NAACP journal, *The Crisis*, that what Downes's assessment "really means is that Negroes must not be allowed to attempt anything more than the frenzy of the primitive religious revival. "Listen to the Lambs" according to Dett, or "Deep River," as translated by Burleigh, or any attempt to sing Italian music or German, in some inexplicable manner, lead them off their preserves and is not "natural." To which the answer is, Art is not natural and is not supposed to be natural. And just because it is not natural, it may be great Art. The Negro chorus has a right to sing music of any sort it likes and to be judged by its accomplishment rather than what foolish critics think that it ought to be doing. (15)

I am not interested in resolving the question of who was right in this quarrel, except to note that Du Bois is surely correct that the tactic of locating "authentic" black cultural expression in a form of primitivism is very often only a false form of cultural appreciation that reinscribes white privilege. What is more fascinating is the consistency in Du Bois's views of black religious music and black religious worship between 1903 and 1933. For Du Bois, what is most authentically artistic and even racial about black religion is its music, which can be decoupled from the social context in which it has been historically and even normatively produced. That normative location is itself barely historical at all, being characterized by the term Frenzy, which is—especially in the formulation of 1933—very nearly subhuman precisely because it is so natural. The Frenzy does not rise to the level of human culture precisely because it does not employ the more considered artifice of artistic creation.

Anderson notes that Du Bois used the sorrow songs—and especially their reproduction in the context of Fisk University Singer art songs—as a means to "underwrite his inheritance claims on the imagined homogeneity or 'unisonance' of black national memory" (29). In other words, racial/national identity rested primarily on a process of reproducing black Christian spiritual forms as black aesthetic forms that were, at least in principle, available to all. I will add the specific and crucial note that in order to imagine this homogeneity, Du Bois first had to render song as sound without language thereby to dispense with the ideology that language inevitably carries. Such an aesthetic effort to establish racial solidarity beyond language erased the specific difference in his own experience—the distance he felt from the Christian faith from which the sorrow songs initially sprang.

One of the remarkable elements of Du Bois's use of the sorrow songs throughout *Souls* is the tendency to invoke only the music and to make minimal if any reference to the lyrics. For Sundquist, this pattern is a clever means of creating a kind of insider status for the community of black readers, as presumably only those who knew the tunes would be able to embrace the music.

> The bars of music posed a pointed challenge to their contemporary audience, for they demanded a familiarity with a cultural language that most whites did not have and that an increasing number of middle-class blacks renounced as an unhealthy reminder of slavery. . . . Hidden within the veil of black life, the music and words of the sorrow songs form a hidden, coded language in *The Souls of Black Folk*, one that recapitulates the original cultural function of the spirituals themselves. (470)

Although I find Sundquist's argument intriguing, to believe this one has to believe that the great majority of Du Bois's readers—black or white—had the ability to sight-read musical notation, a fact that I would be willing to grant but for which Sundquist provides no substantiation. In fact, reading musical notation is a learned skill far less common than reading prose. In general, the average reader will call a tune to mind by seeing words rather than by reading music.

This is the music Du Bois chose to place at the head of the essay "Of Alexander Crummell."[6] Perhaps some people can immediately recognize the tune they see above, but more will recognize the tune when they hear the words "Swing Low, Sweet Chariot." Whether Du Bois intended to create an "insider" community of readers, the decision to leave out the words comports with the general tendency of *The Souls of Black Folk* to quiet the social and cultural setting with which many of the sorrow songs would otherwise be associated: Christianity. The displacement grants room for Du Bois to articulate a newer vision for the twentieth century and to position himself as the true patriarch of the black racial family.

Indeed, when Du Bois does offer the ultimate example of black musical feeling, he embraces a song of ancient Africa that neither he nor his readers can understand, the song sung to his forefathers by his great-great-grandmother. The substance of this song is fundamentally less important than its role in establishing Du Bois as a true inheritor of the spirit of the African motherland. As he says, he knows "as little as our fathers what its words may mean, but [know] well the meaning of its music" (539). Because for Du Bois "the music is far more ancient than the words, and in it we can trace here and there signs of development" (538), knowing the music is a means to racial authenticity that supersedes the use of language. As it develops in the rhetoric of the essay, the words and the music have far less import than the occasion for telling the story of the song. The words are unintelligible to American readers, and the music—written in the difficult key of D flat—is difficult to read as well. What is most memorable about the passage is the tale of its singing:

> My grandfather's grandmother was seized by an evil Dutch trader two centuries ago; and coming to the valleys of the Hudson and Housatonic, black, little, and lithe, she shivered and shrank in the harsh north winds, looking longingly at the hills, and often crooned a heathen melody to the child between her knees, thus:

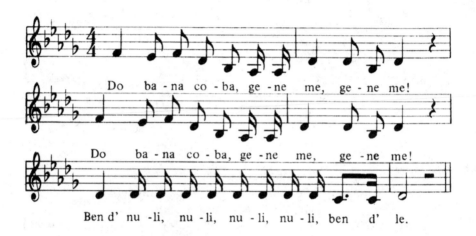

> The child sang it to his children and they to their children's children, and so two hundred years it has traveled down to us and we sing it to our children, knowing as little as our fathers what its words may mean, but knowing well the meaning of its music.[7] (157)

Lamothe also notes the peculiar relationships between sound and language in Du Bois's work. For Lamothe this alliance is primarily a means of reducing masculine privilege rather than enhancing it:

> It is not coincidental that Du Bois so often recounts musical expression emanating from women like his great-great grandmother or the "girl-women" from Fisk, for femininity and emotion are typically linked in patriarchal discourse. Yet at the same time that Du Bois articulates the black male subject's aspiring toward full masculinity through mastery of language . . . , he also problematizes the binary by calling into question the power and authority typically located in language (hence, reason). . . . Du Bois's turn to an artistic, emotive, non-linguistic, and vernacular tradition at these moments suggests the limits of the ethnography and historiography practiced elsewhere in the

volume. Musical soundings, in other words, must do the expressive work
that language fails to achieve. (60)

Although I agree that the emphasis on sound decenters some language, it
is important to note that it hardly decenters all language. Indeed, as my
own reading suggests, the sounds of black worship that Du Bois represents
throughout the text are completely fenced around with language, the language of the text itself through which Du Bois establishes his own mastery.
The only decentered languages are those potentially representing forms of
blackness to which Du Bois is not easily assimilated—that of black folk
religion, that of an ancient African slave.

The story of inheritance in "Of the Sorrow Songs" reveals a Du Bois who
will be best known by the readers not as a musicologist but as someone
whose authority rests on the line of inheritance he here describes. As both
Clare Corbould and Wilson Moses point out in their different ways, laying
claim to Africa and an African inheritance became an important cultural
trope and political pursuit among African Americans in the 1880s through
to the Harlem Renaissance and was perhaps at its height during the period
of Du Bois's coming of age as a scholar at the turn of the century. The figure
of African grandmother allows him to develop a story of racial authenticity
that extends beyond the accidental differences of history and ideological
beliefs into a mythic and nearly timeless African past that exists as an essence, not unlike race itself in the racial ideologies of the period. His ancient
grandmother is metaphorically Africa herself. She is also a female muse who
gifts with language those sons who are most worthy of her blessings. Like
a Black Madonna cradling a Du Bois hidden in the flesh of his long dead
grandfathers, this grandmother establishes Du Bois as the truest inheritor
of her words and spirit. Nevertheless, she structurally inhabits a linguistic
position not terribly different from that of the shrieking devotee or the
Delphic oracle in "Of the Faith of the Fathers." She, like they, cannot speak
for herself but requires an interpreter who, through his act of interpretation,
establishes his superiority to the Frenzy of worship and the claims of the
Preacher, situating himself as the authentic inheritor of an African essence
represented in his ancient grandmother.

To be sure, Du Bois treats the ancient female figure and her song with
even greater sympathy than the wordless sorrow songs. In comparison to
the "heathen melody," the sorrow songs themselves are "naturally veiled
and half-articulate. Words and music have lost each other and new and cant
phrases of a dimly understood theology have displaced the older sentiment.
Once in a while we catch a strange world of an unknown tongue" (159). By

linking the primitive and heathen melodies with his great-great-grandmother, Du Bois associates himself with an original purity that has been lost to the language that the majority of black American Christians were then speaking. On the basis of this purity, Du Bois positions himself as both worthy son and fatherly patriarch. He inherits a mythic station of fatherhood, passing on spirituals received from his father. Du Bois places himself as the inheritor of songs of hope and as the disseminator of hope to future generations.

> Even so is the hope that sang in the songs of my father well sung. If some-where in this whirl and chaos of things there dwells Eternal Good, pitiful yet masterful, then anon in His good time America shall rend the Veil and the prisoned shall go free. Free, free as the sunshine trickling down the morning into these high windows of mine, free as yonder fresh young voices welling up to me from the caverns of brick and mortar below—swelling with song, instinct with life, tremulous treble and darkening bass. My children, my little children, are singing to the sunshine, and thus they sing: "Let us cheer the weary traveler, / Cheer the weary traveler, / Let us cheer the weary traveler / Along the heavenly way." (163)[8]

On one level, Du Bois may be referring to his own children playing some-where in the house below. However, his children surely also represent the African peoples of America, singing a time-honored spiritual. One thinks here as well of the rhetorical convention of African American sermons whereby the preacher beseeches his congregation by addressing them as "My children." By portraying himself as fatherly, and as the preacher of a newer religion, Du Bois completes a reorganization of the patriarchal imaginary begun with "Of the Faith of the Fathers." In that chapter, he establishes the need for a true inheritor of and guide for the people's spirit. In "Of the Com-ing of John," which I will discuss more fully in a later chapter, he positions his allegorical representative as the avatar of black rebellion. In "The Sorrow Songs," Du Bois sees himself as the founder of a home. In "Of the Faith of the Fathers," he is metaphorically homeless, attracted to but distant from the patriarchal figures of black faith. By the end of "The Sorrow Songs," he has become the patriarch of a new faith, hearing "his children" play-ing joyfully in the home he has built for them. Using the rhetoric of faith, Du Bois gives birth to a new self, now not as a foster child far from home but as the father of a people, a man at the center.

Before leaving this chapter, a short coda returning to the question of Du Bois's response to black belief and the structure of his own systems of belief may be valuable, if only because of the immense influence he personally retained throughout the Harlem Renaissance and because of the framing influence *The Souls of Black Folk* exercised on the Renaissance and has continued to exercise to the present. Manning Marable, as I noted above, suggests that Du Bois's religious views are best characterized as a "spiritual identification with . . . black faith" (31). In Marable's development of this notion, and certainly as an implication of my own argument, it is not much of a stretch to say that whatever faith Du Bois had or did not have in the Christian God, he very much had a form of faith in blackness itself and developed this faith as a means of redressing the depredations of white supremacy in the United States and beyond. In his book *Beyond Ontological Blackness*, Victor Anderson points out that there is "a close connection between ontological blackness and religion:"

> Ontological blackness signifies the totality of black existence, a binding together of black life and experience. In its root, *religio*, religion denotes tying together, fastening behind, and binding together. Ontological blackness renders black life and experience a totality. It is a totality that takes narrative formations that emphasize the heroic capacities of African Americans to transcend individuality and personality in the name of black communal survival. (14–15)

As I have suggested, Du Bois had to realize or construct this vision of essential black solidarity in *The Souls of Black Folk* through a narrative that both honors and displaces central forms of black social experience—especially the experience of the Christian religion. This displacement is achieved through a form of aesthetic practice by which religion becomes the occasion for Art, which requires an artist *and* a critic but certainly not a preacher. At once appreciation and displacement, this model of aesthetic practice became one framework through which intellectuals and artists as diverse as Alain Locke, Zora Neale Hurston, and Langston Hughes negotiated their distance from the specifics of Christian beliefs. In this view, art not only sought to achieve recognition for African Americans in the eyes of white patrons, publishers, and other cultural mavens but also enabled a form of secular practice that might have otherwise threatened to divide African American intellectuals from the traditional center of black cultural practice. Art and aesthetics provided a bridge to both travel from and retain connections to the dominant Christian forms of cultural and social life in African America at the turn of the century.

"HE DIDN'T COME TO HELP ME"
Folk Paternity and Failed Conversions in Langston Hughes

In his important study of the use of the folk as a conceptual framework in the Harlem Renaissance, J. Martin Favor notes the contradictory ways in which writers use "the folk" to posit a form of authentic blackness that is at once essentialized in order to provide a ground for a unified black consciousness and performative so that the educated middle and upper middle classes could effectively write themselves into the race. The folk provided a necessary and apparently organic common ground, but that ground threatened to fissure the very racial narratives they enabled along the fault lines of class, educational, and, I would argue, religious differences. As Favor puts it in speaking of Du Bois, "In a series of conscious moves, DuBois writes himself into a folk positionality that lends authority to his explication of blackness in America. Yet 'race' must be, at least in some respects, performative rather than essential to make such a transformation possible" (12).

To put a different spin on this important insight, my last chapter argues that part of Du Bois's purpose in *The Souls of Black Folk* is to authenticate his own prerogatives of leadership. He does so in part by constructing a form of folk life for which he may be an authentic inheritor while establishing a kind of intimate distance from the forms of folk life that he has envisioned. The essence of the folk, in Du Bois's formulation, is freed from the constraints of Christian religion and its written dogma and is characterized instead by a wordless music. Du Bois's leadership is established both by his intimacy with the sounds of black life and by his notable ability to bring those sounds into a modern discursive frame. The language Du Bois deploys at once establishes his intimacy with and his superiority to the tradition he constructs—not least his superiority to the specifics of black religious faith as embodied in the preacher and his female acolytes.

Although many writers of the Harlem Renaissance disputed this and that about Du Bois's philosophy or took serious issue with his perceptions of the laboring masses, the basic structure of *The Souls of Black Folk* became, in many respects, a paradigmatic frame for other writers and intellectuals to write themselves into the race and to effectively negotiate a fraught relationship with the black church and its leadership. In case after case, writers developed pictures of what was essentially important about black experience, visions that sometimes varied significantly from Du Bois's own. They struggled to articulate that essence as it relates to black religious practice, and they established their own imaginative authority by positing various levels of intimacy and distance from the essences that they construct. Moreover, this simultaneous construction and decentering of black religious life was very often achieved not by direct argument and critique so much as by a form of aestheticization whereby religious life was turned into a form of aesthetic practice and therefore a precursor to the artistic life pursued by the aesthetic saviors of the race who came of age in the Harlem Renaissance.

Perhaps no poet disagreed more with Du Bois in his evaluation of the native worth of the laboring classes than did Langston Hughes. Not only did he dismiss the Victorian moral superiority that Du Bois located in the educated class, but he also came quite close to the romantic assertion that the native expression of the men and women in the streets was a form of poetry that needed no formal intervention. Nevertheless, reading Hughes through the lens of his gendered responses to African American Christianity suggests that Hughes, like Du Bois, navigated a tension with his relationship to significant parts of black culture. The specifics of this negotiation with the problem of black Christian faith are in some respects quite different, a difference that reflects his disputes with Du Bois. But no less than Du Bois does he need to articulate a form of African American life that exists comfortably apart from black faith, no less than Du Bois does he articulate that relationship in gendered terms, and no less does he attempt to find recourse in the power of aesthetics to narrate his own artistic and even political practice in terms that are continuous rather than straightforwardly confrontational with Christian belief. In this chapter, I will first look more deeply at the notion of the folk as it developed in the period and especially how Hughes both posited himself and was posited by others as voice of the folk. Second, I will look closely at the problem Christianity posed for Hughes and so the problem it posed for racial representation. Finally, I will look at the resolution that Hughes attempts in trying to become the voice of the people, a resolution that was ultimately only partially successful as Hughes sought ways to represent himself not as the vanguard of the people but as a voice in their midst.

THE VOICE OF THE PEOPLE:
LANGSTON HUGHES'S IMMERSIVE POSE

No poet did more to create the image of the folk and situate them in aesthetic discourse among African Americans than Hughes, who is regularly taken, even in contemporary assessments, as the common man's most steadfast and persistent voice. Certainly in his own day—and until quite recently—there was no more widely accepted dictum than that which defined Langston Hughes's poetry as springing from the depth and singularity of his attachment to what he called the "low-down" Negro: the poor, the working class, the common, the marginally educated. His attachment, in short, to that secular congregation called "the folk." This view was, in part, created by early reviewers seeing in black writers the voice of collectives rather than of individuals. But it was also cultivated by Hughes himself, as his various autobiographical self-portraits make clear.

Hughes opens his autobiography, *The Big Sea*, with the startling image of throwing his library into the sea, an act Hughes clearly ties to his coming of age: "And I felt that nothing would ever happen to me again that I didn't want to happen. I felt grown, a man, inside and out. Twenty-one" (31). This image unsettles many readers because the destruction of books has typically been taken in Western cultural discourse as a sign of cultural ignorance at best, political repression at worst. At the same time, however, there is a strong strain of Romantic liberation that founds itself not in Enlightenment engagement with learning but precisely in freeing oneself from the dead weight of the past in favor of an allegiance to the truth of the present. American writers, especially, have resisted the notion that book learning is the best background for becoming a writer, with authors from Melville to Whitman to Sandburg to Hemingway insisting that vital writing came from encountering the school of life and not the school of schoolmen. In the Romantic tradition of Emerson or Wordsworth, Hughes identifies this destruction of his books as liberating because, as he puts it, "books had been happening to me" (31). The destruction of his library, characterized only by the title of one white patron of the arts, H. L. Mencken, signals a movement into adulthood and self-possession, into action and experience, away from the passivity of received (white) traditions. The destruction of his books, of course, opens an actual journey to Africa aboard a ship where he is immersed in the life of working class African and other Americans. However, first he recounts how his act of book destruction culminates what seems to be a lifelong struggle with books and book culture.

Much of the ensuing two-dozen pages describes Hughes's struggle for experience and his struggle with books. He was born, in several respects, into an African American literary culture. He describes theatre performances with his mother, which he mocked and sought to escape; his mother's publishing career and the history of a family whose members were book writers; his own required recitations of poems in church, a task he notably had refused to complete. He describes his connection to the poetry of Paul Laurence Dunbar and his attachment to the novels of Harold Bell Wright and Zane Grey (46). His mother introduced him to the library at the age of six, and Hughes comes to identify libraries as a source of both comfort and safety but also a source of conflicted allegiance: "[Even] before I was six, books began to happen to me, so that after a while, there came a time when I believed in books more than in people—which, of course, was wrong. That was why, when I went to Africa, I threw all the books into the sea" (46). Hughes opposes his love of books to his love of people and especially, in the repeated reference to Africa, to his love of black people. Books had become a distraction from a prior and more important allegiance.

As if to reemphasize the point, Hughes returns to this particular moment yet a third time at the conclusion of the first section of the autobiography, equating liberation from books and the culture they represent as the sign and symbol of his entrance into manhood. Books represented all the things he wanted to flee. "I wanted to be a man on my own, control my own life, and go my own way. I was twenty-one. So I threw the books in the sea" (94). The image of books as imprisoning or things that had to be escaped is somewhat peculiar for a man of letters and particularly for a writer who, by 1940, was surely viewed as *the* leading African American poetic voice of his generation. Certainly this opposition was at odds with dominant notes in the history of African American letters. For Frederick Douglass, books and reading are the signs and symbols of liberation and arrival into a full-bodied manhood—at least as important as his physical confrontation with his slave master—as they are for Olaudah Equiano and, in a different way, for Phyllis Wheatley. For Du Bois and for James Weldon Johnson, books formed one part of a utopian aspiration, and somewhat later, for Richard Wright, learning to read was a way of lifting himself out of the false consciousness of inferiority. As I shall point out later in this book, there is a tradition of anti-intellectualism among African Americans, as there is in American culture in general. But it is an unusual note to sound for one so obviously a part of the Harlem literati. Moreover, as Hughes portrays it, his attachment to books impeded his attachment with people, and his attachment to people is, by extension, his attachment to blackness. The journey aboard ship is pictured as a form of immersion in people—black people—and thus a story of immersion with the common folk that Hughes sought to repeat on multiple occasions in his autobiography, in his poetry, and throughout his life.

It's hard, of course, to know how much of this Hughes possibly knew when he threw his books into the sea at the age of twenty-one, looking back on the moment in 1940. However, it is fair to say that what I will call the "immersive pose" that Hughes strikes in this narrative actually had come to characterize his reception from the earliest day, a characterization that Hughes embraced and through which he found significant poetic power. His critics—both black and white—certainly felt this or found this in Hughes's earliest work and were remarkably consistent in their attribution of Hughes's poetic genius to a general racial voice rather than to any kind of literary inheritance or even to individual gift; indeed, the idea of a black literary inheritance seems to be hardly a part of the equation at all. What Hughes has inherited is the voice and culture of the underclass. In 1927, DuBose Heyward wrote of *Fine Clothes to the Jew*, "The outstanding contribution of the collection now under review is the portraiture of the author's own people. Langston Hughes knows his underworld. He divines the aspirations and the tragic frustrations of his own race, and the volume is a processional of his people given in brief, revealing glimpses" (8). Heyward continues by remarking on the "folk quality" of a number of the poems (9). Margaret Larkin, reviewing the same text, comments on the blues poems as "charming folk ballads" (10). This discourse in the early reviews culminates in Alain Locke's review of *Fine Clothes*:

> Here . . . there is scarcely a prosaic note or a spiritual sag in spite of the fact that never has cruder colloquialism or more sordid life been put into the substance of poetry. The book is, therefore, notable as an achievement in

poetic realism in addition to its particular value as a folk study in verse of
Negro life.

   The success of these poems owes much to the clever and apt device of taking folk-song forms and idioms as the mold into which the life of the plain
people is descriptively poured. This gives not only an authentic background
and the impression that it is the people themselves speaking, but the sordidness of common life is caught up in the lilt of its own poetry and without
any sentimental propping attains something of the necessary elevation of art.
("Common Clay" 115–116)

Taking Locke literally, Hughes is primarily a documentarian or aesthetic an-
thropologist guided by the effort to collect and preserve an archive. Hughes's
achievement in this view is his invisibility. His work is notable for realism,
for being a study, for being descriptive, for providing authentic background,
for letting the people speak for themselves. The sordidness of common life
is "its own poetry" rather than Hughes's creative intervention. It seemingly
attains the "necessary elevation of art" all by itself without any work by
the writer at all. Hughes dissipates, rendered into airy insubstantiality by
the cauldron of the folk idiom.

   These constructions of Hughes need, of course, to be viewed cautiously.
As Whalan points out, much of the critical temper of the period was driven
by the "Young American" movement with Waldo Frank at the vanguard.
But while Frank could envision himself as a cosmopolitan intellectual mar-
shaling all of the multicultural voices into an American whole, the general
expectation for African Americans like Hughes was that they retain and
represent an allegiance to their race alone (*Manhood* 154). They voiced
their race, in some respects. It was this kind of limitation that Du Bois had
railed against two decades earlier in insisting on his own cosmopolitan
vision of walking arm and arm with Aristotle or in his angry rejection of
those who hinted at the impropriety of turning spirituals into art songs.
However, Hughes himself invested in this link between voice and race. He
sought aesthetic power through identification with—and even submersion
in—what he perceived as folk forms and genres.

   Drawing on Raymond Williams, Whalan notes that genres are conventions
that speak by and to and through communities of discourse. For Whalan,
genre is

one of the most significant conventions within which... social relationships
exist in cultural production. Genres do have an important function in social
interaction and informal shared range of understanding about literary typol-
ogy within specific communities of readers and writers. Genre represents a

site of constant, and specific, negotiation—between author, text, and reader,
between expectations that exist around collective 'conventions' and individuals, between discourses and communicative forms. (17)

By tossing his books into the sea, Hughes signals something not only about
form but also about identity and about belonging, and specifically about
his identity and his mode of belonging to a people characterized by many
things but not primarily by books, especially not works of literature.

The largest issue here is not so much the accuracy of this view of Hughes's
poetic voice as the degree to which Hughes and other modern intellectuals create the conception of "the folk" to meet the needs of modern urban
people, as Hughes's constructs "the folk" in particular ways that reflect
his own needs, convictions, and predilections. That "folkishness" takes on
a quasi-religious status in cultural discourse is a well-established point in
discussions of nationalism that need not be developed fully here. George E.
Kent, in his study of Hughes and folk tradition, expresses this mystical
character aptly, if uncritically, when he says, "From the animal tales to the
hipsterish urban myth-making, folk tradition has is-ness. Things are" (17). In
this view, the essence of the folk is at once more concrete, real, and specific
than any particular individual. At the same time that essence is universal and
trans-historical. Rampersad's view is more circumspect and complicated,
suggesting that Hughes's attraction to the folk is at least partially due to his
sense of isolation from them, driven by the need to write himself into the
folk, as it were (22). Nevertheless, most readings tend to retain this view of
Hughes—that the folk simply are there to get in touch with, to rediscover,
to serve as a ground of being, or to serve as black poetic muse.

By contrast, Favor suggests that this givenness of the folk tradition should
be critically examined not to understand the structure of its metaphysical
qualities but to think through its deployment in discourse. Therefore, in
Hughes's work, the folk and their ways are as much a matter of invention
as they are of documentation. Even if we were to agree that Hughes is in
some measure an archivist of the folk voice, we must also admit that every
archive sculpts a great array of possibility, fashioning an interpretation if
only through the selection and arrangement of materials. "The folk" are always put into discourse rather than being a self-evident ground of discourse.
In this view, Kent is misguided in positing the folk as ground. Folk tradition
does not have is-ness; it is always constructed and performed, sometimes by
those who perceive themselves as folk and sometimes by those who wish
they were. Even Hughes's reviewers demonstrate the ways in which "the
folk" are framed differently by the different discursive and rhetorical needs

of those who turn to them. For Heyward, the essence of the folk is their tragic frustration; for Larkin, it is their charm; while, for Alain Locke, it is their sordidness—which, in an unfortunate turn of Locke's logic, seems to become the essence of the folk Negro. What needs to be understood, then, is not so much the ways in which Hughes speaks for the folk but the ways that the folk—as he creates them in his poetry and prose—speak for him.

SALVATION, SINNERS, AND SOCIAL DEATH: WRITING THE MASCULINE AND SECULAR FOLK

We could say, then, that ideas and images of the folk did not tell the working class or the rural poor about themselves so much as they participated in a contest to tell the cosmopolitan literary class what it meant to be a New Negro when all signs pointed to a gap or fissure between the literati and the working classes. In Hughes's summary of the New Negro Renaissance, after all, "The ordinary Negroes hadn't heard of the Negro Renaissance" (*Big Sea* 178). In some significant ways, this judgment on the Renaissance is continuous with Hughes's construction of the official culture of books and art throughout *The Big Sea*. As Favor points out, this effort to identify—and, in that sense, homogenize—African American experience was articulated through a narrative that imagined the folk as the clue to authentic blackness upon which African American aspiration had to be founded (1–14).

This struggle for identity is multiform, and discourses of religion and gender play a significant role. Favor notes that, with important exceptions such as Zora Neale Hurston, much writing coming out of the Renaissance defines the folk—whether rural or urban—as a repository of a virile masculinity opposed to the homogenizing and dissipating—that is "feminizing"—tendencies of modernity (16–18).[1] The difficulty of this structure is that the defining religion of the folk was primarily Christianity, which many cosmopolitan New Negroes regarded with varying degrees of intensity as inauthentic, politically ineffectual, or, following the gender hierarchies of the day, plainly effeminate. Christianity, in other words, obscured the virile folkishness through which they sought to define the essence of the New Negro, and perhaps even the essence of blackness itself.

This tension between the folk as virile ground of being and African Americans as inauthentic Christians is caught in the well-known narrative of Hughes's faux conversion in *The Big Sea*. In a short and funny section entitled "Salvation," Hughes recounts his first and only trip to the altar to experience salvation during a revival meeting at his aunt's church. Mary and James Reed, with whom Hughes lived after the death of his grandmother, were working-class folks whom Hughes loved enthusiastically. James Reed

was, by Hughes account, "a sinner." Mary Reed was officially Methodist Episcopal, but regularly attended Warren Street Baptist Church, which
Rampersad describes as more "down-home" than St. Luke's Methodist Episcopal (16). In short, living with his aunt, Hughes was temporarily raised
in a religious atmosphere that represented the gamut of African American
Christianity. Moreover, his childhood religious life reflected the diverse and
even contradictory social framework that he would negotiate as a mature
poet: proper Christian domesticity dominated by powerful women and
buttoned-down men, bluesman sinners who are the repository of wisdom,
and down-home Christian shouters whom Hughes finds compelling despite
his inability to believe what they believe.

While Hughes doesn't name the church in which he responded to the
altar call, the depiction of the worship verges toward the ecstatic experiences broadly common to revivalist Protestantism and fairly typical of a
"down-home" church like Warren Street Baptist. His humorous account of
salvation opens with three difficult-to-reconcile statements that otherwise
appear to announce a straightforward anecdote. "I was saved from sin when
I was going on thirteen. But not really saved. It happened like this" (41). The
opening statements give with the one hand but take back with the other.
Saved from sin. But not really. The sentences cloud the following statement
"It happened like this," because we can no longer be certain of what exactly
"it" is, nor can we read the narrative that follows with certainty that what
we are reading is really happening, having been told that the story is, in
some way, not real, after all.

The narrative that follows opens a gap between expectation and fulfillment, between public interpretation and private experience, and ultimately
between the people whom Hughes loves and Hughes himself. The adolescent
Hughes arrives at the meeting fervently expecting in some literal and childlike fashion to see Jesus; indeed, the innocence of this expectation adds to the
charm and humor of the passage for readers familiar with the conventions
of the revival meeting since "seeing" Jesus is ultimately a matter of inward
sight and, even more, a matter of having oneself seen by others by responding
to the call to get up, come to the altar, and pray. Hughes's inability to see
Jesus, however, prevents him from responding to the preacher's invitation
or to the prayers of the women and old men who surround him. "I kept
waiting serenely for Jesus, waiting, waiting—but he didn't come. I wanted
to see him, but nothing happened to me. Nothing! I wanted something to
happen to me, but nothing happened" (42).

Unable to pass through to salvation and, in sociopsychological terms,
at risk of a kind of social death in being unable to meet the community's
insistent demands, Hughes attempts to close the public gap between his

unfulfilled expectations and the unfulfilled desire of the community. Looking to the front and seeing Westley, another mischievous pre-adolescent who had lied about his salvation in order to escape the attention of the old men and women, Hughes decides to act on what he sees, the evidence of his experience, and pretend to be saved:

> So I got up.
>   Suddenly the whole room broke into a sea of shouting as they saw me rise. Waves of rejoicing swept the place. Women leaped in the air. My aunt threw her arms around me. The minister took me by the hand and led me to the platform. (42)

The comedy of this passage springs again from the gap between contradictory interpretations of event; apparent connection—Hughes's conversion leading to full membership in the community—is in fact an even more emphatic disconnection. The humor here is the humor of experience, a knowingness that depends, on some level, on our laughing along with him at the congregation's ignorance of his duplicity. Whereas early descriptions of the revival vividly display a fervent religious life, emphasizing the "wonderful rhythmical sermon" of the preacher, the depictions of the congregation's joy at the conversion suggests a kind of judgment that, if not so harsh as Hughes's condemnations of the bourgeois church in other work, nevertheless points a finger at what he takes to be a lie, and a lie much more profound than Hughes's pragmatic attempt to escape the religious spotlight on the mourner's bench. If this duplicity could be true of Hughes, and if it could be true of Westley, could it not be true of everyone, and could we not dispense with the pretense after all?

The gap opened by disappointed religious expectations widens as the narrative concludes. Hughes cries in bed at night. His aunt believes that he has experienced the second blessing of the Holy Spirit while Hughes knows that he is crying over his inability to achieve the experience that would guarantee his social belonging. The disparity of interpretation points to a tremendous cultural gap, one that is metaphysical and not just linguistic in nature. A kind of conversion has occurred, but not the one that his aunt assumes. Rather, Hughes is converted firmly to the camp of Westley and his "rounder" father. Like them, Hughes is converted finally to unbelief because he "hadn't seen Jesus, and . . . I didn't believe there was a Jesus any more, since he didn't come to help me" (43).

Understanding the social and cultural work of autobiography in general, as well as its specific role in African American and religious life, may help illuminate the gravity of Hughes's failed conversion, a gravity somewhat covered over for nonreligious readers by the comedy that Hughes deploys.

Autobiography can be schematically divided into two forms. The dominant and most familiar form to Western readers focuses on the romantic individual as distinct from or even opposed to the larger social world from which the individual springs. But an older tradition—also thoroughly Western—which we can call Augustinian autobiography, represents individual experience as solidifying one's relationship to a larger social world or cosmic reality.[2] Augustinian autobiography is kindred in spirit to the testimony narratives common to different branches of the Christian church wherein an individual narrates his or her unique experience of a common and communal affirmation of the divine reality of salvation. To tell the story of salvation is not simply to affirm a unique relationship with God; it affirms a form of collective belonging through which the community is regenerated and perpetuated.

In African American autobiography of the early twentieth century, this tension between social belonging and individual desire manifests as a negotiation between the religious forms and expectations of sacred traditions and the individual desires of a writer's (most often) secular self. "Negotiation" is the appropriate term here since it is easy to fall into a stale opposition between church-going repression of the self and secular authentication of the individual. Such an opposition misses the ways in which religious forms themselves give shape to the individual self. The importance of the personal encounter with Jesus, the importance of the individual telling his or her own story, the need to step outside of more faceless social roles to take center stage—all of these portray a spirituality that emphasizes individual experience and individual authenticity over and against collective action. Indeed, some critics have argued that such an individualistic tendency is at the center of the Christian conversion narratives per se and so necessarily at the center of the Western autobiographical tradition. When Maxine Hong Kingston published her memoir, *The Woman Warrior*, Frank Chin accused Kingston of a kind of ethnic self-hatred that manifested in the form of the autobiography itself. Kingston had, Chin believed, declared herself a Christian by choosing to traffic in an individualistic form that traced its roots to Augustine. Kingston was choosing, according to Chin, individual salvation over her responsibility to her collective ethnic identity.

Nevertheless, reducing autobiography to individualism misses its status as a social and cultural form that meets a variety of social, not just individual, needs. To recall my note on Raymond Williams earlier in this chapter, genre depends on, deploys, and manipulates social codes, seeking at once to achieve recognition and create new possibilities. This complicated interaction between affirmative social purpose and individual assertion is found to varying degrees and in different ways throughout Western autobiography, and it is certainly at the center of the tradition of African American life writing. Peter Dorsey points out that despite the obsessively inward gaze of the Augustinian conversion narrative, the individualism and solitude it invokes are usually redirected both by iterating a conventional form and by the fact that individual conviction and conversion result in a call to religious and social vocation (1–43). That is, Augustinian inwardness ultimately serves the purpose of group belonging, social cohesion, and socialization because the stories of individual conversion follow recognizable narrative patterns that religious communities "read" and approve. Religious conversion resulted not in individual uniqueness so much as in a vocation to fulfill one's purpose in the larger social or religious context of the church. While conversions and confessions are conceived as intensely personal and even individualistic experiences, they follow ritual patterns and serve the purpose not only of individuation but also of cementing the individual's membership in the tribe.

Perhaps this generic structure suggests why Hughes's rendition of his youthful misadventures at the mourner's bench ends not with the comedy he invokes at the outset but in melancholy, tears, and a sense of isolation. To fail at conversion is to be alone. And in darkness. Indeed, Hughes underscores the trauma of his failed conversion by associating it with two other signature traumas of his first thirty years: his hatred of his father and his break with Charlotte Osgood Mason. Although Rampersad makes much of these other two watershed moments, the failed conversion is largely passed over. However, when Hughes recalls his failed conversion at the end of *The Big Sea*, the tone belies the apparently innocent and humorous miscommunication that could be read into the passage on its own. Speaking of his break with Osgood Mason, he says,

> That beautiful room, that had been so full of light and help and understanding for me, suddenly became like a trap closing in, faster and faster, the room darker and darker, until the light went out with a sudden crash in the dark, and everything became like that night in Kansas when I had failed to see Jesus and had lied about it afterwards. Or that morning in Mexico when I suddenly hated my father. (243)

Even the imagery of the meeting with Osgood Mason echoes the revival meeting tale since, as they make their way to the meeting, Hughes's aunt tells him that when he is saved he will see a light. And both evenings end with Hughes crying alone in the darkness. Choosing the lonelier road of agnosticism, Hughes has opened a gap between himself and the very folk whom he perceives as nurturers of his sense of self and his creativity, roles played in different ways by his father and Osgood Mason as well.

Linking these three events not only highlights the significance of the religious narrative in Hughes's sense of personal identity. It also re-emphasizes the ways in which Hughes, no less than Du Bois, is constructing a version of what Favor calls "authentic blackness," and one that must be understood in fundamentally secular terms or at least in terms in which participation in a religious cosmos was not a means of authenticating racial belonging, a means of achieving racial voice. Both the abandonment by his father and the rejection by Osgood Mason in the autobiography are tied to antiblack prejudice. In the case of Hughes's father, this took the form of racial self-hatred in which he held himself above the common run of black people or people of color of any kind—evident in his repeated slurs against both African Americans and Mexicans throughout the first part of the book. Although Hughes never states it quite so baldly in the narrative itself, his father has symbolically fled blackness for Mexico where he can play the role of whiteness otherwise denied him in the American context. Racism manifests differently in Osgood Mason, primarily through being a sponsor who controls her artists through romantic and primitivist expectations. While philo-Africanism, like philo-semitism or other racial romanticisms, may have the wash of cross-racial appreciation, no less than straightforward bigotry do they construct the racial other in terms comfortable to the dominant class. No less than Hughes's father does Osgood Mason make the folk into something that they aren't to serve her own purposes and sense of self-empowerment. By linking his failed conversion to these other two autobiographical traumas, Hughes further suggests that the authentic folk may be many things, they may even be Christians, but they are not necessarily so. And so, when we see Hughes embark onto a voyage into his people, his journey takes him less to the many churches where many African Americans thronged on Sunday mornings than to the streets of Harlem, the African American clubs of Paris, the dockworkers and dishwashers, the laborers and the unemployed—many of whom, of course, may or may not have been religious but are certainly not depicted as being so. Rather, they are the secular congregation for whom Hughes became a persistent and perspicacious voice.

NEGOTIATING THE FAITHFUL:
HUGHES AND THE IMPOSSIBILITY OF ATHEISM

Having noted these links among the three great leave-takings that Hughes posits in *The Big Sea*, it is still worth noting that while Hughes sometimes regrets separation from his father and from his godmother, Osgood Mason, he never backtracks or attempts to renegotiate the terms of that separation. The same cannot be said so straightforwardly of Hughes's break with African American Christendom. Indeed, it is arguable that *The Big Sea* is, in part, an effort to repair the rupture with official Christian culture that had occurred in the previous three decades of his life, and one which in three to four years prior to *The Big Sea*'s publication had become especially fraught and damaging for Hughes's reputation as the voice of African Americans.

Rampersad argues, persuasively to my mind, that Hughes's true gods, as represented in *The Big Sea,* are poetry and the folk. Explicating the scene in Mexico where Hughes's father disparages his intention of becoming a writer, Rampersad writes,

> Having led the young black Christ-poet up to a high place, Satan has threatened him with poverty and ignominy, then offered him the world in exchange for his soul. But Langston remains true to his God, which is poetry and the black folk, two elements seen by him as virtually one and the same. His admission that he hated his father establishes for the black reader the depth of his will to be a writer and his undying love of the black race. What his father detests, the son loves; thus Langston Hughes almost subliminally whispers to his black readers, his ultimate audience in spite of the realities of the marketplace and the intentions of Knopf, that his life is completely devoted to their own. For them, he had "killed" his own father. And killed his mother, too, who wished him to work and support her, instead of singing the black race at the price of poverty. In *The Big Sea*, Carrie Clark is praised a little but more often (although gently) ridiculed and dismissed. (378)

Though Rampersad does not say so overtly, the rhetoric of patricide and matricide here suggests that Hughes creates for himself a new familial line located in "the folk" who are at once muse and poetic/aesthetic object. However, even in positing poetry and "black folk" as his gods, Hughes puts himself in some sense at a very far remove from the everyday reality of many of the actual black folk upon which his being putatively depends.

Hughes's open repudiation of his father, and his declaration of independence from both his biological mother and his poetic Godmother, results implicitly and explicitly in a fairly straightforward declaration of allegiance to the "low-down" Negro and his or her needs. His refusal to convert results in a much murkier and less straightforward relationship to the object of his devotion. In declaring earlier in the biography that the stories of Jesus told by his black church are a lie, Hughes places them in the same category as his father, whose racial hatred of American Negroes he finds repugnant and false throughout the autobiography. But at the same time, he cannot utterly abandon the people without being cast finally adrift into the loneliness that, according to Rampersad, characterized and dominated his emotional life. Indeed, it is worth noting that, in some respects, the failed conversion may be the primordial rupture in Hughes's life that threated his aesthetic status in ways that his father and Mason could not. Hughes explicitly repudiates his father's internalized racism and embraces black folk as the source of his imagination. Hughes explicitly repudiates Osgood Mason's racialized patronage, recognizing in her efforts to control his imaginative life a variation on a theme of white privilege and oppression. Again, choosing black folk over their disparagers. Nevertheless, Hughes makes no such self-confident repudiation of the Christian faith of the folk even despite the fact that Jesus had not come to help him in his hour of need.

Certainly, in my view, one important way of understanding the whole of *The Big Sea* is not as a summative statement of independence—at least not independence from the religion of black folk—however much it may be a manifesto of independence from the social expectations of his father and the cultural expectations of white patrons. Rather, *The Big Sea* is, in some respects, an effort at recovery and reconciliation, not so much a recovery of faith but a renegotiation of the terms of his relationship with those who had remained steadfastly religious in the three decades since his failed conversion. *The Big Sea,* after all, comes at the end of a phase of life that Langston Hughes leaves nearly unremarked upon in the autobiography itself, one of explicit tension and even conflict with central features of black faith, a conflict that culminated in a rupture with his black audience and one that damaged what I have called his immersive pose: the publication of "Goodbye Christ" and its popular reception.

By the time Langston Hughes publishes "Goodbye Christ" in 1932, the respect that Du Bois felt intellectuals owed to the Christian church had been destabilized, though not dismantled. In this well-known and controversial poem, Hughes opposes revolutionary Marxism to Christianity and employs the rhetoric of failed masculinity against the central figure of Christianity rather than against his failed representatives. The suspect masculinity of Christ leaves him a far distance from the concerns of black Americans.

Goodbye,
Christ Jesus Lord God Jehova,
Beat it on away from here now.
Make way for a new guy with no religion at all—
A real guy named
Marx Communist Lenin Peasant Stalin Worker ME—

I said, ME! (*Collected Poems* 166–67)

Early in the third stanza, the invocation of the Christian God, "Christ Jesus Lord God Jehova," moves from the relatively familiar figure of "Christ Jesus" to the increasingly remote "Lord" and "God," ending finally in the archaic and anglicized name for God from the King James Bible, "Jehova," a syntax indicating distance and alienation. Jehova is displaced by "Marx Communist Lenin Peasant Stalin Worker ME," a progression that moves in contradistinction to the historically and philosophically remote Marx to the more immediate and personal "Worker ME." This "Worker ME" is a "real guy" in comparison to the ghostly, worn out, and archaic Christ. Indeed, Christ is worn out because he has become little more than a commodity through which religious figures make money. Judas's betrayal of Christ—the first time Christ is sold—is a sign of Christ's weakness, a capitulation to worldly powers.

> The popes and the preachers've
> Made too much money from it.
> They've sold you to too many
>
> Kings, generals, robbers, and killers
> Even to the Tzar and the Cossacks
> Even to Rockefeller's Church
> Even to THE SATURDAY EVENING POST.
> You ain't no good no more.
> They've pawned you
> Till you've done wore out. (166)

In Hughes's poem, Jesus is an empty signifier controlled by powerful men of the world, a commodity to be exchanged even as money was used to exchange Jesus's life in the gospel stories. Christ is ultimately associated with holy people the speaker sees as passive, ineffectual, or duplicitous: Ghandi, Becton, McPherson, Pope Pius. Rather than being a "real man" who resists the system, Christ is the currency upon which the system ultimately depends.

In some respects, "Goodbye Christ" is an exceptional poem in Hughes's oeuvre, but it doesn't stand alone. It is the high water mark of his increasingly direct criticism of Christianity itself, criticism framed through the same kind of masculine rhetoric deployed in many plays and stories. Early in his career, he regularly celebrated the possibility of physical resistance to oppression as preferable to Christian long-suffering. For instance, in his early signature poem "I, Too Sing America," the speaker's imposing physical presence, as much as his recognized gifts and abilities, guarantee him a seat at the table of American democracy. Hughes is consistently and increasingly concerned with the ways in which Christianity blunts this quest for human dignity or simply is inadequate to the needs African Americans are facing. The poem "Gods" ridicules human religion as something made up by human beings. "Prayer for a Winter Night" pleads with God to simply bring death since he doesn't seem to bring anything else. "To Certain 'Brothers'" chronicles Hughes's deep suspicion of the clergy as persons hypocritically leeching off the goodwill of others:

> You sicken me with lies,
> With truthful lies.
> And with your pious faces.
> And your wide, out-stretched,
> Mock-welcome, Christian hands.
> While underneath
> Is dirt and ugliness,
> And rottening hearts,
> And wild hyenas howling
> In your soul's waste lands. (*Collected Poems* 55)

Besides "Goodbye Christ," by the 1930s, Hughes represented the failures of Christianity as the failures of men in poems such as "A Christian Country."

> God slumbers in a back alley
> With a gin bottle in His hand
> Come on, God, get up and fight
> Like a man. (*Collected Poems* 136)

The failed masculinity of God means, finally, that African Americans must make their way on their own, much as Langston Hughes says he had to make his way on his own at the end of the first section of *The Big Sea*, without the reassurances and obligations of books and culture and parents and schooling, and certainly without the reassurances of a god who has proven himself unworthy of so much patience and devotion. "Goodbye Christ," then, was the culminating point of a long movement away from Christian faith and even aggressive opposition to it, an explicit opposition that an older generation of writers like Du Bois and James Weldon Johnson never voiced, or at least voiced only *sotto voce*.

Nevertheless, Hughes never felt completely reconciled to this rejection. His letters to Carl Van Vechten and others suggest that he fretted repeatedly about the publication of "Goodbye Christ" and the ensuing uproar among Christians, black and white. Although the most famous protester against Hughes's poem was the white evangelist Amee Semple McPherson, she was joined in sentiment by countless African Americans offended by Hughes's ridiculing of the Christian God. Hughes found the popular rejection of the poem so traumatic that he spent much of the rest of his life backtracking. The poem itself and the entire episode go unmentioned in *The Big Sea*. Hughes did not include it later in his collected poems and did what he could to disown the poem that had gone perhaps a step too far in repudiating the most traditional form of black religious faith. As Rampersad puts it: "The Christmas season, 1940, was haunted by the ghost of 'Goodbye Christ' and Hughes's desire to repudiate this extreme evidence of his radical past. In a fateful step, he spent several days laboring on a statement about the poem which he sent to everyone who mattered," a statement that included repudiations of his socialism and an assertion that he had withdrawn the poem from circulation (392-33).

This retraction won Hughes no friends among his communist fellow travelers, who eventually repudiated Hughes (394–95). As Hughes's career progressed, he continued to repair his relationship with the black church, writing a number of gospel plays and musicals that were designed to be performed in church. Whatever the status of belief in Hughes's later life, it seems clear that he found the stance of intimate distance difficult to perform and maintain and the stance of critical cultural outsider impossible to endure. Indeed, *The Big Sea* is one part of this effort to articulate a peace with African American religion. Although my earlier reading points out the ways in which *The Big Sea* establishes a necessary separation from Christianity in articulating a secular folk voice, it is also the case that Hughes's criticism of Christianity is far more muted than the strident criticism in several of the poems mentioned above. In articulating his love for his Uncle Reed, "a sinner," he mentions his love for his aunt and his enjoyment of the church scene. He is careful to note that "both of them were very good and kind— the one who went to church and the one who didn't. And no doubt from them I learned to like both Christians and sinners equally well" (41). This careful expression, of course, cuts several ways. On the one hand, in the context of a Christian group increasingly angry and vocal about poems like "Goodbye Christ," it serves to reassure the folk of his genuine affection. It also has the effect of creating a more encompassing and universal sense of black humanity than even the church accomplishes with its metaphysical morality. His humor in articulating his failed conversion is unmistakable, as is his sorrow and anguish at the separation that he feels, an ambiguous emotional tenor that, again, both provokes sympathy and blunts the edge of separation between the sinners and the saved. These renderings, with their ambiguous tone and careful nuance, are a far cry from the aggressive declarations of "Goodbye Christ," and are but one part of a bridge that

Hughes sought in the last half of his life to rebuild with the faithful many, sometimes at the cost of his relationship with the enlightened few.

This is not to say simply and straightforwardly that Hughes abandoned his doubts or made a declaration of faith. It is to say he sought an aesthetic form that made his distance from faith a less dramatic factor in his poetic persona than it was in "Goodbye Christ." Indeed, in some respects he returned to an earlier form of seeing the church's forms as a resource for aesthetic play. This became Hughes's own means of negotiating the question of intimacy with and distance from black faith. Donna Haraway points out that blasphemy is something quite different from utter abandonment or indifference. Instead, the blasphemer remains within the accepted discourse of the community at hand even while questioning or rejecting the very language one feels compelled to use (2269–70). In repeated letters to Carl Van Vechten, Hughes plays this role as he reports on visits to revival services or other religious goings-on much as both of them reported attendance at the latest play. Moreover, he is able to use distinctions between class-based forms of religion to affirm the popular religion of the working class even when he himself does not take the claims seriously. Writing from Lincoln, he tells Van Vechten, "We are now having a revival out here. I went tonight with the intention of being saved, —but it was such a highbrow meeting that nobody shouted, —so I sat there unmoved and am still a sinner. Have Mercy!" (*Remember Me* 60).

In these and many other passages Hughes is construing blackness and folkishness in particular ways that are inescapably tied to his experience of black religious practice. His allegiance to his uncle, "the sinner," serves as a synecdoche for his general effort to establish a new and authentic ancestry and to remain both within and without the practices of the people he claims to represent; he establishes a new paternity for himself, different from the racial self-hatred of his biological father but different too from the religiosity of female aunt and grandmother. Truth, and true blackness, and his own true identity can be traced to the father he has created for himself, his sinner uncle, or more generally to blacks who are sinners. In declaring himself a sinner, Hughes was able to lay claim to an identity and a purpose made possible by the folk who were his object of devotion. Sinners are those who are both within and without, intimate with and yet distant from the discourse of the sacred community. To be a sinner, after all, is to hold out—perhaps unceasingly—the possibility of salvation.

"ARTIFICIAL MEN"
Anti-intellectualism, Christianity, and Cultural Leadership

When Arnold Rampersad suggests that Langston Hughes wrote as both an insider and an outsider to the race (13), he is describing an intellectual self-consciousness that held true for almost all the writers of the Harlem Renaissance, not least because their status as intellectuals often marginalized them in relationship to the discourses of faith that animated so many African Americans during this period. To note this tension with the broader African American populace is not of itself new. Indeed, suggesting that the intellectual occupies a difficult insider/outsider status has been a common trope of black intellectual self-definition since Du Bois. Beginning with Du Bois's evocation of the talented tenth, extending to Harold Cruse's essentially critical account of the failure of black intellectuals to negotiate the racial mountain of white power, and on to Cornel West's clarion call for a black insurgent, organic intelligentsia, the difficulty of being both spokesperson and exception, of being both intimate and distant, has been a defining tension in black intellectual life in the United States. West summarizes this dilemma, noting:

> The choice of becoming a black intellectual is an act of self-imposed margin-
> ality; it assures a peripheral status in and to the black community. The quest
> for literacy indeed is a fundamental theme in African-American history and
> a basic impulse in the black community. But for blacks, as with most Ameri-
> cans, the uses for literacy are usually perceived to be for more substantive
> pecuniary benefits than those of a writer, artist, teacher, or professor. (59)

Du Bois, Hughes, Cruse, and West contribute important analyses of this tension in black intellectual life, laying it variously to the ground of numerous
forms of white oppression and its educational legacy, American capitalism
and its exploitation of black labor, or to the organization of American civic
and institutional life in forms that marginalize black intellectuals within
the academy and strain their connections to black communities. None of
these important voices, however, explicitly identifies the repeated images of
tension with black evangelical faith that *Goodbye Christ?* has been chart-
ing. Heretofore, I've looked primarily at the consequences of belief and
unbelief and the efforts of intellectuals like Du Bois and Hughes to negotiate the problem of belief in their own quest to narrate a form of racial
authenticity. However, tension between intellectuals and the faithful came
not simply from the absence of faith among the intelligentsia but also from
the commonly benign disregard for—and the sometimes-aggressive assault
upon—intellectual work on the part of the faithful.

To be sure, there are important exceptions that the ensuing chapters seek
to nuance. And I should also say emphatically that the intellectual life of
African Americans as it developed cannot be easily separated from its roots
in the educational work of churches. The education upon which the idea
of a talented tenth depended was largely achieved through church-founded
or related institutions such as Fisk, Wilberforce, Spelman, Morehouse, and
many others. Even independent Howard University saw ministerial training
as central to its mission. Moreover, the development of a secular African
American intelligentsia cannot be meaningfully separated from its roots in
the work of church intellectuals. Indeed, Dorrien has noted that it is, by
now, a convention of historiography to believe that "religious intellectuals
no longer mattered by the end of the nineteenth century. In that case, black
religious intellectuals [in the twentieth century] did not matter whether or
not they existed" (9). The importance of social gospel pioneers like Reverdy
Ransom is barely noted, and nineteenth-century precursors like Alexander
Crummell and Henry McNeal Turner are forgotten or marginalized in their
importance to the developments of early twentieth-century African American culture. As I have mentioned, even the fact that Frederick Douglass
was an ordained minister in the African Methodist Episcopal Zion church

is often forgotten or usually found unremarkable. Nonetheless, West is surely correct when he notes that a high value placed on basic and even higher education can effortlessly exist alongside a familiar American form of anti-intellectualism. The broadly anti-intellectual stance of the churches called in to question the legitimacy of intellectual and artistic pursuits as a black vocation. In the ensuing chapters, *Goodbye Christ?* will investigate the consequences of this form of anti-intellectualism for black intellectual life, especially the efforts of black intellectuals to counter its effects by constructing the intellectual as a culture hero.

Anti-intellectual elements in African American culture in many respects reflect the anti-intellectualism of American culture at large while demonstrating a variety of specific differences. Given the facts of having been denied access to education, the manifest empowerment that came from basic education, and the history of degrading stereotypes such as that of Zip Coon that derided the desire for learning, African Americans had a spur to education that was and has remained a pronounced part of common culture. Ross Posnock among many others points out the degree to which the cultivation of black intellect could be seen as an explicitly political activity:

> [*Black*] *intellectual* is a disturbance that encloses another, prior one—the very fact of black literacy. This was a specter that filled white Southerners with consuming fear throughout the nineteenth century. "To stamp out the brains of the Negro!" said Alexander Crummell in 1898, was the South's "systematized method" of subjugation (Destiny 291). If caught reading a slave might have fingers or hands chopped off. "For Coloured people to acquire learning in this country, makes tyrants quake and tremble," declared David Walker in his Appeal of 1829 (31). "Educating the coloured people," he implies, ignites a train of dire consequences: not only does it spell the end of submission and the publicizing of slavers' "infernal deeds of cruelty," but, most important, it explodes the white image of blacks as "talking apes, void of intellect, incapable of learning" (61–62). On all these counts, Walker's Appeal is a nightmare, its very existence shocking proof of prodigious black intellectual capacity. Little wonder that to distribute it was a crime of sedition (one white sailor was convicted) or that it had to be sewn into the coats of sailors for surreptitious distribution. (Posnock 50)[1]

Posnock's declaration is powerfully persuasive on its own terms. In the immediate aftermath of the Civil War, missionary teachers reported a high degree of zeal for learning the basics of reading and writing, and many scholars emphasize the centrality of literacy narratives to African American literary history (Banks 33–47).[2] Nevertheless, there were important constraints and limits placed upon the image of the educated man in

African American popular culture, perhaps especially as that image related to religion. These attitudes should be understood in the broader context of attitudes toward intellectual activity in the United States among both whites and blacks. "Learning" in a generic sense was esteemed among both whites and blacks and was understood by most African Americans as a way of uplifting the race. But for most Americans of the late nineteenth and early twentieth century, valuable learning had a deeply practical cast, one that viewed "higher" intellectual activity with some suspicion.[3] Literature by Anglo-Americans is arguably dominated by characters for whom book-learning is an ambivalent value at best: one thinks of Huck Finn, the main characters of the stories of Stephen Crane or Jack London, the tendency of Hemingway's heroes to prefer action to ideas. Faulkner's great intellectual characters are either mad or suicidal or both. Attitudes toward college-educated intellectuals among white Americans were and have remained various but could hardly be described as secure and exalted. Intellectuals in European American literary history often are ineffectual milquetoasts (Ichabod Crane), heartless scientific fascists (Rappaccini), or sexual predators (Humbert Humbert). The seminal authority on anti-intellectualism in American life, Richard Hofstadter, points out that intellectuals were often viewed with great suspicion and beginning in the late nineteenth century were consistently characterized as impractical and effeminate, men incapable of political leadership precisely because their learning had left them less than manly:

> It was not enough for the politicians to say that the reformers were hypo-
> critical and impractical. Their cultivation and fastidious manners were taken
> as evidence that these "namby-pamby, goody-goody gentlemen" who "sip
> cold tea" were deficient in masculinity.[4] They were on occasion denounced
> as "political hermaphrodites". . . . The waspish Senator Ingalls of Kansas,
> furious at their lack of party loyalty, once denounced them as "the third
> sex"— "effeminate without being either masculine or feminine; unable ei-
> ther to beget or bear; possessing neither fecundity nor virility; endowed with
> the contempt of men and the derision of women, and doomed to sterility,
> isolation, and extinction. . . . They have two recognized functions," the sena-
> tor said of the third sex. "They sing falsetto, and they are usually selected as
> the guardians of the seraglios of Oriental despots."[5] (188)

In the gender codes of the late nineteenth and early twentieth centuries, the assertion that intellectuals were of a "third sex" translates loosely into a denigration that they were homosexuals in a heteronormative culture—in some sense worse than either men or women because they could neither "beget" as a man or "bear" as a woman, failures at achieving the normative and defining features of human sexuality in the period. Although these quotations focus on the late nineteenth century, Hofstadter makes a convincing case that this stereotype of intellectual activity as unmanly, impractical, and perhaps traitorous endured through the Cold War.

Looking at a parallel African American history, some distinctions are in order. There is an enduring image of the African American "bad man" as well as mythical physical giants like John Henry who secure the dignity of the race through physical dominance.[6] Later in this book, I will explore the ways in which some African American writers deployed the male body, its strength and desires, as a means of envisioning alternatives to received Christian faith. Nevertheless, such images have not been accompanied by a simultaneous denigration of basic learning on the order of Huck Finn. The tradition of literacy narratives to which Cornel West alludes above points to reading and writing as signs of freedom, and teachers in African American history are often portrayed as liberating figures rather than impediments to imaginative freedom. Nevertheless, images, narratives, and ideologies that caution against intellectual pursuits are evident in African American cultural history. Posnock himself points out that Booker T. Washington's aggressive critiques of intellectual activity drew on images of effeminacy and unnaturalness:

> Washington recalled the early plans for Tuskegee and sympathized with white anxiety about starting a black college. He remarked that those who had questioned the wisdom of creating Tuskegee had in their minds pictures "of what was called an educated negro, with a high hat, imitation gold eye-glasses, a showy walking stick, kid gloves, fancy boots and what not— in a word a man who was determined to live by his wits."[7] The men and women of Tuskegee stood in merciful and stark contrast to this effeminate urban fop borrowed from the minstrel tropes of black dandy lore. . . . In 1903 Washington assailed those who disrupted a speech of his in Boston as "artificial" men, "graduates of New England colleges".[8] And in his 1911 recounting of the incident, which had become known as the Boston riot, Washington gave a name to his unnatural enemies—"people who call themselves 'The Intellectuals.'" They live "at a distance," in a world of "theories, but they do not understand" people and things.[9] (58–59)

Posnock suggests that in characterizing intellectual activity in this way, Washington is assailing both Du Bois and William James, who worked hard to give the term "intellectual" a positive meaning in the American context. Washington's negative image in our contemporary moment, especially in relationship to his extended conflicts with Du Bois, makes it hard for scholars to give credence to his criticism. However, it's worth saying

that many people with a wide variety of intellectual, cultural, or political
programs repeated variations on Washington's main theme: that intellectuals lived at too great an imaginative remove from the common person to
be any common good. Such critics included writers like Hughes, who, as I
noted in my last chapter, made the distinction between books and people a
central opposition of his autobiography, ironically positioning his allegiance
to people and against intellectual culture—even the culture of the Harlem
Renaissance itself—as the root of his intellectual and artistic achievements.
Zora Neale Hurston, while possessing a degree from Barnard and having
completed extensive graduate work at Columbia in anthropology, nevertheless tended to root her authority less in the fact of intellectual pedigree and
academic accomplishments and more in her immersion in the nonacademic
practices of the folk. Even in Du Bois, the exaltation of practicality is evident
in defenses of higher learning for the talented tenth, defenses that turned on
the practical benefits to the race that would ensue. His definition of art as
propaganda—a thesis that infuriated the bohemian element of the Harlem
Renaissance—certainly rested on the notion that cultural work needed to
have identifiable cultural benefits to be justified.

The presence of such tropes and elements even in the work of leading
intellectual figures may well be due to the efforts to negotiate the cultural
tension of black intellectual life that West calls the dilemma of the black intellectual; they also surely indicate the continuing strength of anti-intellectual
discourse on the American scene among European and African Americans
alike. Well before the term "intellectual" came into vogue, suspicions of
higher learning characterized much of American life, including a good deal
of the American educational system, which saw itself as fitting most people
for the practicalities of commerce and politics, not to walk in the halls of
learning with Aristotle and Du Bois. Recognizing this is not to diminish the
racist cast of white attitudes toward black intellectuals or to diminish the
ideological problems with Booker T. Washington's efforts to accommodate
the violent realities of the Jim Crow South. It is to say that the quest for
a higher intellectual vocation in the arts or humanities was very nearly an
idiosyncratic bent in American life, one viewed with a suspicion that was
often cast in gendered terms.

In this light, Posnock's conflation of the terms "literacy" and "black intellectual" should be unpacked since it overrides the very different historical
periods of the literacy narratives with the newly developing social position of
intellectuals and the intelligentsia in the early twentieth century. It also elides
the very different social positions of the person who is functionally literate
or even generally educated in American society and those who came to be

called "intellectuals" in the first years of the twentieth century. To be literate so that one could read the Bible in order to hear the voice of God for oneself, or to be adequately educated in order to read the newspaper and participate in elections, was a crucial advance in African American life. It was also a very different thing from being an intellectual in the Du Boisian sense of that term. While white Americans, especially in the South, viewed black literacy with suspicion and black intelligence with disbelief, it doesn't follow that black championing of literacy made one an automatic champion of intellectuals. Booker T. Washington's arguments about education never denied the need for literacy. He did question the immediate need for higher schooling in literature, philosophy, languages, sciences, and other things that the modern academy was coming to associate with the term "intellectual." In doing so, he stood on the same ground as many white American businessmen who doubted the need for higher education among white Americans. It was impractical and distracted intelligent men from useful social and economic activities.

Besides the dominant arguments of American utilitarianism against the intellectual life, there are also serious religious roots to American anti-intellectualism. The suspicion that the deracinated intellectual might be disloyal to country or to race was in some respects a secularized version of an earlier and long-enduring suspicion among American Christian sects that learning led to disloyalty of a different and more metaphysical sort. Like many Americans, African Americans sometimes saw higher educa-tion as an impediment—if not outright obstacle—to Christian devotion. While intellectual leaders of the Harlem Renaissance sometimes lamented the tendency of African Americans to give very large amounts of money to churches and a pittance to education or other cultural work, pious African Americans were much of the time living out an African American version of Billy Sunday's admonition to the white Americans of the period who made up the majority of his revival audiences: "Thousands of college graduates are going as fast as they can straight to hell," said Sunday. "If I had a million dollars I'd give $999,999 to the church and $1 to education." And, "When the word of God says one thing and scholarship says another, scholarship can go to hell!" (Hofstadter 122).[10]

To be sure, the prestige of literacy among African Americans sometimes forestalled a descent into the know-nothing-ism that could characterize the revivalist factions of fundamentalist Christianity. Sometimes not. Like their white counterparts, many black clergymen were outspoken in their opposi-tion to Darwin or to higher criticism of the Bible. To the contrary, calls for higher levels of education among African American clergy most often came, unsurprisingly, from intellectuals or from other members of the educated elite.[11] Occasional calls for more highly trained clergy were issued by conventions of various churches or church-related groups. Nannie H. Burroughs, in a report on the work of Baptist women in 1920, excoriates the male Baptist ministry on the grounds of inferior mental development and puts this problem in the context of speaking to an increasingly educated people:

> The next fact prominent in the study of the Survey is the inadequate mental equipment of the men who are trying to lead the people from spiritual darkness into the knowledge of God's word. The statement that, "His activity is usually confined to preaching with homely, natural eloquence and emotional fervor," is too true. The day for such leaders is past. The laymen are taking advantage of opportunities for education and are demanding men in the pulpits who are mentally, morally, and spiritually equipped. Jesus pointed out the danger when he reminded his disciples that, if the blind lead the blind both shall fall in the ditch. The blind cannot lead the blind and those who have sight will not allow the blind to lead them. An educated pew will not be led by an ignorant pulpit. Noise might attract people, but noise alone will not hold them nor will it mold character. (380)

I'm sure most intellectuals nod approvingly at Burroughs's criticisms and prescriptions. It's worth pointing out, however, that some lines of her criticism turn perceptions by Du Bois, Hughes, and James Weldon Johnson on their head when they note that the preacher's power lies not in education or intellectuality but in rhetoric, performance, even musicianship. There were few fervent demands from the unlettered masses in the pews that their preachers be more informed about trends in German criticism, Biblical linguistics, or the abstractions of theology or philosophy. Even many of the ecclesiastical elite were cautious about the newly developing intellectual class. In 1917, the council of Bishops in the AME church—a church group often, in fact, associated with the cultural and intellectual elite among African Americans—exhorted its flock to "not be mystified by the voices and sounds of those who would acclaim that religious standards and doctrines can no longer be relied upon." The address implicitly links skeptical intellectual speculation with pool halls, saloons, and prostitution as dangers to the race, dangers that the Bishops describe as a "new form of bondage" (AME Bishops 361–62). They urge their followers to understand the superior example of Jesus as a teacher in comparison to the intellectual class:

> Our age is full of skepticism. Many who are regarded as the intellectual lights of the world can least be trusted in things spiritual, and yet their commanding position among men demands for them a respectful hearing upon all subjects: this makes them therefore all the more dangerous in their influence upon society.

But the world's greatest teacher, who alone is the light of the world, is the only safe guide. His truths have been tested in all the ages past, and still stand impregnable, and will endure forever. Walking in this light, and in this truth, the humblest of earth may feel secure. (362)

Such language contrasts the stout and reliable shoulders of Jesus with the deceptive and unreliable doctrines of men. If this unease came from a Christian denomination with a strong record of advancing the cause of education, how much more was this the case in rural or storefront congregations less known for serving the educated classes. In some respects, this statement reflects Carter Woodson's analysis that the church resists theological or ritual modernization:

> Inasmuch as God changes not, and is just the same to-day as yesterday, how can a minister of Jehovah advocate such innovations? 'Give me, therefore, that old time religion,' they say, 'it's good enough for me.' The rural Negro minister, then, will not proclaim a new thought. He will preach the same gospel in the same way. He has not changed and never intends to do so. (418)

Woodson suggests that he is analyzing the religion of the "backwoods Negroes," but the statement from the House of Bishops suggests that different versions of this idea were pervasive throughout African American Christianity as they were through much of American Christianity at large. On the whole, intellectuals recognized that the success of all but a few elite churches seemed to depend little on intellectual training. Such training could even be viewed as counterproductive in the immediate terms of the preacher's ecclesiastical success. William Banks points out that, although black intellectual activity in the nineteenth century was overwhelmingly associated with the educated clerical elite, this elite was very far from the norm in the early decades of the twentieth century.

> [Few] black ministers were educated at seminaries or universities. More frequently, blacks assumed the role of preacher after having been "called." Such persons claiming divine selection usually had a rudimentary knowledge of the Bible, but their position and mobility in the black church depended more on their ability to evoke religious emotions in the congregations than on their grasp of theological arguments. Untrained preachers came to rest in the pulpits of churches with poor and uneducated congregations. (60–61)

Such congregations had much greater need of practical religion than of theological systematizing and intellectual speculation. As C. Eric Lincoln has suggested:

> For [black people] religion is personal—almost tangible; it is never an abstraction disassociated from the here-and-now, the experiences that shape the life situations of real people who are suffering and dying and struggling against

forces they don't understand. Black Christians have never learned to rational-
ize God; rather they personalize Him and include Him in their life situations.
Hence, a Black God is not only logical—He is practical. (*Since Frazier* 149)

This practical cast, in itself, tended to push black Christianity, like all American evangelical Christianities, toward anti-intellectualism, whatever other
sources of practical strength and validity it may have had.[12] This tendency
put it at odds with the cultural and intellectual programs that dominated
the New Negro writers of the first decades of the century.

Both black and white intellectuals decried such religious anti-intellectualism and regularly excoriated it in terms that associated religion as an
atavistic holdover from an age superseded by the modern intellectual. H. L.
Mencken, intellectual mentor to many in the Harlem Renaissance, is typically extreme in his statements associated with the Scopes trial but not
unusual in the structure of his argument:

> The so-called religious organizations which now lead the war against the
> teaching of evolution are nothing more, at bottom, than conspiracies of the
> inferior man against his betters. They mirror very accurately his congenital
> hatred of knowledge, his bitter enmity to the man who knows more than he
> does, and so gets more out of life. Certainly it cannot have gone unnoticed
> that their membership is recruited, in the overwhelming main, from the
> lower orders — that no man of any education or other human dignity be-
> longs to them. What they propose to do, at bottom and in brief, is to make
> the superior man infamous — by mere abuse if it is sufficient, and if it is not,
> then by law. ("Homo Neanderthalensis")

Few African American writers display Mencken's frank embrace of the
Nietzchean ethos at the root of this excerpt, though the rhetoric that posited
Old against New Negroes as well as those that inverted typical racial hierarchies sometimes lent themselves to similar forms of argument. Nevertheless,
Moran has suggested that many African American intellectuals embraced
the Menckenian position on the Scopes trial and saw in it an opportunity
to advance the causes of science in order to ridicule and overturn racial
superstitions. Mencken himself was unabashed in suggesting that devotion
to preachers was among the greatest problems facing African Americans.
Charles Scruggs points out that a great deal of Mencken's advocacy for
black American intellectuals during the twenties turned on a vision of the
anti-intellectual quality of African American religion, as did that of one of
Mencken's African American disciples, George Schuyler:

> Mencken kept hoping that blacks would see the light at the end of the theo-
> logical tunnel. He continued to exhort the race "to reorganize its religious

ideas, to get rid of its lingering childishness and, above all, to deliver itself from the exploitation of frauds and mountebanks." He wrote one piece in which he noticed signs of rebellion against "the hog wallow theology" that had entrapped blacks, and he encouraged George Schuyler to write an article for the *Mercury* in which these signs had become an accomplished fact. In "Black America Begins to Doubt"—a title that Mencken gave Schuyler for his article—Schuyler's main thesis was that the black church was losing its hold on black people as they came of age intellectually. Both Mencken and Schuyler saw themselves as modern Voltaires who were trying to sweep away that mental rubbish that cluttered the Negro's brain so that he might take one long leap from the Dark ages into the twentieth century. (Moran 44–45)

The characterization of the childishness of belief and the general narrative of historical progress were common intellectual tropes for describing the inferiority of religion, figures that pointed to the superior and usually masculine maturity of the knowing intellectual. Although some Harlem intellectuals were warier of Mencken than was Schuyler, for the most part, they quietly and sometimes loudly agreed with Mencken's thesis.

Given this context, it does seem to me that the cultural and especially religious distance that Posnock tends to celebrate as an instance of race transcendence in African American intellectuals in fact posed a terrific problem. I am not persuaded that men like Du Bois or Woodson or Johnson were interested in transcending race so much as transforming it and transforming it in such a way that their own cosmopolitan forms of racial identity could inhabit stations of cultural leadership. In a quest for cultural leadership, they hoped cosmopolitan and secular intellectuals could be imagined as culture heroes, as men at the center of a group of men. Writers and artists of the period sought to transform the image of the educated African American in the hopes that such transformation would be one step in the transformation of the race as a whole. Writers sought to negotiate the necessary tension that their position evoked in different ways, sometimes by inhabiting the forms of Christian language while emptying them of their specific social and ideological resonance. As I have already shown, Du Bois's approach to African American Christianity is a difficult combination of both aggressive repudiation and transformative recognition, seeing Christian institutions and dogmas as having largely negative or problematic histories in the African American context, even while seeing in the music of the sorrow songs, bereft of language, a form of authentic blackness that could be deployed both to enhance the image of the race and establish his own claims to leadership. In this latter vein, intellectuals could honor religious traditions while revealing that newer secular intellectual movements had displaced those very same traditions.[13]

Perhaps the epitome of this approach to traditional forms of African American culture is found in James Weldon Johnson. Johnson's *God's Trombones,* published at the height of the Renaissance in 1927 epitomizes the nuanced effort to produce work rooted in African American Christian culture even while transforming that culture through principles of high art. Johnson's astonishing achievement in the collection of poetry was to produce a work that is taken by many to be a full-blooded rendition of religious art—one that is used to the present in Christian worship—even while Johnson himself made very clear throughout his adult life that he was an agnostic and rooted his agnosticism in his intellectual and artistic pursuits. Johnson vigorously promoted a secularist version of African American identity even while working closely with New Negro church leaders such as Frederick Asbury Cullen.

In the preface to the *God's Trombones,* Johnson recalls the inspiration for what became his most enduring work of literary art. Although manifestly intended as a tribute to the folk artistry of the black preacher—an artistry that Johnson describes as superior to his own—the moment of inspiration also reflects the tensions and uncertainties that arose in the Harlem Renaissance when cosmopolitan intellectuals engaged with or reflected upon the black religious culture. Johnson tells of one visit to a church, where he sat exhausted at the end of a long day of official activities. A couple of perfunctory introductory sermons gave way at last to the main event, a sermon by a famed visiting preacher:

> At last he arose. He was a dark-brown man, handsome in his gigantic proportions. He appeared to be a bit self-conscious, perhaps impressed by the presence of the "distinguished visitor" on the platform, and started in to preach a formal sermon from a formal text. The congregation sat apathetic and dozing. He sensed that he was losing his audience and his opportunity. Suddenly he closed the Bible, stepped out from behind the pulpit and began to preach. He started intoning the old folk-sermon that begins with the creation of the world and ends with Judgment Day. He was at once a changed man, free, at ease and masterful. The change in the congregation was instantaneous. An electric current ran through the crowd. It was in a moment alive and quivering; and all the while the preacher held it in the palm of his hand. He was wonderful in the way he employed his conscious and unconscious art. He strode the pulpit up and down in what was actually a very rhythmic dance, and he brought into play the full gamut of his wonderful voice, a voice—what shall I say?—not of an organ or a trumpet, but rather of a trombone, the instrument possessing above all others the power to express the wide and varied range of emotions encompassed by the human voice—and with greater amplitude.

He intoned, he moaned, he pleaded—he blared, he crashed, he thundered. I sat fascinated; and more, I was, perhaps against my will, deeply moved; the emotional effect upon me was irresistible. Before he had finished I took a slip of paper and somewhat surreptitiously jotted down some ideas for the first poem, "The Creation." (6–7)

The tone of this passage, as of the entirety of the preface, suggests both intimacy and distance; not a little of the imagery invokes Du Bois's description of his experience of backwoods southern worship in "Faith of The Fathers," one that included both deep emotional appeal and intellectual distance from that appeal. Johnson is a "distinguished visitor," literally but also metaphorically since he no longer shares the religious culture here on display. Johnson's memories are personal but hazy, worn away by time and circumstance as well as by the author's own changed religious convictions. He is proximate to the various preachers on the podium, but he is also removed, not counting himself among the exhorters so much as occupying a separate space. He is there not to preach but to give a "talk" or an "address." Johnson is moved emotionally "against his will," something that testifies both to the power of the folk sermon and to the existential distance of Johnson's stance.

Johnson translates the emotional appeal of this sermon, and so in some sense controls and displaces it, by pausing to take notes for a future written text, in contrast to the preacher whose spiritual effect depends on his having abandoned the written text altogether in order reach the people of his congregation. The preacher's artistry and the culture to which it speaks are necessarily oral. In most respects, the preacher abandons the typical trappings of intellectual work in order to reach the masses of his congregation. He becomes, in Johnson's rendering, not so much a mind as a voice. While Johnson insists persuasively on high levels of intelligence among the folk preachers, this intelligence is not manifest in intellectual reflection or argument. Indeed, Johnson's formulation closely follows Richard Hofstadter's distinction between intelligence and intellect in American discourse, a distinction that highly praises intelligence as a practical force while intellect is cold, distant, and disconnected from the life of the people (Hofstadter 25). For Johnson, the clearest manifestations of the old-time preacher's nonintellectual behavior are also the surest marks of his communal virtues:

The old-time Negro preacher of parts was above all an orator, and in good measure an actor. He knew the secret of oratory, that at bottom it is a progression of rhythmic words more than it is anything else. Indeed, I have witnessed congregations moved to ecstasy by the rhythmic intoning of sheer incoherencies. He was a master of all the modes of eloquence. He often possessed a voice that was a marvelous instrument, a voice he could modulate

from a sepulchral whisper to a crashing thunder clap. His discourse was
generally kept at a high pitch of fervency, but occasionally he dropped into
colloquialisms and, less often, into humor. He preached a personal and an-
thropomorphic God, a sure-enough heaven and a red-hot hell. His imagination was bold and unfettered. He had the power to sweep his hearers before
him; and so himself was often swept away. At such times his language was
not prose but poetry. (5)

And somewhat later:

Gross exaggeration of the use of big words by these preachers, in fact by
Negroes in general, has been commonly made; the laugh being at the exhibi-
tion of ignorance involved. What is the basis of this fondness for big words?
Is the predilection due, as is supposed, to ignorance desiring to parade itself
as knowledge? Not at all. The old-time Negro preacher loved the sonorous,
mouth-filling, ear-filling phrase because it gratified a highly developed sense
of sound and rhythm in himself and his hearers. (9)

Here, Johnson enunciates one important strain of New Negro thinking about
art that is deeply romantic when it figures the unlettered folk as the truest
artists, recalling Wordsworth's insistence that the language of the shepherd
was, by nature, poetry, untainted by the formal rules of textual traditions.
The preacher, while himself literate, must abandon the trappings of the written word in order to become an artist to whom the people can respond. The
passage in which the preacher sets aside his book and steps forth to speak
in the language of the people echoes in several important respects Hughes's
decision to cast his books into the river as a symbol of his desire to connect
more deeply with the voice of the people. Johnson's formulation similarly
carries all the ironies of the Romantic tradition generally, one felt not simply
in the pervasive past tense of this elegy but also in the transformation of
daily practice into formal art without explicitly revealing the ideological
distance such a transformation entails.

But more important for my purposes are the subtle contrasts that Johnson
draws between the life of books and the life of sermons. In Johnson's rendering, the preacher is most himself, and most able to reach the people, when
he leaves behind his formal text, when he closes up his written book—in
this case the Bible—and launches not into argument but into intonation,
into song. Like Du Bois in "Faith of the Fathers" and in "The Sorrow
Songs," Johnson locates racial authenticity and connection in sounds rather
than in texts or even in language generally. Nevertheless, Johnson himself
is addressing people of the book, fellow text-bound intellectuals, writers,
and readers like himself. Johnson's rationale for writing assumes that the

preacher's world has been superseded, not least by the world of the book of which Johnson himself is the representative. Both literally and symbolically, the sermonic tour-de-force is a figurative preliminary, not unlike the two short sermons that made way for it, preparing the way for the superior "distinguished" visitor on the platform who makes no pretense of putting texts aside, who, in fact, begins creating texts while on the podium rather than being moved to the holy shouting that occurs around him.

Toward the end of the preface, Johnson figures both his own belatedness and his own necessity: "The old-time Negro preacher is rapidly passing. I have here tried sincerely to fix something of him" (11). Johnson's paean to the folk preacher is both celebration and eulogy. It is also compensatory; Johnson wants to "fix" the folk preacher in the obvious sense of making him permanent, but Johnson also seeks to "fix" the preacher in the sense of making him and the sermons in the poetic volume fit for public intellectual consumption that is the condition of the new era that Johnson as the distinguished visitor heralds. Like Du Bois in "Faith of the Fathers," Johnson's poems testify to a religious greatness that has been, but which is now displaced by the cosmopolitan intellectual and urban activist, one who writes books that treat preaching as a form of music rather than a form of truth, a transformation that the preachers themselves would reject.

In his introduction and in other works such as his autobiography, *Along This Way*, Johnson is his own leading character in a drama of racial leadership. He is not only imagining and creating art through the aegis of black Christian culture but also envisaging and narrating the superiority and future role of the African American intellectual. This dramatization of the racial role of the intellectual was a repeated narrative response to the anti-intellectualism of American culture, a response directed both to its racist manifestations in Jim Crow denigrations of black intellect and to the suspicions with which intellectual labor could be greeted by the African American rank and file. In pursuing a new construction of the black intellectual, writers like Johnson and Du Bois drew on existing strengths within African American culture, even while deploying them in ways that work against the grain of existing anti-intellectual strains within the faith, and perhaps even against the grain of the faith itself.

For instance, although anti-intellectualism was a feature of African American life as it was pervasive in the rest of American life, Posnock's basic thesis that there is a long history of the literate African American as culture hero is surely correct. The quest for at least basic literacy from slavery to World War I was coextensive with the quest for freedom, sign and symbol of the African American's full humanity in the face of white supremacy. Although

I believe Posnock unhelpfully conflates the literate person with the intellectual, the image of literacy as liberating was also, surely, a heroic image
cultivated and promulgated vigorously by the aspiring intelligentsia. It gave
a ground on which to build. In the "Wings of Atlanta," Du Bois draws on
this tradition and, in the early portions of the essay at least, positions the
preacher and the teacher as twin pillars of resistance to the debasing pursuit
of material gain without spiritual development:

> In the Black World, the Preacher and Teacher embodied once the ideals of
> this people—the strife for another and a juster world, the vague dream of
> righteousness, the mystery of knowing; but today the danger is that these
> ideals, with their simple beauty and weird inspiration, will suddenly sink to
> a question of cash and a lust for gold. (*Souls* 57)

Du Bois's assertions reflect the value long placed upon preachers and teachers
in African American culture, a value that someone like Booker T. Washington
shared even while he tried to distance himself from developing notions of
the intellectual.

Writers of the twentieth century do, however, articulate the role of the
educated man differently. Prior to the twentieth century, preachers and teachers shared the same social and institutional spaces. Indeed, churches often
also served as schools. Intellectuals that we point to as founding fathers of
African American intellectual, literary, and even political traditions were
most often ministers. However, later writers position the intellectual as a
distinct figure, separate from and even opposed to the Christian leaders who
otherwise captivate the minds and spirits of the African American populace.
In *Souls of Black Folk*, the preacher may be a man at the center of a group
of men, but through the course of the book, he is gradually displaced by the
educated man as the true center and benefactor of African American culture.

Hofstadter and others point out the ways in which the social roles associated with higher education became increasingly rationalized at the turn of
the twentieth century through the processes of professionalization. Although
my own use of the term intellectual is more expansive than Hofstadter's,
including literary artists, teachers, and others, it does seem to me that a
similar process occurs among the African American intelligentsia. Indeed,
upon Du Bois's resignation as editor of *The Crisis*, the board of the NAACP
recognized as one of his significant contributions the creation of a black
intelligentsia where one had not existed before (Du Bois, *Crisis* 429). This
could not reasonably be taken to mean that there was no black intellectual
work prior to Du Bois but rather that "intellectuals" or "the intelligentsia"

did not exist as a recognizable social group independent of other social groups, especially the church.

In creating this new status, New Negro intellectuals from 1900 to 1940 divided the world between superior intellectuals and inferior proponents of religion, even if this discourse was usually milder than the antireligious screeds of white counterparts like H. L. Mencken. This is seen even in statements that acknowledge the role of Christian faith such as "Wings of Atlanta." As I have suggested, Du Bois initially positions the preacher and the teacher as allies in opposition to the corrosive effects of mammon. Gradually, however, religion is relegated to an inferior position:

> The function of the university is not simply to teach bread-winning, or to furnish teachers for the public schools or to be a centre of polite society; it is, above all, to be the organ of the fine adjustment between real life and the growing knowledge of life, an adjustment which forms the secret of civilization. Such an institution the South of today sorely needs. She has religion, earnest, bigoted: —religion that on both sides of the Veil often omits the sixth, seventh, and eight commandments, but substitutes a dozen supplementary ones. . . .
> The Wings of Atlanta are the coming universities of the South. They alone can bear the maiden past the temptation of golden fruit. They will not guide her flying feet away from the cotton and gold; for—ah, thoughtful Hippomenes!—do not the apples lie in the Way of Life? But they will guide her over and beyond them, and leave her kneeling in the Sanctuary of Truth and Freedom and broad Humanity, virgin and undefiled. (60)

Du Bois's messianic view of university life is almost astonishing given our common contemporary discourses about the failures of higher education. The educator is a savior, particularly saving the virgin purity of the race. Religionists in *Souls of Black Folk*, by contrast, have already shown themselves to be defiled and unworthy of the task of protecting the virginal purity of the South (and even more specifically the African races of the South) in having regularly violated the injunctions against murder, adultery, and theft. In Du Bois's framework, religion is one of the primary violators of Southern purity. While the focus is surely on the violation of African America by white bigotry, Du Bois is clear that those responsible for this violation exist on both sides of the veil. Although the "wings" of Atlanta are not clearly gendered, the gendering of the South in the virginal Atlanta readily suggests a tradition of female purity in need of protection. Education, intellect, culture: these virtues and, by implication, the men associated with them are the worthy guides and saviors of the new race.

Imagining the intellectual as a distinguished visitor who is not at home is a form of discourse about intellectuals that first took shape during the New Negro Renaissance. It is, however, a discourse that continued to shape thinking about black intellectual work through Harold Cruse and the Black Arts movement to contemporary thinkers such as Cornel West. Consistently, this discourse troubles the question of the intellectual's authenticity as a person of, by, and for African American people, and prescriptions concerning appropriate forms of black intellectual labor attempt to negotiate the distance between the concrete experience of the average African American and the reflective activity of the intellectual. Writers and intellectuals between 1900 and 1940 sought a form of intellectual labor that could be regarded as genuinely African American and genuinely useful, this in the midst of an encompassing white American culture at large that doubted the intellectual abilities of African Americans in the first place and that considered intellectual activity in general to be impractical when not impious. Nevertheless, the intellectual's role as hero was not easily and straightforwardly imagined. In the ensuing chapters, *Goodbye Christ?* will look more closely at New Negro efforts, often frustrated efforts, to achieve narrative closure and resolution to the conflicts that arise around the complicated figure of the black intellectual.

"LEAVE ALL THAT LITTLENESS AND LOOK HIGHER"
The Educated Man as Hero and Martyr

> The contemporary black intellectual faces a grim predica-
> ment. Caught between an insolent American society and an
> insouciant black community, the African American who takes
> seriously the life of the mind inhabits an isolated and insulated
> world. This condition has little to do with the motives and in-
> tentions of black intellectuals; rather it is an objective situation
> created by circumstances not of their own choosing.
>
> —Cornel West

One outcome of the complicated social positioning of the African American intellectual is that New Negro narrative is preoccupied with analyzing and resolving the tensions of that social position. Much critical attention has been focused on the dilemma of the black intellectual in what is not only an insolent American society but also often an aggressively dismissive and racist one. Somewhat less attention has been given to what Cornel West once described as an indifferent black community, especially as conflict with that community is represented in fiction. As my last chapter suggests, African American intellectuals and artists faced not simply indifference but suspicion, if not outright hostility, toward their work. Wary church leaders and lay men and women saw the secular pretensions of intellectuals as not only threatening to the faith but, by extension, as a betrayal of the race they had rooted in a specifically Christian mythos. At the turn of the twentieth century these conflicts were especially intractable. Although intellectuals felt higher academic and artistic work could redress or at least ameliorate racism in the United States, that very pursuit drew African American intellectuals ever further from the ground of their intellectual vocation in and to a specific religious people.[1] It is one thing to assert the preeminent stature of the intellectual life as Du Bois does in "Wings of Atlanta." It is another to envision realistic means of creating that stature in a social world, even a fictional one. In the next two chapters, I will look at New Negro efforts to render the preeminence of the intellectual life in a racial world ambivalent in its attitudes toward that life. In the fiction of Du Bois, Hughes, and Jean Toomer taken up in this chapter, I look closely at the distance between two factors: on the one hand, the narrative of immersion and return that sought to establish the Northern, educated intellectual as an authentic spokesperson and, on the other, the actual difficulty of establishing such connection. Ultimately, New Negro narratives of the intellectual hero tell the story of men who are partial successes but also partial failures, deferring fulfillment to a future that can be intuited but not grasped.

DU BOIS AND THE PROBLEM OF THE RELIGIOUS PAST

While W. E. B. Du Bois was a man of some doubt and uncertainty when it came to the specifics of Christian faith, he was a man of great confidence in the powers of education and of intellectual work particularly to meet and overcome the social ills plaguing African Americans in a racist society. For Du Bois, the entire edifice of racial progress rested on the foundation of the talented tenth, which itself lay on the bedrock of educational achievement, which in turn ultimately depended upon the leadership of an intellectual class. Nevertheless, the plausible coherencies of educational, social, and political theorizing proved less certain in the more prosaic encounters with real life on the ground of American racism and anti-intellectualism. The overwhelming popularity of Booker T. Washington at the time of the writing of *Souls of Black Folk,* as well as Du Bois's own sense of distance from religious, class, and cultural realities of many African Americans, left Du Bois uncertain, if not of the significance and truth of his own theories, then of how to implement them effectively with the rank and file of a community unprepared to receive them. In order to bridge the distance between his gospel of enlightened education and a community living behind a veil of racism that made that gospel incomprehensible, Du Bois regularly adopts a discourse of heroic martyrdom that underscores the moral and spiritual authority of his educational message while deferring its realization to a future not yet revealed, a method that allows Du Bois to rearticulate material failure as a more fundamental success.

Du Bois's wrestling with the role of the intellectual within the African American community is vividly charted in "Of the Coming of John," the story of a young black man from the South who has gone north to study, much to the delight of black folk and to the dismay of white folk in his hometown. Upon his return, whites censure John for teaching things to young black children that shouldn't be taught, reflecting the tensions over education and racial domination. He is also censured by blacks for putting on airs that seem to raise him above the common run of folks and especially for having forgotten the religion of his people. The Methodist preacher says he "'Peared kind o' down in the mouf," and a Baptist woman says that he "Seemed monstus stuck up" (148). Some readings of this story suggest that the focal point is John's education and his inability to connect to the community, but such readings seem to underplay the ways in which Du Bois emphasizes the fact of religion as a shaping force in the community. Otherwise the specific references to a Methodist preacher and a Baptist woman seem mostly gratuitous. Including this specification points out that it is John's loss of faith, or at least his changed and modernized faith, that precipitates social alienation in spite of communal pride at his accomplishments.

As with "Faith of the Fathers," distance from religion is a complicated phenomenon in this short story. It is both a source of alienation and a source of power. He transcends the provincialism of religion that holds the culture captive. He is also a lonely and isolated figure as male messiahs usually are in American popular culture. The "real man" in this tradition is beset on all sides by false traditions and other oppressors but maintains his beliefs and integrity against the odds, delivering the people from both their oppressors and their baser instincts. Such is the American Adam from Natty Bumpo to Clint Eastwood in his spaghetti Westerns to epic narratives in films like *Unforgiven*. Most of these lonely American heroes, however, have not been intellectuals, and Du Bois's rendering of John as such is a creative turn on that tradition. In Lewis's words, "No one could make a virtue of loneliness better than Du Bois" (*Biography of a Race* 134). Drawing on a masculine discourse of isolation and loneliness, Du Bois is able to offer a rationalization for his distance from the emotional, spiritual, and imaginative horizons of the black folk he represents, even while that distance becomes itself the source of a promised communal redemption and transfiguration. Loneliness is a source of trouble, but it also certifies power and promise.

Consistent with the larger themes of *Souls*, John establishes his claim to manly distinction through his superior use of language, but even this "superiority" marks out the great chasm that exists between the educated and enlightened Du Bois and the community of his attention. In "Faith of the Fathers," the shrieking women and the preacher spewing words both require the calm interpretive activity of the intellectual Du Bois speaking to a more composed reading audience. "The Coming of John" evinces a similar dynamic. At the church service celebrating John's return, various denominations of black Christians are present, putting aside for the moment their religious disagreements. John's presence, not unlike the presence of James Weldon Johnson as a "distinguished visitor" in the preface to *God's Trombones*, seems to discombobulate the three local preachers, who all falter and fail to varying degrees. The Methodist doesn't elicit an "Amen"; the Presbyterian draws no response; the Baptist gets so confused he stops early. John, however, is thoughtful and erudite; he is also dismissive of values the community holds dear:

> "Today," he said with a smile, "the world cares little whether a man be Baptist or Methodist, or indeed a churchman at all, so long as he is good and true. What difference does it make whether a man be baptized in river or washbowl, or not at all? Let's leave all that littleness and look higher." (149)

These lines resonate with Du Bois's confrontations with the religious leaders of Wilberforce, Fisk, and Atlanta University. Throughout his life, Du Bois pleaded with the church to downplay doctrinal beliefs and make a place for the intellectual. In *The Crisis*, Du Bois outlined a plan for improving the churches that called for "Bending every effort to make the Negro church a place where colored men and women of education and energy can work for the best things regardless of their belief or disbelief in unimportant dogmas and ancient and outworn creeds" (*Crisis Writings*, "The Negro Church" 333). The fact of such pleading suggests the degree to which the educated African American did not find the church to be such a place. The "unimportant dogmas" and the "ancient and outworn creeds" were fundamental signs of the "Old Negro" unfit for the new world.

Such ideas sound common and unremarkable to the academic ear; they elicit aggressive responses from John's audience. Following John's talk—it could not be called a sermon—a lay preacher pronounces judgment:

> Then at last a low suppressed snarl came from the Amen corner, and an old bent man arose, walked over the seats, and climbed straight up to the pulpit. He was wrinkled and black, with scant gray and tufted hair; his voice and

hands shook as with palsy; but on his face lay the intense rapt look of the
religious fanatic. He seized the Bible with his rough huge hands; twice he
raised it inarticulate, and then fairly burst into the words, with rude and
awful eloquence. He quivered, swayed, and bent; then rose aloft in perfect
majesty, till the people moaned and wept, wailed and shouted, and a wild
shrieking arose from the corners where all the pent-up feeling of the hour
gathered itself and rushed into the air. John never knew clearly what the old
man said; he only felt himself held up to scorn and scathing denunciation
for trampling on the true Religion, and he realized with amazement that all
unknowingly he had put rough, rude hands on something this little world
held sacred. He arose silently and passed out into the night. (149–50)

Sundquist sees in this portrait "the quality of faith that Du Bois located in
the slave generation" (523) and endorses Du Bois's portrayal of the preacher
as simple realism, calling it "brilliant" (524). Sundquist says, "His 'sermon' if
one may call it that, takes John as its text, and with the passion, frenzy, and
extraordinary vocality characteristic of the fundamentalist black preacher,
denounces all that John stands for, his educational and social aspirations
forged at once of assimilation and alienation" (524). Sundquist reads the
text as a straightforward denunciation of John, one pole of a long and
conflicted critical reception of the story. Sundquist's reading, perhaps the
dominant pole, focuses on the ways in which assimilated intellectuals failed
to actually connect with and understand the black community. They fail at
authentic blackness in some sense precisely because of the education they
have pursued. I find this reading understandable but finally implausible,
primarily because John reflects in almost every instance Du Boisian values for
the intellectual. He particularly reflects Du Bois's general critique of existing
black religion as an impediment to progress rather than an authenticator
of culture. If John is unable to connect effectively with the community, the
failure rests at least as much in the community's inability to listen and hear.
The story embodies the dilemma that Cornel West articulates and Du Bois
repeatedly expresses: John's education has left him homeless—in part, yes,
because he has assimilated the norms of Western educational priorities but
also because the community cannot receive intellectual work per se, especially not work that calls into question its fundamental and—in this case,
unthinking—values.

Daphne Lamothe largely agrees with Sundquist when she argues that
Du Bois is characterized by an "unwillingness to accept the notion that 'the
folk' as primitive subalterns, cannot speak. This unwillingness is illustrated
by his depiction of the tension existing between literate and illiterate, cosmopolitan and tribal, representative and represented" (65). In this reading,

John fails because he believes the folk cannot speak, or at least he cannot comprehend what they speak of. However, this reading, like Sundquist's, ignores that religious folk in the story do very little speaking at all, at least about the religion that matters to them. Indeed, Sundquist's reading gives us a great deal about the text of the sermon that we can't find in the story itself. What stands out is that the preacher is inarticulate and can't be understood; certainly not by John and not by the reader. The lay-preacher snarls and climbs over the seats in front of him. He has the palsy and sways and trembles much like the quivering preacher in "Faith of the Fathers." He raises the Bible aloft twice but cannot speak, as if the book itself is making him silent. He does finally "burst" into words that the narrator describes as "eloquent." However, this eloquence is opaque and unintelligible. John himself "never knew clearly what the old man had said." Neither does the reader. We hear instead Du Bois's eloquent description. The people respond with shrieking and wailing. However, this shrieking is not narratively connected to the preacher's words but to his inarticulate body as it quivers, sways, and bends while the congregation moans, weeps, wails, shouts, and shrieks.

An early version of this story included a full-blown representation of a black preacher's rhetorical eloquence, a sermon Bernard Bell has called "one of the earliest and, even in its unpolished state, most effective imaginative reconstructions of the fiery blend of Old and New Testament biblical imagery and the soul-stirring participatory drama of a black chanted sermon in 19th century American and Afro-American literature" (117). The published version gives us none of this. I agree with Sundquist and Bell regarding Du Bois's masterful control of prose in this story; however, in view of that mastery, the existence of a fully developed sermon implies a narrative choice. Du Bois could have, for instance, chosen to represent the sermon itself much as James Weldon Johnson represented sermons in *God's Trombones*. He does not do so, choosing to represent black religion primarily through chaotic physicality rather than through a form of folk intellectual or artistic discourse. And, as James Weldon Johnson's poems make clear, this intellectual and artistic discourse did surely exist. As a consequence of its absence in this story, we can only judge black religion through the consciousness of the modernist, intellectual skeptic, John, who cannot understand the preacher.

This focus on John's superior intellectual and rhetorical gifts, of course, privileges the significance of education in the ideological frame of the story. However, it also reveals a gap between word and action that intellectual work itself is unable to close. If a people cannot understand you and is not moved to action by your words, of what use your superiority? While John evinces the superiority of education on the one hand, he also reveals its problematic ineffectiveness on the other. Is John merely a speaker of the word, or is he also a doer of the word? The narrative as a whole seeks to emphasize a link between rhetorical competence and effective liberatory action while leaving the final achievements of those actions in an ambiguous and deferred state, a state that John's martyrdom underscores even as martyrdom is evoked in order to overcome the gap between educational ideals and pragmatic action.

The narrative most clearly endorses John as the male worthy of emulation in his role as protector of his first disciple, his sister Jennie. Upon leaving the church service, he is followed and embraced by his sister as they speak of the sad but necessary superiority of learning to religion. They represent the beginning of a small community of the educationally redeemed. Late in the story, John is on the verge of giving up in the face of white racism and black disdain. While walking out toward the sea, he sees his sister struggling in the arms of the white judge's son who is attempting to rape her. John's response is immediate and decisive:

> He said not a word, but, seizing a fallen limb, struck him with all the pent-up hatred of his great black arm; and the body lay white and still beneath the pines, all bathed in sunshine and blood. John looked at it dreamily, then walked back to the house briskly, and said in a soft voice, "Mammy, I'm going away, —I'm going to be free."
>
> She gazed at him dimly and faltered, "No'th, honey, is yo' gwine No'th agin?"
>
> He looked out where the North Star glistened pale above the waters, and said, "Yes, mammy, I'm going—North." (153)

In the face of stereotypes of passive male intellectuals, John is the man who acts, the true inheritor of the Danish blacks and the fierce Maroons. Indeed, it is worth noting that John "said not a word" but begins immediately to act. That he is already well established as a man of words, however, tends to reinforce rather than diminish a connection between education, rhetorical power, and material action. While the inarticulate preachers are swaying and quivering, provoking the people to an ecstasy that leaves them submissive to white domination, John acts boldly. Whereas his own father is absent, John asserts himself as the protector of the family—the new patriarch who protects his sister. He takes up a fallen limb and strikes out against his sister's attacker. Unlike the quivering and palsied body of the lay preacher, John's "great black arm" embodies hatred and material strength and energy directed outward against a foe.

This scene dismantles the conventional distinction between the man of words and the man of action. As my last chapter suggested, much of the public rhetoric surrounding intellectuals during Du Bois's career was that they were ineffectual and impractical at best—artificial men who were not up to the task. By contrast, John, the articulate and erudite man, is the effective battler on behalf of his family and his race. The absent body of his father, the palsied bodies of the black preachers, and the shrieking bodies of the black women who are their communicants do nothing to rescue the spirit of the people. Only the intellectual leader of the race strikes out.

John's defense of his sister results in more word play as John goes home to tell his mother he is going to be free. The mother's hesitant insistence that he is going north promotes ironic affirmations by John; he is going north—the traditional land of freedom—but he is also going to the North Star, or to heaven—that other land of freedom longed for by the Negro church. The ironic wordplay represents John as the truest masculine leader, one who can use words rationally, playfully, and movingly, but also a man who raises his strong right arm.

There are, of course, other strong readings of the text that suggest John is anything but a culture hero. Lamothe suggests that the

> powerful image [of John's lynching] captures the acute irony of John's situation, lauding on the one hand art's universality; yet on the other hand implicitly condemning his classical education for not equipping him with the means to navigate the treacherous waters of the racist and uncivilized Southern society to which he returned. (67)

I agree with the broadest elements of Lamothe's interpretation that John's efforts are in some sense a "failure" if by failure we mean that John did not immediately achieve the liberating effects that he and his entire community longed for. On the other hand, I cannot agree with Lamothe that Du Bois is implicitly rejecting or condemning the classical education that John received—one that Du Bois championed so passionately and repeatedly throughout *Souls of Black Folk*. John's humming of Wagner's "The Song of the Bride" is a repetition of Du Bois's formal operations throughout *Souls of Black Folk*, linking classical education to black experience—and here to the primordial and agonizing experience of racial violence in the lynch mob. It is analogous to Du Bois placing the tunes of spirituals alongside references to classical poetry. Such links suggest a form of racial and intellectual utopianism in which the black intellectual can combine and unify the contradictory elements of both cultures in one body as an avatar of the future.

Viewed in this light, John's "failure" is less a judgment on him than a judgment on the present order. John, like many messianic figures who precede him, is a prophet who cannot be received in his own country. The surest sign of his success is his own martyrdom. The lynching that concludes the story is not so much a sign of failure as an ironic affirmation of his masculine apotheosis. Indeed, we might say that lynching in general represents a particularly horrific tableau through which black masculinity has been asserted. For Trudier Harris, lynching ritualized an emasculation that the rebellious black male has apparently forgotten:

> The image of the harmless darky came to epitomize the black man who was socially and psychologically emasculated. Hand-me-down hat in hand . . . stooped shoulders, head bowed, without sexual consciousness or ability, eyes forever on the tip of the master's shoe, a 'Yessuh' forever on the tip of his tongue, this character soothed white consciences and justified their claims to superiority. (*Exorcising* 29)

If the submissive "darky" is already an unambiguous symbol of emasculation, the lynched male body perversely affirms the masculinity of the black rebel by the very rage with which that masculinity is attacked. The lynched body signifies a man who has not stayed in his place, who has either forgotten or rejected his emasculation in a racist society. Because John's body threatens white domination, it must be destroyed. Ironically, because John's is the body that whites fear, John the intellectual is affirmed as the symbol of potential liberation. The old black preacher, by comparison, may evoke sympathy or even a limited admiration; he does not, however, inspire emulation. One expects he will grow old and die in his church, not in battle.

The final segment of *The Souls of Black Folk*, "The Sorrow Songs," supports this reading. Here, Du Bois specifically links the ancient song of his great-great-grandmother, "Do bana coba gene me," to the story and music of John Jones. "This was primitive African Music: it may be seen in larger form in the strange chant which heralds 'The Coming of John': 'You may bury me in the East, / You may bury me in the west, / But I'll hear the trumpet sound in the morning,' —the voice of exile" (157). Du Bois specifically references the headnote to the story. Given the ways in which Du Bois deploys music throughout *The Souls of Black Folk*, the "heralding" of John affirms John, an affirmation that Du Bois can articulate not through the material success of liberation but through the spiritual figure of martyrdom. Paradoxically, John's death affirms his power. The distance between John's educated life and the religious life of his community collapses through the sounds of the spiritual—"the trumpet sound in the morning"—that promise resurrection, the form of ultimate liberation for the redeemed. Formally, the spiritual and the Wagnerian opera are conflated in ways that symbolically close the distance between the martyred prophet and his people.

In other fiction and poetry, Du Bois was drawn to figures of martyrdom both to articulate present resistance and to defer the instantiation of its material success to an apocalyptic future. Images of crucifixion and of Black Christs are recurrent, especially in the collection *Darkwater*. In the story "Jesus Christ in Texas," a black man arrives in town and experiences a form of martyrdom as he seeks through his own death to take the place of the death of others. He is portrayed explicitly as having "the voice of a white man" (63), perhaps suggesting a formal education in the racial codes of the day, but certainly linking two cultures in much the way that John Jones links two cultures in the story written two decades earlier. The lynching of this particular black prophet suggests the possibility of liberation and redemption, certainly for the black race, and perhaps for white persons who will recognize Christ in those they crucify. A white woman who claimed to be attacked by a different black man recognizes the crucifixion in the lynching:

> A fierce joy sobbed up through the terror in her soul and then sank abashed as she watched the flame rise. Suddenly whirling into one great crimson column it shot to the top of the sky and threw great arms athwart the gloom until above the world and behind the roped and swaying form below hung quivering and burning a great crimson cross.
>
> She hid her dizzy, aching head in an agony of tears, and dared not look, for she knew. Her dry lips moved:
>
> "Despised and rejected of men."
>
> She knew, and the very horror of it lifted her dull and shrinking eyelids. There heaven-tall, earth-wide, hung the stranger on the crimson cross, riven and blood-stained, with thorn-crowned head and pierced hands. She stretched her arms and shrieked.
>
> He did not hear. He did not see. His calm dark eyes, all sorrowful, were fastened on the writhing, twisting body of the thief, and a voice came out of the winds of the night, saying:
>
> "This day thou shalt be with me in Paradise." (64)

Here the crucified Christ is identified with the black thief who is being lynched, and the prayers of the white woman are not heard as this Christ attends to the violence and pain and suffering of the lynched black man. The white woman's awakening may, indeed, have come too late for any effective salvation. However, provoking awakenings is the role of martyrdom, bearing witness to a wider and larger truth than the immediate "failure" attending the loss of life. A similar structure of lynching as martyrdom that awakens and bears powerful witness can be found in the poem "The Prayers of God," wherein, again, the identification of black suffering and lynching with the person of Christ serves to awaken, if not transform, the white perpetrators of injustice.

In the ideological structure of martyrdom, putative "failure" bears witness to a broader story of success. Stories of Christian martyrs sustained the church during persecution, giving narrative and psychic strength to those who did not have the material power to control the narrative of an oppressive culture at large. Du Bois's story structure uses martyrdom as a powerful bridge to overcome the alienation that John felt in the opening of the story. Creating martyrs to epitomize manhood is a common trope, one that draws self-consciously on Christian roots. In African American literature and popular culture, the lynched black man is repeatedly figured as a crucified Christ. Frequently, in the twentieth century, these lynched men are portrayed as intellectual men, or at least men educated to the point that their education conflicts with the white community. By placing the educated man at the center of lynching narratives, black writers revised a white Southern imaginary that regularly carried out lynching on specious charges of rape or molestation, playing on the image of uncontrollable black sexual potency. This revision on the part of Du Bois and black intellectuals is striking because it displaces the common image of the intellectual as effete and impractical with an image of dangerous political virility.

The discourse of martyrdom is a particularly powerful method for negotiating the divide between the intellectual labors of the talented tenth and their uncertain reception among the working classes. On the one hand, the suffering of the martyr establishes him or her as one of the faithful. Or, in the terms developed in Du Bois's short fiction and poetry, it establishes the intellectual as one with the people because he suffers as they suffer. His intellectual heroes testify to what it means to be a black man in a racist society. At the same time, martyrdom establishes the transcendence of the martyr by becoming an exemplar for the faith or, in the case of Du Bois's short stories, for the race. Du Bois's crucified/lynched Black Christs are especially singled out because they threaten or undermine the forces that cause black suffering in the first place. To live as an old, inarticulate man like the black preacher in "Of The Coming of John" is to live out an expected script in the narratives of white power; to die because you bothered to resist that power is to establish your own manly authority. The superiority of the intellectual in this discourse is established most firmly by the violence with which it is extinguished rather than through the material changes he is able to achieve. Finally, the discourse of martyrdom enables a writer like Du Bois to negotiate the immediate question of the effectiveness of the intellectual life in that martyrdom is always tied to future hope. One dies as a martyr in testimony to a world that is to come; the promise of a utopian future gives meaning to a death and life that might otherwise seem random or inconsequential.

LANGSTON HUGHES AND THE AMBIGUITY OF MARTYRDOM

Theologian James Cone has noted the pervasiveness of lynching narratives in African American literary history as well as their recurrent connection with images of crucifixion and, more broadly, of martyrdom. For Cone this connection between lynching and crucifixion—a fundamentally religious image—was far more pervasive among the agnostic literati than among preachers and theologians, even in the black church, a fact he attributes to the lesser imaginative capacities of theologians and ministers (95–96). Nevertheless, Cone seems to assume the naturalness of this connection and elides the question of aesthetic choices and ideological urgencies. Why did this narrative form prove particularly attractive or compelling to writers like Du Bois, Hughes, and Cullen? As Candida Moss points out in *The Myth of Persecution*, accounts of martyrdom from Socrates and Jesus to the Anabaptists of the *Martyrs Mirror* are not simply factual accounts in the historical archive; they serve ideological purposes. Martyrdom stories are particularly powerful tools for supporting the validity of belief. "[There] was no better argument for the sincerity of an individual's belief than the fact that he or she was prepared to die for it. . . . [Martyrs] were powerful spokespersons for the church" (19). Moreover, Moss notes that martyrs were particularly powerful because they were in some sense ordinary:

> [Martyrs] were deeply cherished by the Christian laity. Martyrs were ordinary people—slaves, women, and children—as well as bishops and soldiers who had risen above the constraints of their circumstances to display exceptional courage. For those who experienced hardship and heard stories of the sufferings of martyrs, these Christian heroes were deeply personal sources of inspiration. . . . In a world in which social mobility did not exist, they lived a dream that many dared not imagine. (19)

Martyrs, in short, are exemplars in the sense of being both an exceptional ideal of faith to imitate and one person among many, an example *for* the faithful and an example *of* the faithful. This general structure serves the purpose of exalting the position of the educated man in the face of the manifest failure of the ideologies of education as uplift. That is, if education and cultural development were designed to overcome racism, the continuing facts of racism and the inability of intellectual work to resolve them threatened the status of the educated man, as did the cultural gulf created by education itself. As my readings so far have suggested, this narrative of return is fraught with contradiction and complication. The educated man is not only rejected and threatened by the white society around him but also rejected or misunderstood by the black community to which he returns—a prophet without honor in his own country. In the narratives of return that I have looked at so far, martyrdom serves the peculiar purpose of both giving meaning to black suffering by making the educated man an exemplar and covering over the very real fact of a failure to reconnect. In death, the martyr becomes a leader the people can follow because they can see his moral superiority in his courageous willingness to suffer to the point of death. Martyrdom effects unity with the common folk that is otherwise impossible to achieve among the living because of the gulf created by education itself. Authentic blackness is signified through nothing else if not suffering at the hands of whiteness, and so the black intellectual certifies his oneness with the "insouciant" masses through a spectacular and exemplary death at the hands of common white persecutors.

Such negotiation of various divides suggests why this kind of martyrdom narrative proved useful to other writers, even those who were not so driven by their perception of talented tenth superiority. Langston Hughes draws on this view of the educated person, though to somewhat different and even more ambiguous ends. As I have pointed out, Hughes, of all the Renaissance writers, did more to project himself as the writer at one with the common man and woman. This immersive pose left him, at times, ill at ease; he seems halfway apologetic that he went to college at all, and he wears the mantle of the poet lightly, at times, uncomfortably. He famously repudiated the learned life in his autobiography when he recounts throwing his collected library into the sea. This is a constructed fiction since the testimony of his biographers and even of his own letters suggests that he kept up an active reading life. But that it was a fiction Hughes chose to employ does suggest that Hughes had little interest in walking arm in arm with Du Bois and Aristotle across the color line.

At the same time, Hughes clearly felt the distance and tension that pursuing the work of a literary intellectual could entail, tensions both with white power structures and with black social and cultural expectations. If anything, he felt it more acutely. His famous early essay "The Negro Artist and the Racial Mountain" charts the travails of being a black artist in a racist culture. Like "Of the Coming of John," it registers the failure of the black community to embrace the black artist. Much of his criticism is leveled at middle-class African Americans whom he accuses of "aping things white"

(*Essays* 32), and this racial mimicry itself seems deeply connected to forms of Christianity that long for "an Episcopal heaven." However, an aside in the essay points out that the "low-down folks" seem largely satisfied in a world of their own making and have little need for the makings of a poet. "And perhaps these common people will give to the world its truly great negro artist, the one who is not afraid to be himself. Whereas the better-class Negro would tell the artist what to do, the people at least let him alone when he does appear. And they are not ashamed of him—if they know he exists at all" (32–33). This last uncertain note prefigures Hughes's judgment on the Harlem Renaissance as not making that much difference to the "ordinary Negro" (*The Big Sea* 178). The inconsequentiality of intellectual work, even of Hughes's own poetry, is striking. Nevertheless, Hughes did not rest with a judgment on the inconsequentiality of his art or its irrelevance to even the low-down folk who didn't care about it. No less than Du Bois, Hughes saw writing and intellectual labor as having a special role in achieving the freedom of African Americans and, perhaps even more than Du Bois, cast that role in terms of political and other material achievements. Between the swelling individuality of "The Negro Artist and the Racial Mountain" and the self-deprecating tone of *The Big Sea*, Hughes argued passionately for the life-changing and transformative power of writing and its special role in realizing a future world. For instance, his address to the American Writers Congress in 1935 emphatically insists on the responsibility of African American writers and white writers alike to make a difference: "We want an America that will be ours, a world that will be ours—we Negro workers and white workers! Black writers and white! We'll make that world!" (*Essays* 133).

Thus, even Hughes felt drawn to this discourse of the educated man as culture hero and martyr as he negotiated the practical invisibility of the artist to the vast majority of African Americans. He investigates this image most clearly in the story "Father and Son," written in the early 1930s as a revision of his play *Mulatto*. The two narratives were written roughly in the same period as Hughes's growing political activity, the play early and the story late, the latter coming near the high water mark of his rejection of the Christian God in "Goodbye Christ." Although the language of martyrdom is itself rooted in imaginative forms drawn from Christianity, "Father and Son" suggests developing concern with the contrast between political passivity induced by Christian obedience and masculine rebellion encouraged by education. Like "Of the Coming of John," martyrdom in "Father and Son" closes the gap between the community and its educated hero. However, Hughes's grappling with the material and communal dynamics of racism is far more pronounced than that of Du Bois, and consequently the success of martyrdom as a revolutionary strategy is ultimately far more suspect.

Hughes's story recounts the return to the Norwood Plantation of Robert Norwood, mulatto son of Colonel Norwood and Cora, his black mistress. Robert has been away at college and, upon his return, believes that he should be treated with the same respect as any white man. Colonel Norwood's refusal to recognize him as a son leads to Robert killing the colonel. The consequences are predictable, but Robert frustrates the designs of the lynching party by shooting himself before the mob's desires can be realized.

Both the story and the earlier play from which it is drawn expound upon Hughes's concerns with metaphorical and literal homelessness in the United States as a feature of racial identity. Robert's self-assertion is partially articulated through laying claim to his whiteness, a theme at the center of the play *Mulatto*, but more muted in "Father and Son." In the original play, education is tied closely to Robert's apparent desire to be white. In the later short story, by contrast, his mixed racial heritage is more muted, and his rebelliousness is driven primarily by his education, his learning driving him to refuse the common tactics for ameliorating racial pain and division.

In the play, Robert rejects his mother's pleas that he return to his subservient ways by asserting his mixed racial identity:

ROBERT: (Angrily) And I'm not black, either. Look at me, mama. (Rising and throwing up his arms) Don't I look like my father? Ain't I as light as he is? Ain't my eyes grey like his eyes are? (*Plays* 35)

Such moments signal an ambivalent racial identity. Colonel Norwood provokes this ambivalence in a final confrontation.

ROBERT: (After a pause) I'd like to kill all the white men in the world.
NORWOOD: (Starting) Niggers like you are hung to trees.
ROBERT: I'm not a nigger.
NORWOOD: You don't like your own race? (ROBERT is silent) Yet you don't like white folks either?
ROBERT: (Defiantly) You think I ought to? (39)

These passages resonate with Hughes's "Racial Mountain" essay published two years before he began to write *Mulatto*. In some respects, the educated Robert is not unlike the nameless black poet in Hughes's essay who, in Hughes's judgment, really wants to be white. Robert's silence at his father's question concerning racial identity produces an ambiguity. On the one hand, of course, he could simply be rejecting Norwood's conflation of the slur "nigger" with racial identity. For Norwood, to be black is to be "a nigger,"

and Robert's silence could be a rejection of that term. However, his defi-
ant "You think I ought to?" could apply to his disaffection for both white
people and, possibly, for black people. These ambiguous moments evoke,
in some respects, the anguished longing for racial approval and belonging
that, according to Rampersad, shaped Hughes's career and may also reflect
Hughes's judgment on his father's racial self-hatred (378).

This ambiguity is also present in the short story. For instance, Robert
refuses his sister's imprecations that he be a bit more docile in expressing
himself to the Colonel: "'Why should I be?' Bert asked 'I'm the old man's
son, ain't I? Got white blood in me, too?'" (*Short Stories* 138). However,
this general issue is much more muted in the story, and much more significance is given to the fact of Robert's education as a motive force for social
change. Robert makes far fewer references to his light skin, his grey eyes,
or his "whiteness" in general. Whereas the play roots resistance in Robert's
biological status, as seen in Robert's claim to the privileges of having "white
blood," the short story is more clearly trained on establishing a form of resistant black masculinity rooted not in blood but in education. For instance,
conflict with the postal employee turns on Robert's superior ability to work
with simple math. Bert corrects her efforts at counting change and insists
"You owe me twelve cents more":

> The girl looked at the change and realized she was wrong. She looked at
> Bert—light near white nigger with grey-blue eyes. You gotta be harder on
> those kind than you have on the black ones. An educated nigger, too! Besides
> it was hot and she wasn't feeling well. A light near-white nigger with grey
> eyes! Instead of correcting the change, she screamed, and let her head fall
> forward in front of the window. (142)

After a scuffle in which Bert bloodies one white man's mouth, he leaves the
Post Office, and soon the woman "was telling everyone how Bert insulted
her" (143), a racial code accusing Bert of making a sexual advance. In the
furor that follows, the postmaster, Higgins, accuses Colonel Norwood of
bad behavior, especially for having educated his black children.

"Father and Son" underscores Robert's rebellious force by contrasting
it with other African Americans who are defined as "white folk's niggers"
(138), blacks who are subservient and docile. The story emphasizes that
Robert's siblings, Willie, Bertha, and Sallie, are biracial as well but draws
strong distinctions between them, distinctions that turn on differences of
education and religion. Willie and Bertha both proved unfit for the college
in Atlanta. His younger sister, Sallie, has been educated but seems much

more in the mold of her mother and other traditional "plantation Negroes" in urging her older and rebellious brother to be cautious and obedient.

These characters are also clearly devout Christians, the narrative emphasizing that Christianity serves the purposes of white supremacy through emasculation of the black male. Willie, Bert's brother, is marked as a praying man, but also a humbled and fearful one. "Willie and the Colonel got along fine, because Willie was docile and good natured and nigger-like, bowing and scraping and treating white folks like they expected to be treated" (138). After a tense confrontation between Bert and the Colonel, the narrator describes the tension among the black plantation laborers. "In his cabin Willie prayed, too, humble, Lord, humble. . . . Bow down and pray in fear and trembling, go way back in the dark afraid; or work harder and harder; or stumble and learn; or raise up your fist and strike—but once the idea comes into your head you'll never be the same again" (139). The narrator, writing close to Bert's consciousness in these passages, links Christianity to servility and quietism before the rhetoric moves from learning to physical action: stumble and learn, raise up your fist and fight.

The story goes on to more emphatically imagine the abandonment of Christianity as a prerequisite for forceful action after Colonel Norwood orders the local black minister to begin a revival with the explicit purpose of distracting servants from their complaints, trusting in spiritual fervor to help them forget "the troubles of this world":

> Poor over-worked Jesus! Somehow since the War, he hadn't borne that cross so well. Too heavy, it's too heavy! Lately, negroes seem to sense that it's not Jesus' cross, anyhow, it's their own. Only old people praise King Jesus any more. On the Norwood plantation, Bert's done told the young people to stop being white folks' niggers. More and more, the Colonel felt it was Bert who brought trouble into the Georgia summer. The revival was a failure. (140)

Newly discovered aggressiveness occasioned by the war is linked to abandonment of Old Negro masculinity associated with the Christian minister. As with Du Bois's "Of the Coming of John," Bert's resistance as an educated man suggests that the development of the intellect results in practical and aggressive action, an imaginative move that both displaces the Christian minister as community leader and overturns the image of the educated man as effeminate or impractical.

Nevertheless, the ambiguities of the educated man as a culture hero are more pronounced for Hughes than for Du Bois, and the differences may lie in Hughes's more acute and troubled sense of the intellectual's relationship to the larger social order. Whereas Du Bois's John actually saves his sister and, by implication, his community, Bert saves no one in particular. He battles white power structures largely through pursuing his own rights and self-interest and, like John, seems pronouncedly separate from the rest of the community by virtue of his education. Moreover, his killing of Colonel Norwood in the short story results not only in his own death but also in that of his brother, a lynching that is noted in the local papers:

DOUBLE LYNCHING IN GEORGIA

A large mob late this afternoon wrecked vengeance on the second of two Negro field hands, the murderers of Colonel Thomas Norwood, wealthy planter found dead at Big House Plantation. Bert Lewis was lynched last night, and his brother, Willie Lewis, today. The sheriff of the country is unable to identify any members of the mob. Colonel Norwood's funeral has not yet been held. The dead man left no heirs. (153)

The final line of the story casts an ambiguous pall over both Colonel Norwood and the other dead men of the passage, Bert and Willie. On the one hand, there is a prophetic judgment that Norwood is the end of a line. On the other hand, and ironically, both Willie and Bert are his progeny, his putative "heirs," at least in a fantastical world in which race does not count as it does in the United States.

Willie's death also demonstrates the ambiguity of casting the educated man as racial martyr, one that Du Bois's story elides by stopping just prior to the lynching. Willie's lynching may merely underscore the fact that Christianity cannot save you in the racist South. However, it also casts a shadow over Bert's character and over martyrdom as a political ideal, implicitly critiquing the romantic exaltation of intellectual resistance to white power that motivated Du Bois's story. By concluding "Of the Coming of John" just prior to the lynching itself, Du Bois leaves us with a vision of the heroic male and with the memory of his recent victory over white oppressors. This conclusion obscures the social reality that Hughes's story exhibits. That is, lynchings were not only assaults on individual heroes; they were assaults upon entire communities. They were forms of social violence and political control rather than instances of individual retribution against individual men. Indeed, lynching regularly played out in the fashion suggested by Hughes's short story. While individual black men alone might be lynched, their families and in many cases their entire communities were often assaulted and lynched in the bargain.

The irony of the educated man as martyr is that his apotheosis might guarantee him a place of communal honor. It might just as easily result in communal terror and death. The ambiguity of martyrdom in Hughes suggests the ambiguity of martyrdom generally as a narrative strategy. Although Du Bois's narrative encourages us to imagine the intellectual in the pantheon of racial heroes, and indeed insists on placing the African American culture hero cheek by jowl with the cultural heroism of the West in general, it is ironic that the intellectual's racial authenticity can only be guaranteed through his death. Hughes—more uncertain from the start about the role of intellectual pursuits that seemed to impose a distance from the wisdom of the common folk—raises the question of whether the intellectual sees and understands the nature of his own relationship to the racial politics of the Southern folk. Does the quest for individual intellectual achievement guarantee either racial belonging or racial advancement? Martyrdom in both stories creates heroic images of resistance to racial oppression, but neither ultimately finds a place for the educated man within the social life of an ongoing racial community.

JEAN TOOMER AND THE IRONY OF MESSIANIC MANHOOD

The male protagonists of Hughes's and Du Bois's stories play out a complicated engagement with two intertwined narratives that were central to African American cultural production as well as to the production of masculinity in the United States between the World Wars. First, they are enacting a form of masculine apotheosis through martyrdom; through heroic deaths, alienated intellectuals seek reintegration with the Southern folk they are supposed to represent, lead, educate, and free. Second, they are enacting a narrative of return: on the one hand a return to primal cultural roots and on the other a return to enact a messianic mission through education. This narrative of return to the South was pervasive throughout the period, with missionary impulses to promote and seek racial uplift tangled with a complicated sense of return to authenticity through a reconnection with roots, always defined as the more primitive, simpler, and blacker Southern experience. To this degree, the ideology of return ironically reinforced intellectual alienation as educators from the North returned to the South, both to "reconnect" with a lost homeland and to turn the denizens of that homeland into people more like themselves.

Indeed, the ambiguous martyrdoms of characters in Du Bois and Hughes are designed to overcome this contradiction, and their very ambiguity suggests that this form of martyrdom depends upon the presumed value of reconnection. It assumes, in other words, that the intellectual apart from the common folks is deracinated, inauthentic, or otherwise without significant meaning. Reconnection is imperative, both to certify the racial authenticity of the educated leader and to effect the process of racial uplift that education is supposed to provide. In *Cane,* Jean Toomer questions these assumptions even while he both uses the framework of the narrative of return and invokes and manipulates the image of the intellectual as a martyr or potential martyr. Ultimately, Toomer ironizes the figure of the intellectual as hero nearly to the point of burlesque as his educated heroes are neither missionaries nor martyrs but, depending upon their orientation to the past and the future, can become nearly pathetically disconnected figures who have undertaken a delusional quest into the past instead of facing firmly toward an as-yet unrealized future.

To note the complications in Toomer's return narratives is not in itself unique; it is very nearly now a staple of Toomer criticism, dividing those who see in Toomer himself a racial champion from those who see him primarily as a racial Judas. On this score, I am in broad agreement with Robert Arbour's argument when he questions reading Toomer as an avatar of folk spirit as did many of his earlier reviewers or, alternatively, as a champion of racial modernization through the aegis of the intellectual as do Mark Whalan or Martin Favor. I agree with Arbour that Toomer "proposes an aesthetic and subjective reconnection with a Southern folk identity accomplished through metaphor, a project consistent both with his interest in the construction of a new American race and with the redefinitions of the folk during the Harlem Renaissance" (308). The critical point of emphasis here is metaphor. Although it is clearly the case that Toomer invokes the mythos of return to roots, such images of return in Toomer are aborted when they are literalized. Return is an imaginative or intellectual sympathy with what one cannot possibly become rather than the organic or immersive continuity some intellectuals imagined. As metaphor, the Southern African American can be carried forward by an intellectual who resolutely faces a future only partially realized.

What seems to me to be missing from Arbour's and other similar accounts is an adequate view of the relationship between spirituality, intellectualism, race, and future hope in Toomer's work. That is, too little attention has been paid to *Cane* as a "spiritual" text, one that reflects Toomer's persistent interests in a form of spirituality that he viewed as not opposed to Christianity so much as beyond it. *Cane* prefigures Toomer's later intellectual and spiritual development rather than being fundamentally opposed to it, as so many commentators have believed. Indeed, Toomer's letters are replete with evidence that he is already concerned with the spiritual ideas that developed in his later thinking. His letters make clear that his late poem

"Blue Meridian," a spiritual manifesto of sorts, was begun at least three years prior to the publication of *Cane,* though it was not finally published until thirteen years after his signature work. So the works were in many respects conceived simultaneously. *Cane* is clearly an initial groping toward the kind of vision of human integration that was far more overt in the later work. This is only evident if Toomer's views of spirituality and religion are foregrounded in the reading rather than taken as incidental examples of folk culture and its problems.

This recognition also clarifies some elements of Toomer's views of both intellectual work and Southern black Christianity. Toomer understands the ascent of the intellectual not as an apotheosis of black progress but as a way station on the road toward higher spiritual fulfillment. Rather than embracing Enlightenment reason, whereby the exercise of intellect dispels the clouds of religious mystery, Toomer sees at least certain forms of the educational and intellectual process as inimical to integration, part and parcel of the process of mechanization and alienation that he otherwise perceives as a modern disease. He imagines an alternative spirituality that intellectual work could, but did not necessarily, further. This emergent and yet-to-be-manifest humanity could live a fully integrated life-body, intellect, imagination, and spirit together. Nellie McKay suggests that the overriding concern of Toomer's work from the beginning has been a quest for integration, a quest to "bring the physical, emotional, and intellectual parts of himself into harmony." Viewing *Cane* as part of that quest posits that it is not a singular flowering distinct from the later work but the first extended effort to imagine such integration. Integration, however, must be oriented toward a future state of emergence rather than toward the typical narrative of a return to roots or a spiritual identification with the folk. To attempt to place one's identity in past roots is to embrace a false image of primitive authenticity that leaves the present incapable of authentic self-possession. Abandoning the self to the past is an impossible fantasy that prevents the possibility of fully embracing and owning oneself for the future.

The destructive potential of a fantasy of return is vehement in a number of stories throughout *Cane,* such as "Esther" and "Box Seat." These themes are especially pronounced in the concluding story of the book, "Kabnis." The eponymous main character, Kabnis, typifies the intellectual on the road of return to the South, return on the one hand to fulfill the *noblesse oblige* of the educated classes on an educational mission but on the other to demonstrate a racial unity that would guarantee the authenticity of his art. Since Waldo Frank's early review, *Cane* has been read as a pastoral in which alienated modern man rediscovers the roots of his humanity. In this view, Kabnis is a New Negro counterpoint to Eliot's Fisher King on a journey of return, baptizing himself in the great river of Southern blackness. In the 1960s, when *Cane* was rediscovered, this reading was revitalized to emphasize the need for connection to racial heritage in a way that made Toomer surprisingly accessible to the imperatives of the Black Arts movement. Indeed, so enduring is this explanatory narrative that it influences the portrait of Toomer's biography as such, with critics implying that the later Toomer had not followed the wisdom of his own artistic achievement in abandoning race for the theosophical vagaries of the religious mystics Gurdjieff and Ouspensky.

That the racialist underpinnings of this narrative have yet to be abandoned is more surprising given the fact that the text offers so little support for them. What is repeatedly true of the educated Northern pilgrims to the South from the narrator of "Fern" to Kabnis himself is just how elusive if not deluded the hopes of such return and reintegration really seem to be. Kabnis is an ironic, almost satirical, reminder that far from messianic fulfillment or atavistic restoration, a "return to roots" is a nearly pathetic mistake, one that can lead at best to a purging of the self to gain an orientation toward the future. Like similar stories from Du Bois and Hughes, the impossibility of return is partially predicated on the facts of education and the gulf created by that experience. Nevertheless, within "Kabnis," the focus is primarily on just how ignorant his education has left him, particularly in delivering him to the grip of fantasies of the South very far from the lived experience of African Americans in the region.

Unlike the protagonists of "Father and Son" and "Of the Coming of John," who were born in the South and are literally enacting a story of return, Kabnis knows nothing of the deep south except what he has heard through family stories and gossip, not terribly unlike the narrator of Cullen's poem "Heritage," who listlessly thumbs picture books of Africa in order to establish some kind of connection to an imaginary homeland. Early in the story, trying to justify and confirm his desire for connection, Kabnis resorts to the myths of the idyllic South, myths promoted primarily by the plantation school of white American fiction. The other men of the story caution Kabnis against his romantic views and suggest he's not completely fit for the South as it actually exists. He emphasizes his family connections, as if to draw on a biological or biographical connection to the culture from which he is so obviously alienated. The preacher/teacher Layman cuts Kabnis off with the reminder that a family tree is "Nothin t feel proud about" (89). Halsey and Layman point out that this very belief in racial roots dissolves the vision of Southern hospitality in which Kabnis wants so desperately to believe:

HALSEY: . . . An Mr. Kabnis, kindly remember you're in the land of cotton—hell of a land. Th white folks get the boll; the niggers get the stalk. An don't you dare touch the boll, or even look at it. They'll swing y sho.

KABNIS: But they wouldn't touch a gentleman—fellows, men like us three here—

LAYMAN: Nigger's a nigger down this way, Professor. An only two dividins: good an bad. An even they aint permanent categories. They sometimes mixes um up when it comes t lynchin. I've seen um do it. (89)

Kabnis, in such passages, comes across as an educated man divorced from effective self-awareness and cultural knowledge. He presumes that his status as an educated gentleman is a shield against the violence of Southern white racism while his Southern black counterparts understand that the capriciousness of violence makes no such distinctions. If anything, the fact of his education may make him more of a target, as my earlier discussion of the threat that education poses to white supremacy may suggest. Unlike the protagonists of Du Bois's and Hughes's stories, the educated man is not posited as a heroic exemplar over and against the religious ignorance of the masses. To the contrary, Toomer wrote extensively and critically about the role of education in the uplift of African Americans. In "The Negro Emergent," he comes very close to the Bookerite critique of higher education and echoes distantly the judgment that education—at least in its modern forms—is a "white thing" that has nothing to do with authentic Negro existence:

[The] Negro has become a victim of education and false ideals. In terms of mastery, the results have been both ludicrous and pathetic. But this is true of most educational attempts, though it is less apparent in white examples. For Negroes had a special cause for their submission and desires: the white man claimed that the Negro was mentally inferior. Here was a chance to disprove that statement. The Negro would cram his brain with theories, dates, the Greek alphabet, and become equally civilized. He has done so: he is beginning to question the profit of his efforts. For he now seeks a balanced life, based upon capacity, wherein all faculties are given the necessary usage. (*Selected Essays* 49–50)

The sarcasm of the passage calls into question the idea that education is the route to uplift, or at least to a form of cultural and social health. The essay does not deny that education has been necessary given the circumstances but regards the forms and intents of that education as misguided in and of themselves. Applied to Kabnis, this might suggest that the hero has yet to abandon the image for reality. He is crammed with theories—or at least stories and fantasies—of human behavior, but he doesn't see the world as it exists around him. More than this, however, Toomer questions whether mastery of "white" forms is an appropriate end to seek. The problem with education in this vein is that it is an imitation of the imbalanced and mechanistic life that has developed in modern civilization as a whole, producing not so much spiritually whole and integrated human beings as cogs in a machine. Indeed, "The Negro Emergent" goes on to chart not simply the fact of false consciousness among an oppressed people but a broader concern with the forms of modern life. Toomer argues, "The mass of whites, save in the single instance of racial oppression, are as bound and determined as the mass of blacks." The apparent advantages and opportunities of educational and material advancements disguise a more fundamental alienation and unfreedom, one that extends, in a startling passing statement, even to the facts of violent racial oppression itself: "It is assumed, among other things, that the white man voluntarily oppresses the Negro, that he freely hates him, that white mobs are acting from free will when they lynch a Negro" (*Selected Essays* 50). It is not a dramatic convolution of the essay to say that Toomer sees that the forms of education promoted by movements for racial uplift were themselves unconsciously continuous with rather than opposed to the lynch culture they sought to counter—a view that, as I shall suggest in my next chapter, Toomer holds in common with Nella Larsen. Toomer construes lynching and racial hatred as signs of compulsion and constraint from which education, on its own, delivers no one. Intellectual pursuits as normally conceived and unintegrated with other elements of body mind and spirit are merely another part of the problem rather than an avenue toward wholeness.

This unconscious continuity between the culture of the Southern lynch mob and the culture of modern education suggests the limitations of most critical responses to the story, which cast *Cane* either as a pastoralist argument for the politics of return or as championing modern educated New Negro. It is simultaneously a criticism of both because neither the mission of racial uplift nor the deliverances of religious salvation in its Christian mode can orient human beings toward the future as Toomer imagines it. Thus, while critical camps either see Toomer embracing one or the other, he is, in my view, questioning both since neither an archaic folk religion and culture nor a fragmented intellectual knowledge is sufficient to the necessities of the human future.

Therefore, Kabnis's inability to graft himself to the roots he hopes to find in Southern culture is represented as a failure. However, it is a failure of conception rather than evidence that Kabnis needed to be more receptive to the wisdom of the folk. He is especially disturbed and repulsed by the Christianity that pervades the region, identifying as he does religion with the most negative and degrading aspects of his existence. Because Kabnis is himself a relatively unsympathetic character, it is tempting to believe the story endorses the folk Christian culture Kabnis rejects. At one point, Halsey mocks Kabnis's nervousness about a church service, suggesting that Northern African Americans are most interested in regulating the experiences of others that they don't understand:

> Singing from the church becomes audible. Above it, rising and falling in a plaintive moan, a woman's voice swells to shouting. Kabnis hears it. His face gives way to an expression of mingled fear, contempt, and pity. Layman takes no notice of it. Halsey grins at Kabnis. He feels like having a little sport with him.
>
> HALSEY: Let's go t church, eh, Kabnis?
>
> KABNIS: (seeking control): All right—no sir, not by a damn sight. Once a day's enough for me. Christ, but that stuff gets to me. Meaning no reflection on you, Professor.
>
> HALSEY: Course not. Say, Kabnis, noticed y this morning. What'd y get up for an go out?
>
> KABNIS: Couldn't stand the shouting, and that's a fact. We don't have that sort of thing up North. We do, but, that is, someone should see to it that they are stopped or put out when they get so bad the preacher has to stop his sermon for them.
>
> HALSEY: Is that th way youall sit on sisters up North?
>
> KABNIS: In the church I used to go to no one ever shouted—
>
> HALSEY: Lungs weak?
>
> KABNIS: Hardly, that is—
>
> HALSEY: Yankees are right up t the minute in telling folk how t turn a trick. They always were good at talking. (91)

The irony of this passage is that it embodies the simultaneous critique of religion and of education that I have been suggesting. On the one hand, Kabnis is criticized by Halsey, a man who is himself hardly a sympathetic character. As Barbara Foley points out, he is likely based on the figure of Lucius Holsey, a well known black minister who was an apologist for white supremacy in Sparta, Georgia (180). Simultaneously, however, we are almost inevitably alert to Kabnis's lack of the sort of empathetic imagination he needs to appreciate the power and emotion of black Southern religion. His discomfort with emotional and spiritual experience suggests he is a truncated man, certainly not the whole and integrated man that Toomer tried to imagine in his more spiritual and philosophical writings.

Toomer's search for an integrated solution to personal and social problems—what he described as a search for a "new vital religion"—does not mean that he was enamored of religion per se. He was raised in a fairly irreligious household, his mother a nominal Catholic, and he held fairly typical modern attitudes toward religious groups. He claimed to have felt

> no bias for or against any faith, sect or creed. Nothing could be more remote
> from or abhorrent to my nature than that I take part in those perversions
> which are not ashamed to bear the names of religious persecutions and reli-
> gious wars. But I have hated and I do hate the vices and vanities, the thirsts
> for power, the crafty acquisitiveness, that hide under religious cloaks. I do
> hate the oily piety, the sweet sugar frosting, the hypocrisy, the infidelity. And
> I do hate the organized religious machine. The majority of my contacts with
> conventional religion have caused mechanical pain or suffering. (*Wayward* 65)

Toomer's characterization of religion as mechanistic sounds a common re-frain that modern institutions turn men in to machines.[2] Indeed, throughout his life, Toomer was inspired by various religious philosophies, not simply those of Gurdjieff but by any religion that he viewed as primarily experi-ential and antithetical to the rationalization of modern organized faith. His views of the Negro Church varied. While his depiction of Halsey may recall forms of accommodation to racism that existed in Southern churches, at other points, Toomer saw in black religion the kind of holistic, integrated life that he imagined should be sought for the future. Toomer asserts that, unlike the Puritans, "[The] Negro finds that the poverty of creed has not killed his religious impulse. He is on earth, so placed; somewhere is God. The need to discover himself and the desire to find God are similar. Perhaps that strange thing called soul, hardly an existence, rarely mentioned nowadays above a whisper, the Negro in his search may help uncover" ("Emergent" *Selected Essays* 52). Toomer appreciates the cultural dynamism of the folk and their religion, suggesting later in "The Negro Emergent" that "The Ne-gro has found his roots. . . . And something of their spirit now lives within him. He is about to harvest whatever the past has stored, good and evil" (54). Nevertheless, just as the narrative repeatedly questions the adequacy of Kabnis's education and the politics of uplift on which it is based, his narrative consistently questions the adequacy of this religious formation to the problems of the present, an interrogation that takes the form of a critical vision of different permutations of religious manhood. Characters who fail to recognize the temptations of return violate both the past and the present at the cost of immense destruction to themselves and others. Taking "Kabnis" and "The Negro Emergent" together, we may say that neither the road of antique spirituality nor the road of modern education provides a pathway forward for African Americans; the one tries to apply an effective solution of the past to a very different present while the other tries to address a holistic human problem with a truncated vision of education, this itself drawn from a white model that has served the purposes of the very white supremacy it is designed to overcome.

Kabnis himself seems unable to negotiate this problem, having both a romantic and therefore ahistorical view of Southern folk life and being unconscious of his own allegiance to what Toomer would judge as fragmented and despiritualizing views of the mind. As Toomer says himself in judgment of Kabnis:

> The elemental pulse of a peasant people, together with the impalpable fog of white dominance and its implications which the raw sensibility of Ralph Kabnis (the protagonist) spreads over the entire countryside, are too strong and oppressive for his depleted energies to successfully grapple with. Hence Kabnis progresses downward from rejection and defiance to a passive acceptance of them. Such acquiescence, in a man potentially capable of directing life, signifies frustration and defeat. This drama is then the tragedy of a talented Negro whose forces have been dissipated, whose remaining strength is unequal to the task of winning a clear way through life. ("The South in Literature," *Selected Essays* 15)

I agree with Barbara Foley that such a judgment militates strongly against positive readings of Kabnis; certainly it suggests that Kabnis is not the strong intellectual male hero figure on the order of the characters from Du Bois and Hughes and Johnson that we have examined so far. Moreover, I think Foley is correct that the secondary character, Lewis, is a stronger candidate for a New Negro character who is not tragic but has an opportunity to find a clear way through life. But whereas Foley sees Lewis as Toomer's ideal because of his socialism, it is more important to note that Lewis embodies a nuanced effort at integration, one that respects and learns from the past as a model, but retains a fundamental orientation toward the future as the site of an authentic humanism, one that neither old style religion nor New Negro educational uplift can effectively achieve (168).

Lewis, like Kabnis, does not seem interested in embracing Southern black religious expression for himself. Late in the story, he remarks to Kabnis on the conflicts that he has had with the community over his own lack of religious convictions, especially with regard to the passivity he believes Christian traditions of good and evil and final judgment induce. Regarding such stories, Lewis says, "Interesting, eh, Kabnis? But not exactly what we want" (101). Lewis honors the framework of the religion of the folk without embracing its specific manifestation. What is "interesting" in the narrative of sin and judgment and the Second Coming is the apocalyptic promise of

newness. The fracturing of existent social order makes room for new possibilities, for the metaphorical "New World Christ" that Dan Moore announces
in "Box Seat." Yet, it is "not exactly what we want" because, ironically, this
announcement is primarily backward-looking and closed off from possibility.
People are too weak. Every question is shut down by a preexistent answer
that allows for no genuinely new creation. As such, Lewis cannot imagine
himself "returning" or "reconnecting" to the South; he has no apparent
counterpart to the family in Georgia that Kabnis dubiously romanticizes.
Indeed, Lewis does not seem interested in fitting in at all because such fitting
in would be undesirable in the end. Fitting in would inhibit the emergence
of the New Man and substitute an old Christ that delays the emergence of
the "New Christ," the new man for a new generation.

Lewis's complex attitude toward black religion is evident in his response
to Father John. While Kabnis is contemptuous of the old man, calling him
a "black fakir," Lewis reads Father John into a story of emergence. When
he first sees the old man in the fifth section of the story, he alone gives attention and a form of dignity to the old man:

> To the left, sitting in a high-backed chair which stands upon a low platform,
> the old man. He is like a bust in black walnut. Gray-bearded. Gray-haired.
> Prophetic. Immobile. Lewis' eyes are sunk in him. The others, unconcerned,
> are about to pass on to the front table when Lewis grips Halsey and so turns
> him that the candle flame shines obliquely on the old man's features.
>
> LEWIS: And he rules over—
> KABNIS: Th smoke and fire of th forge.
> LEWIS: Black Vulcan? I wouldn't say so. That forehead. Great woolly
>   beard. Those eyes. A mute John the Baptist of a new religion—or a
>   tongue-tied shadow of an old.
> KABNIS: His tongue is tied all right, an I can vouch f that.
> LEWIS: Has he never talked to you?
> HALSEY: Kabnis wont give him a chance.
>   *He laughs. The girls laugh. Kabnis winces.*
> LEWIS: What do you call him?
> HALSEY: Father.
> LEWIS: Good. Father what?
> KABNIS: Father of hell.
> HALSEY: Father's th only name we have fer him. Come on. Lets sit down an
>   get t th pleasure of the evenin.
> LEWIS: Father John it is from now on...

Slave boy whom some Christian mistress taught to read the Bible. Black man
who saw Jesus in the ricefields, and began preaching to his people. Moses-
and Christ-words used for songs. Dead blind father of a muted folk who feel

their way upward to a life that crushes or absorbs them. (Speak, Father!)
Suppose your eyes could see, old man. (The years hold hands. O Sing!) Suppose your lips. . . . (106)

Foley notes that the conclusion lends itself to the wide variety of readings
that have attended it, including arguments for Kabnis's quasi-spiritual redemption, and criticism of Lewis since he leaves the story entirely. I agree
with Foley that the conclusion of the story is ironic, but not precisely with the
kinds of judgments that Foley makes on the characters in the text, especially
on the Christian characters who seem to end the story on an oddly positive
but static note. Of these characters, Foley says the following:

> Carrie K. and Father John remain in the basement where, Kabnis notes,
> "they used to throw th old worn-out slaves" (113); the folk Christianity
> embraced by the young girl and the old man is part of a "buried culture"
> that will remain buried. Carrie Kate's "nascent maternity" is, in this reading,
> merely metaphorical; the preservation of her chastity may satisfy the needs
> of the brother of Mamie Toomer, but—sequestered in her brother's basement
> and bound to the past—she is one more Black Madonna who will not give
> birth. Moreover, while Father John's long-awaited words of wisdom may
> not warrant Kabnis's cynical response that the former slave is an "old fakir,"
> through Kabnis—indeed through Cane—it has been repeatedly suggested
> that "white folks" have "made the Bible lie": the blind prophet's pronounce-
> ment conveys no startling insight of use to those subjected to the rigors of
> present-day Jim Crow. (184)

Foley is clearly correct about the buried status of Kabnis and the others
at the end of the text. I cannot possibly read Kabnis's exhaustion and loss
of hope as a prefiguring of redemption simply because they take place in
rays of a sunrise. This would suggest that the conclusion is an unnuanced
instance of the pathetic fallacy. However, I do think it is important to read
the final scenes, and especially the figure of Father John, in light of Lewis's
interpretation of the old man, and especially in light of his bidding him to
speak and to sing. Indeed, the man speaks shortly after Lewis, the avatar of
an integrated futurity, bids him to speak. Moreover, what he speaks finally
is precisely what Lewis has recognized: a prophetic word against the corruption of the existent Christianity of which he is a part. Lewis recognizes
the prophetic potential within the old man seeing both the testimony to
oppression and prophecy of new possibility. Unlike the old preacher in
"Of the Coming of John" or the fearful Christians of "Father and Son,"
Father John is not simply a tongue-tied shadow of an old religion but a
John the Baptist of a new religion, of a new world Christ. This possibility
of emergence is traced in Lewis's narrative of the old man's engagement

with language. Learning from a slave mistress, the old man in Lewis's story takes that language to make his own new creation, his own new possibility. Black Christianity, for Lewis, is the story of words made new for new circumstance, enabling the upward struggle toward self-realization of a muted folk. When Lewis imagines what might be possible if the old man could see or speak, he is wondering what new creation might be possible now—how would the old give birth to the new if the old were not sunk in mute and sightless stasis? What can be drawn from the old man, then, is a story of hope for a new creation. The usable past is not the specifics of Christian belief but the monumental act of taking something that is old, dead, or oppressive and making it new.

Foley notes that earlier versions of the story gave Father John a larger and more voluble role (185). To some degree, it seems to me the silencing of Father John in the story works in similar ways to the silencing of the preacher in "Of the Coming of John." The ability to use language well and effectively is a sign and symbol of imaginative and spiritual power. Father John is mute, but in a certain sense so is Kabnis throughout the text—a writer who cannot write because he cannot find his way to the future. But Father John has clearly spoken in the past, using the Christianity he received in new ways for what was at that time his new day. In this process of discovering the essentially liberating aspects of past cultural forms, Lewis sees a model for his own form of prophetic activity, one that endorses the culture of folk religion without perpetuating it. Ironically, both the old Christian man, Father John, and the New Negro man, Lewis, are more adept at this poetical "making new" than is Kabnis, the writer who rejects what he cannot understand. Because Kabnis can only imagine the new as absolutely split from the old, or engagement with the old as a form of atavistic return into worshipful silence, he remains trapped in the cellar, oscillating between rejection of the past and its embrace. Lewis, by contrast, recognizes that the past may be embraced insofar as it testifies to the emergence of the new. Lewis alone among Toomer's characters is able to embrace the past without falling victim to it because in it he finds a trajectory toward the future. Lewis, as the New Man—perhaps the "Blue Man" that Toomer projected into the future—cannot remain in the story because to do so would calcify the story of return to authenticity. The blackness of Southern folk life cannot be recovered or returned to, but it can be learned from. To believe otherwise is to become a pathetic figure like Kabnis, stumbling in the darkness, buried in a cellar.

"THAT GOOD MAN, THAT GODLY MAN"

Abusive Ministers and Educated Lovers in Oscar Micheaux and Nella Larsen

In the writers examined in the last chapter, educated men and intellectuals take center stage, which moves Christian figures such as preachers to the periphery. Even while the success of such men is deferred into an unrealized future, in the representational economy of a short story, drama, or novel, it is their story to which we attend, their failures and successes that matter. Their representation of racial identity and loss and triumph carries out a kind of metonymic action in which the story of the intellectual man serves as the common reference point for the whole. In our imaginative engagement with them as readers, we assent, at least for the period of our reading, to their primacy and claims on our attention while Christian figures like Father John or the growling preacher in "Of the Coming of John" become part of the furniture of their larger secular drama.

Nevertheless, neither Du Bois, Hughes, or Toomer portrayed Christianity as a positive evil, focusing instead on the ways in which Christianity passively retarded racial development in its resistance to education or in its affirmation of virtues like patience, long-suffering, and otherworldliness. Father John is superseded because he is old, ineffectual, and out of touch, not because he is malicious. The Christian folk in *Mulatto* and "Fathers and Sons" are primarily frightened rather than bold. They are not positively advancing the race; they are also not actively wounding it. A fairly mild version of this critique of Christian faith is found in James Weldon Johnson's *Autobiography of an Ex-Colored Man*; the protagonist, reflecting on the Christian faith he sees around him and especially in Harriet Beecher Stowe's *Uncle Tom's Cabin,* says: "For my part, I was never an admirer of Uncle Tom, nor of his type of goodness; but I believe that there were lots of old Negroes as foolishly good as he; the proof of which is that they knowingly stayed and worked on the plantations that furnished sinews for the army which was fighting to keep them enslaved" (39). This criticism is consistent with Du Bois in "Faith of Our Fathers," wherein the Christian faith of the enslaved led to passive acceptance of their lot rather than activating a desire for freedom. Throughout the period, however, a grimmer analysis perceives in Christian faith not only ineffectiveness or irrelevance but conscious or unconscious malice as well as active collusion with the enemies of the race. This chapter looks closely at this specific critique of African American Christianity as it is found in the work of Oscar Micheaux and Nella Larsen. Negative portrayals of Christian faith by these two artists open other more secular means of envisioning racial experience, culture, and meaning, especially focusing on the figure of the educated man. However, Micheaux and Larsen differ significantly both in their portrayal of a pernicious Christian faith, and in their hopes for a racial future. Micheaux's celebration of the educated and professional bourgeoisie is consistent with the celebration of educated classes found in Du Bois, even if Micheaux's own racial politics were more clearly Bookerite. By contrast, Larsen's work evinces a bitter disappointment with the promise of education and the arts, at least as it is lived out by the Du Boisian talented tenth. In Larsen's vision, the deliverances of education are compromised in that they simply mirror, and so perpetuate, patriarchal domination by means less metaphysical but no less sure than the dominant forms of African American faith.

CHRISTIAN CORRUPTION AND CINEMATIC
STEREOTYPES IN OSCAR MICHEAUX

Few writers make the malicious effect of Christian faith, and especially the male leaders of that faith, as central to artistic and political vision as Oscar Micheaux. Micheaux despised the clergy with a vitriol that makes Hughes and Du Bois seem pious, a well-documented criticism of his work. Explanations for this bitterness tend to focus on personal biography. Bowser and

Spence, like many others, note that depictions of preachers who are lecherous, violent, greedy, and grifting, and especially who were enemies of the race, were likely born out of Micheaux's personal experience with having his marriage broken apart by a disapproving father-in-law who was a clergyman (*Writing Himself* 187). For Bowser, this critique is narrowly focused on the clergy without extending to the church or to questions of theological conviction. Discussing church scenes in *Within Our Gates*—during which Ol' Ned, a typically corrupt Micheauxian preacher, manipulates his congregation into a religious frenzy—Bowser and Spence suggest that "Micheaux is not attacking the institution of the church, or even the emotional catharsis of the Black folk sermon, but condemning those who, under the guise of moral authority, lead the group astray" (150). This strikes me as an overly generous reading when looking at Micheaux's work as a whole. I see little evidence that Micheaux sought to redeem the church or that he made a separate judgment of the church in comparison to the evildoers within it. He does not replace evil Christian men with better Christian men; he does not counter manipulative sermons with artistic or inspiring sermons on the order of those in James Weldon Johnson or Zora Neale Hurston. Rather, the preachers are culpable in their manipulation and greed, and the congregations are culpable in their gullibility. In portraying the black preacher and his congregation as he does, Micheaux's work is continuous with a larger New Negro Renaissance project of moving Christianity from the center of African American experience to be replaced by the figure of educational achievement.[1] While Micheaux's views on education tended to be Bookerite, and while he had a strong preference for the ideals of the self-made and individualistic man over racial solidarity, Micheaux saw the future of the race embodied in an ideal of educated masculinity that could overcome the superstitious and abusive practices he associated with the church.

Indeed, Micheaux's aggressive critique of the church and mockery of the people who could support it were part of his effort to achieve a larger bourgeois ideal for the race. This contrast between Micheaux's middle-class ideals and his mockery of the race has left critics unable to settle on an image of Micheaux as either a racial champion or a racial traitor. For bell hooks, Micheaux's manipulation of the relationship between audience and spectacle decomposes stereotypical images of African Americans, while for Joseph Young, Micheaux is guilty of the most egregious forms of internalized racism. In a scathing denunciation, Young declares Micheaux a "white racist," saying of his films and novels,

> Micheaux was . . . influenced by what was happening in literature. The
> impact of the local color school and the plantation school on Afro-American

literature . . . forced many black literary artists to accept the conventional image of Blacks as quaint, picaresque, and exotic. Although Micheaux's black characters are not quaint, picaresque, or exotic, their flaws are exaggerated to such an extent that they almost mirror the basic Plantation mythical image of Blacks, which deprived them of dignity, maturity, and any mental capacity for independent judgment. (9)

Surveying the conflicted judgments that Micheaux's films provoke, Jane Gaines offers the obvious but still true observation that "the jury is still out on Oscar Micheaux (243).

Bowser and Spence attempt to negotiate Micheaux's regularly difficult and troublesome depictions of common black folk by arguing that Micheaux provides them with forms of character development that go beyond stereotypes as well as by noting how the use of stereotypes was usually for a larger moral purpose, the stereotype having a powerful rhetorical force that enabled black Americans to confront internal dilemmas and contradictions.

Racial stereotypes are usually analyzed in the context of racist motivations or effects: to justify and maintain white domination, aggression, and privilege. However, if we look at Eph and Old Ned as discourses from within the Black community, as part of the Grand Narrative, and examine the social voices speaking through these characters, we see that Micheaux's strategic use of the stereotypes was not meant to dehumanize or subordinate but to posit moral instruction, as examples of misplaced values and low self-worth. (153–54)

Such a reading is clearly consistent with the argument of this book that the period of the New Negro Renaissance is as much an argument about religion as it is about the confrontation with racial oppression. Certainly, as an artist, Micheaux can't be critiqued for having a stake in that important discourse. Moreover, there is clearly something to be said for this reading in that there are moments in Micheaux's films when evil or deluded Christians have moments of insight. Ol' Ned in *Within Our Gates* has a moment of guilt in which he is disgusted with himself for his willingness to use his position for material gain. But these moments are few. And the moments when some African Americans are clearly and obviously dehumanized or subordinated to depictions of others are quite abundant.

Focusing on Micheaux's representation of black Christians won't resolve these dilemmas, but an examination of two of his films, *Within Our Gates* and *Body and Soul*, will suggest that the ideological purposes that these stereotypes serve bring Micheaux into more intimate contact with the main currents of the New Negro Renaissance between 1900 and 1940 than is usually thought. His depictions of black Christians lack the nuance and complexity of almost every other artist of the period, but they nevertheless are connected to a similar ideological effort to question the pervasive definition of black life as inherently Christian and to exalt a definition of African Americans characterized by educational achievement. By bringing Micheaux into the same context as writers like Du Bois and Hughes or Toomer and Larsen, we can understand his work as contributing to a broad and serious effort to reimagine the future of the race rather than simply indulging in stereotyping. Whether that proximity redeems Micheaux from the charge of malicious racial self-hatred is debatable, but it underscores the ideological, cultural, and imaginative tensions that surrounded the subject of black Christian faith during the period.

Body and Soul tells the story of a corrupt black minister, Isaiah Jenkins, played by Paul Robeson. An escaped felon who has hoodwinked his congregation, Jenkins gambles, drinks staggering amounts of alcohol, preys sexually and financially upon the women he holds in thrall, rapes the young heroine of the film, robs her mother, and reaches the nadir when he clubs a young boy to death in the film's most chilling scene. All this occurs while Sister Martha Jane, the heroine's mother, worships him with a barely disguised erotic devotion. When her daughter, Isabelle, attempts repeatedly to tear back the veil that Jenkins has thrown over her mother's eyes, Sister Martha Jane is only appalled that Isabelle would dare to cast aspersions on Jenkins's character, a man whom she calls on several occasions in the film "That good man. That Godly man."

In one scene that some of Micheaux's critics have found particularly disturbing, Reverend Jenkins preaches to a congregation just prior to his melodramatic unmasking as a villain. He holds the congregation in thrall through his sermonizing. As Micheaux presents it, the congregation is seemingly devoid of any substantive spirituality or intelligence. While Jenkins drinks and leers from the pulpit, his congregants are gradually overcome and fall out in a religious ecstasy. As he pounds away at his Bible, the viewer is aware of Reverend Jenkins's viciousness and can only see the congregation as sadly deluded. Viewed in one context, the image of black faith presented here has little to redeem it. Whatever criticisms Du Bois and others leveled at religion, their depictions never descended into the burlesque.

John Burma points out that stereotyping black ministers was one traditional way of attacking the most central and enduring form of black male leadership (624). An interesting feature of Micheaux's work, however, is that it didn't simply and easily win white approval—what we might expect in an era of pop culture that celebrated the minstrelsy of Bert Williams and saw the rise of Stepin Fetchit. The censorship boards required extensive recutting of *Body and Soul*, explicitly requiring that the overt attacks upon Christianity be remediated. Rejecting the film, the New York State Motion Picture Commission described it as follows: "*Body and Soul* is the story of a man, minister of the gospel, whose habits and manner of life are anything but the life of a good man. . . . A story against religion morals and crime. The film is of such a character that in the opinion of the Commission it is sacrilegious, immoral, and would tend to incite to crime."[2] This assessment followed a pattern established by the earlier film, *Within Our Gates*. Indeed, at least some of Micheaux's contemporary audience saw the images as so crude and degrading of Christianity that they provoked protest that breached the racial line. According to Jane Gaines, the Methodist Episcopal Ministers' Alliance of Chicago, which consisted of members of both races, protested to the mayor and the chief of police in order to prevent *Within Our Gates* from being shown (*Fire* 231). Such criticism of Micheaux's work was not limited to the pious. Micheaux was regularly criticized for playing up the most degrading aspects of the race by professional and educated critics (Bowser and Spence 176–82). According to this line of criticism, Micheaux replicates ugly stereotypes that cast African-Americans as ignorant, gullible, and overwhelmed by extreme emotion. Such images suggest that Micheaux is historically important but finally is a negative figure in the history of black filmmaking.

However, with Bowser and Spence, we should at least take seriously Micheaux's self-understanding of his work as a visual riposte to images of African Americans then prevalent on stage and screen. Chapman points out that through the development of the popular culture industry and new technologies of discourse—records and films especially—African Americans had new means to engage in the process of representation and image making. As Chapman puts it, "To an unprecedented degree, African Americans themselves participated in the formation of the racial and sexual discourses forming their world" (6). As many, including Gaines, Bowser, and Chapman have pointed out, *Within Our Gates* responded directly to D. W. Griffith's *Birth of a Nation*, with its images of black men oscillating between happy, servile buffoons and violent and lawless rapists. *Within Our Gates*, by contrast, demonstrates that the white lynch mob is the most obvious symbol of American savagery, with Chapman linking the film closely to the antilynching campaigns that were characteristic of the New Negro era. Similarly, Charles Musser argues that *Body and Soul* responds to and reworks Eugene O'Neill's popular and groundbreaking stage plays *The Emperor Jones* and *All God's Chillun' Got Wings*. His decision to cast Paul Robeson in the lead role sprang in part from the desire to make the relationship between the works clear. When Micheaux is accused of racial self-hatred, such analysis tends to see Micheaux's work as merely replicating the very visual violence he hoped to counteract. It is not impossible, indeed it is entirely likely, that these positive and negative visions of Micheaux are both justified; in doing creative work within rather than apart from a culture and its contradictions, an artist necessarily develops insight through a glass darkly, as it were. However, the idea that Micheaux's work could be viewed as an intervention in the racial imaginary of the period is bolstered when the entire racial context of attitudes toward the ministry and toward Christianity more generally is brought forward. Reviewing images of African American Christianity deployed by Eugene O'Neill and other European American artists of the period helps clarify the visual language that Micheaux engaged and deployed in his own films to advance a specific racial agenda and ideology.

Among white Americans, alongside the tradition of comic denigration of black ministers, an equally powerful image of black Christianity has been the reassuring image of the black Christian as the all-forgiving gentle soul who demonstrates her superior spirituality by suffering, like Christ, in a noble and divine silence. This tradition reached its unequalled pinnacle in Harriet Beecher Stowe's depiction of Uncle Tom and the aftermath of its popular reproduction in an immense variety of copycat novels, Tom plays, and literary rejoinders both positive and critical. Drawing on George Frederickson, Sarah Meer notes that the figure of Uncle Tom, even in Stowe's hands, was deeply linked to a tradition of romantic racialism that posited the African American as inherently Christian, or at least Christ-like. Romantic racialism "characterized black people as inherently innocent, good-natured, and receptive to Christianity. It is for this reason that Douglas Lorimer associates Stowe's text with the philanthropists' racial imagery in his characterization of Victorian ideas of black people as linked either with missionary Bibles or else with minstrel banjos and bones" (13). Meer points out that while this caricature may have reached its height in the 1850s, the figure of Uncle Tom—painted more broadly as the long-suffering man in service to white priorities—endured as an archetype, regularly referenced at the turn of the century and invoked even to the present (253–56). Certainly it was a staple of European American cultural life in the modernist period, perhaps reaching a pinnacle in Marc Connelly's play, and later film, *Green Pastures*, wherein the hyper-spirituality of black folk is visualized—at least in the film of 1936—in that the figure of God and the black preacher are the same person, and the angels of the Lord are hard to distinguish from the happy black children gathered to hear the preacher's stories. Among white modernists, this ideology manifested in Faulkner's character Dilsey in the *Sound and the Fury*. The idea of the inherent religiosity and spiritual superiority of African

Americans was even alluded to—or explicitly suggested—by black writers from Frederick Douglass to Du Bois, sometimes as a generic spiritual ideal and sometimes as an embodiment of a specifically Christian ethic. Black Christians were more truly Christian than their white counterparts. The stereotype of the noble and suffering black Christian has remained part of the furniture of the American racial imagination, a powerful fantasy of black life punctured only partially by the Christian militancy of the Civil Rights movement.[3]

During Micheaux's early career, white writers and filmmakers responded to the transformative potential of the great migration with a combination of curiosity and anxiety. One common response imagined fearsome consequences for blacks who left behind a rural and Christian life for a world of secular ambition, a story that supported white Southern efforts to discourage black mobility and retain a cheap source of agricultural and industrial labor. In O'Neill's *Emperor Jones*, one index of Brutus Jones's pride and inevitable degradation is his cynical and cavalier attitude toward the Baptist faith of his upbringing. He believes that he can leave his religion on the shelf and pick it up as he chooses in time of need. While O'Neill doesn't overtly link Jones to black migration, as a Pullman car porter, Jones is a traveling man who leaves behind the secure and stable world of his Baptist church. These elements emerge even more explicitly in the filmed version of the play produced in 1930. In the film, Brutus Jones—played by Robeson—is interrupted in the midst of leading worship by the whistle of a train, a train that takes him north to the jazz joints and gambling dens that often served as a white image of life in Harlem or more broadly in the secular city. Crucially, it takes him away as well from the stability and containment of ambition symbolized in Christian marriage. Jones's abandonment of Southern Christian simplicity in favor of ambitious dreams ultimately leads him to become emperor of a Haiti-like island in the Caribbean where he gradually loses any last vestiges of civilized decency. Jones's final cries in the film of "Aww Lawd! Aww Lawd!" uttered as he kneels and casts his arms toward heaven in desperate supplication bear testimony to the supposed security of the faith he has left behind, suggesting to the audience that the black Christian man was best in his place at home and in his church.

Similarly, King Vidor imagines the threat of black male mobility and economic independence in film. *Hallelujah* traces the story of Zeke, a good natured and hardworking young man who, in the tradition of Vidor's Southern Agrarianism, happens to love picking cotton. Surrounded at home by a devout mother and a preacher father, Zeke struggles for faith against the surge of seemingly irresistible sexual desire, a near addiction that reduces him on several occasions to a zombie-like state of insensibility. Having brought in a particularly good cotton crop, Zeke heads for town, money in hand, where he meets up with Chick, the femme fatale. Chick, a sexually free and undomesticated woman, represents what Chapman notes is the era's larger freedom for women, "which seemed so capable of destroying, or at least revolutionizing, the vaunted American family and patriarchal authority that ostensibly provided stability and social control" (4). Chick corrupts Zeke's rural Christian innocence in a scheme with her crooked lover by luring Zeke into a gambling den where he loses his hard-earned cotton money and where his younger brother is killed in a brawl.

The balance of the drama in the film is focused on the contest for Zeke's allegiance: a contest between his ruinous sexual passion and his calling to domestic harmony and Christian ministry. Returning home with his brother's body, Zeke feels the call to become an evangelist and marry a young woman from his hometown. He meets Chick again in another town while on a revival tour. In the throes of sexual passion, Zeke leaves behind his wife and ministerial calling to scrape out a living in a lumberyard. Things turn out badly, with Chick dying at the hand of her former lover and Zeke serving a term in prison for killing the lover in return. However, at the film's conclusion, Zeke returns home to the loving embrace of his mother and religion, the demons of urbanism, mobility, and sexual desire finally exorcised.

Such images of black Christian men in films by white filmmakers reassured white Americans of the unchanging and antimodern quality of black American life. Like Faulkner's Dilsey, the good black person demonstrated goodness when he or she didn't move north, didn't show ambition, and only challenged the status quo by remaining silently superior to it. Viewed in this light, Micheaux's depictions of Christian life are more interesting and less straightforwardly stereotypical than they first appear, however controversial they remain. In Micheaux's work, the Christian church is hardly a site for social stability. It is a site of predatory behavior within the race that explicitly supports the environing white supremacy that challenges the uplift of the race. In the frenzied church service in *Body and Soul* described above, the woman in the congregation who is falling out in a religious frenzy says that she wants to be washed whiter than snow, a common religious rhetoric, but one that many in Micheaux's audience would have felt as racially offensive. Elsewhere in the film, Isabelle, the daughter whom Reverend Jenkins rapes, describes him as a "white-livered beast." Finally, on an occasion when Jenkins is robbing Isabelle and her mother of their hard-earned savings, Micheaux cuts into the scene first with an image of Martha Jane ironing—the domestic occupation by which she earns her money—then with an image of freshly picked cotton, and finally with the title description "blood money." Micheaux's visual rhetoric links the Reverend Jenkins to the abusive systems of slavery and sharecropping that characterized black economic oppression throughout the South. The image of the minister to which the congregation gives unthinking devotion is, in terms of this rhetoric, an image of white power rather than black solidarity.

Nevertheless, it is not simply black ministers whom Micheaux attacks; he attacks the entire culture that surrounds and supports abusive ministers. It is this quality of Micheaux's films, rather than his criticisms of the clergy alone, that have led critics to feel that Micheaux's work is marred by its disparagement of the race. Two issues in *Body and Soul* complicate such a thesis. First, Micheaux does offer a counter narrative to the image of corrupt Christian leadership. Sylvester—also played by Robeson—is everything that Jenkins is not: polite, hardworking, creative, self-sufficient, conventionally moral. While a minor character, he offers a different version of black leadership to balance the horrific images suggested by Revered Jenkins. The second element is Micheaux's narrative decision at the conclusion of the film to declare, melodramatically, that the horrors we have just witnessed have all been the nightmare visions of a tortured soul. These two elements come together in the final scene, as Micheaux pushes toward the happy conclusion that melodramatic conventions typically demand. Sister Martha Jane awakens to discover that everything that we've been witnessing has been a horrible dream. Her daughter has not been raped and abandoned and is instead happily engaged to the loving Sylvester, an educated member of the bourgeois middle class who lives in a finely appointed apartment. This scene often elicits impatient groans from contemporary viewers. However, the awkward ending underlines some of the film's major preoccupations. The film is, after all, an interrogation of appearance and reality, of image and substance, of body and soul. The apparently good image of the Christian minister is in reality the embodiment of corruption as the audience knows and Sister Martha discovers in the dream world of her imagination. Our secure sense of Paul Robeson's image of black masculinity is complicated in his playing a double part. Finally, the entirety of the film is refigured as a nightmarish phantasm, an appearance in the mind of a soul tortured by what else than an excessive Christian devotion that had, until the last moment, prevented her from understanding the goodness that Sylvester embodies. Indeed, on the largest scale, we might suggest that Micheaux's film calls into question the appearance of the black Christian body in the minds of many white—and, indeed, many black—Americans, in firm favor of Sylvester's version of the black male soul: rational, educated, and modern.

But if *Body and Soul* challenges the depictions of the African American as essentially religious in favor of a version of educated bourgeois professionalism, Micheaux largely leaves in place the domestication of that male that is envisioned in race movies and plays produced by white Americans during the same period. For instance, although *Body and Soul* questions the domesticating office of the Christian church, Micheaux leaves intact the basic form of domestication in the stable heterosexual family. While threatening aspects of black masculinity are relocated in the figures of Christian ministers, they are especially destructive in the way they threaten the scene of virtuous domesticity. Jenkins, posing as a suitor, is a rapist of young women, despoiler of the work of hardworking mothers, and murderer of small children. The resolution to this scene restores a specifically domestic stability and ideal, not through the pacifying effects of Christian virtue but through the refinement of educational pursuits.

Focusing especially on the film *Within Our Gates*, Erin Chapman demonstrates how this kind of resolution in domestic stability is characteristic of Micheaux's work more broadly. Chapman notes, "[Micheaux's] ideal New Negro man and woman were fixed paragons unassailable by the temptations of urban life and protected by their 'intelligence' from the worst ravages of racial oppression. With these paragons, Micheaux intended to counter the unrelenting stereotypes proffered as black characters in Hollywood films and popular theater and to provide images of African American audiences might venerate and emulate" (27). As a visual rejoinder to the racist epic *Birth of a Nation*, *Within Our Gates* presents white racial violence through scenes of lynching and in the attempted rape of the main character by a white landowner. Unlike *Body and Soul,* there are numerous scenes of varying lengths in which white racism is portrayed in less physically violent forms. While these moments are important and have drawn the most critical attention, Chapman rightly notes that the narrative as a whole is dominated by a family romance as various African American men contest with one another for the right to Sylvia's affections. In various ways, most of Sylvia's suitors—Conrad Drebert, Larry "the Leech" Prichard, and the Reverend Jacobs—fall by the wayside for various reasons in their efforts to either woo or seduce Sylvia, who is described as the "typical of the intelligent Negro of her time."

Sylvia's affections are won ultimately by Dr. V. Vivian, whose very name represents life and vitality in its Latin root. Chapman notes that this success is deeply tied to Micheaux's ideological vision for the New Negro. Here, the successful suitor is the model for a New Negro future in much the same way as the educated activist in Hughes or Du Bois. His enthusiasm is life-giving and, joined with Sylvia, promises the birth of a new black reality. Indeed,

though I have no specific evidence regarding Micheaux's choice in the matter, it seems likely to me that Sylvia is symbolically named after the mother
of Romulus and Remus, the founders of Rome. This matches the rhetoric
of racial motherhood and racial nationalism that Chapman foregrounds in
her interesting study. Sylvia is the New Negro mother of the race but exists primarily for the birthing of men who will build the nation. As I have
suggested, in Micheaux's narrative formation, the scene of domestic nation
building is reinforced rather than questioned. The ideology of domesticity
is secured not by Christian virtues and chastity but by the refinements of
education. Not only are Christian men poor suitors for the New Negro
racial mother—Reverend Jacobs is honorable but old and dependent on
charity from white women that Sylvia must procure—but also they can
be inimical to racial domesticity. The film's other primary representative
of Christian faith, the preacher Ol' Ned, follows the pattern of villainy apparent elsewhere in Micheaux's work. Like Reverend Jenkins of *Body and
Soul*, Ol' Ned depends on his parishioners for money and explicitly frames
his sermons to encourage black passivity in the face of white oppression.
He represents the "ol' time religion," emphasizing the glories of heaven
and suggesting that African Americans forget about things such education,
wealth, and politics and set their eyes firmly on heaven. In the traditions
of anti-intellectual Christian faith, Ol' Ned includes "schooling" as one of
those "vices" of the white man that black Christians should avoid. His direct
and indirect support of white supremacy is underscored grotesquely when
he is lauded by a white southern woman as the man who would keep the
Negroes in their place. The woman says disparagingly, "Their ambition is
to belong to a dozen lodges, consume religion without restraint, and, when
they die, go straight up to Heaven." Shortly after an interlude in which we
see Ol' Ned at work fleecing his congregation—apparently confirming their
gullibility—she notes, "Ol' Ned will do more to keep the Negro in his place
than all the schools put together."

Through such images, Micheaux ironically both questions and reinforces
the domestication of the black male that white filmmakers imagined as a
resolution to the threat of racial uplift. Micheaux certainly questions the
notion that Christianity is another term for civilization, whether through
the brutal murderousness of the preacher in *Body and Soul*, the complicity
of black ministers with white violence or the simple fact that the attempted
rape of Sylvia Landry and the lynching of her parents occur on a Sunday.
However, if Micheaux questions the civilizing function of Christianity, he
does not question the general structure of domesticity as a civilized and
civilizing ideal. Indeed, Micheaux's male villains or quasi-villains in these

two films are all traveling men of one sort or another, or at least are men found in the streets and byways of the town. Reverend Jenkins in *Body and Soul* has come to town after escaping from jail in Texas. Larry the Leech springs on Sylvia from the bushes at the edge of town. Sylvia's mugger assaults her in the streets. Even Conrad Drebert, admirable in some ways until he begins assaulting Sylvia mercilessly, travels the world as an archeologist. By comparison, the heroes of these films are domesticated men of the house. We know about Vivian as much through his office with its eye charts and stacks of books and papers as we do from anything he does. The idealized view of black masculinity that Micheaux melodramatically inscribes at the end of these films is finally the bourgeois ideal of a man close to hearth and home. In the end in these films, Micheaux does not question the paragon of the domesticated male; he rejects Christianity as the means of achieving this middle-class ideal.

CHRISTIAN UPLIFT AND EDUCATIONAL
MISOGYNY IN NELLA LARSEN

Erin Chapman, whom I have already engaged extensively in my reading of Micheaux, is one of many critics who point out that defining the essence of the New Negro, and so the essence of the race and its future, was seen as a masculine privilege and domain. It is not so much literally that "all the blacks are men," to echo Gloria Hull's early important black feminist work, but it is surely the case that women played a subordinate role in the imagined future for most New Negro men and that discourse about the virtues of the race was posited in masculine terms. Indeed, this was true even for a good many New Negro women. Chapman points out that early black feminist uplift ideology of what she calls the Reconstruction generation was focused primarily on the assumption that bourgeois homes were "both women's rightful sphere of influence, and the basis for the civic activism outside the home. This ideology further assumed the creation of such bourgeois homes to be integral to the formation of respectable ladyhood and pure motherhood" (11). The consequence of this formulation and others is that the ascendancy of the New Negro was treated primarily as a contest between men: Christian saint or secular intellectual, bourgeois political activist or bohemian artist, black pan-nationalist or patriotic integrationist, with overlap and many different permutations between these binaries. But in all cases these were presented as masculine possibilities and options with women relegated to primarily supportive roles. The race was to achieve its full manhood in order to achieve its integrity.

What might be called the gendered turn in Harlem Renaissance studies has, of course, pointed out the problematic gender politics in these formulations. At the root of this turn is the recognition that every assertion of racial identity or politics depends on a network of assumptions, assertions, and stereotypes about gender identity and politics. Cultural and racial ideologies are always gendered ideologies, and vice versa. The particular urgency toward defining the masculinity of blackness sprang in some significant part from this prior gendering of the race. I have suggested already that in contradistinction to stereotypes of the black male as especially brutal or animalistic, there was a prevalent discourse concerning the essential spirituality, childlike faith, and Christ-like obedience of the African American—an image repeated in many different popular cultural formats from Tom plays to Broadway shows to the silver screen. Such discourse reinforced the sense that African Americans were safest, most productive, and happiest when they stayed in their place, whether their place was imagined in a white family's kitchen, in the home, in a cotton field, or in a church.

These images exist against a broader back drop of the gendering of African Americans in racist discourse of the nineteenth century, in which black people were portrayed not as hyper-masculine but as essentially feminine. In a misogynistic cultural context, racializing discourse often feminized racial others and perceived this feminine presence in the civic body as destructive to the masculine health of the European or American nation. Homi Bhabha, reading Fichte, notes that for Fichte's seminal views of cultural genesis and flourishing, cultural outsiders were always potentially destabilizing for the masculine strength of the nation. "It is the world of perception—the eye of the mind—that fosters a naturalist, national pedagogy which defines the Menschenfreundlichkeit of the German nation: 'Naturalness [and manliness] on the German side,' [Fichte] writes, 'arbitrariness and artificiality [and effeminacy] on the foreign side, are the fundamental differences'" (59).[4] This formation only grew and flourished over the course of the early twentieth century. In his study of black fascisms, Mark Thompson notes that the ideal image of the fascist is essentially male, with women a threat to national or racial stability (30). This culminates in a view of cultural others as feminine forces that weaken the masculinity of the fascist nation.

It was a short step from this misogynistic understanding of culture to a reading of national minorities as both destructive agents and themselves feminine. As they seduced the hegemonic cultural body with feminine wiles, national minorities infected this body with the disease of the feminine. In exhorting that women know their place and remain at home, fascists by

proxy ordered the strict separation of the nation proper from the national
minorities festering within it. If the hypermasculine national majority were
to regain its potent phallic stature, national minorities, too, would have to
know their place and stay there. (31)

There is, of course, some distance to travel between this kind of fascist vision and the ideology of the "motherhood of the race" that Chapman traces
in the National Association of Colored Women—a women's organization
devoted to racial uplift as well as to some forms of direct political activism
such as anti-lynching campaigns and campaigns for suffrage. Nevertheless,
when Robert Park attempts to imagine the role of Africans in world culture
by designating them "the lady of the races," we need not label him a fascist
to understand that such a designation controls and subordinates Africans
and their descendants rather than meeting them as equal players on the
cultural stage. As Marlon Ross suggests:

> The passage on the Negro as the lady of the races accomplishes a neat
> division of labor within the national economy. Whereas the (male) "Anglo-
> Saxon" is left free for "action" in the world—for guiding the national inter-
> ests and managing the imperial borders domestically and globally—the Negro
> race (gendered male) is left to perform the feminine role of accessory artistic
> expression. . . . As the lady of the races, the Negro, we can infer, needs a man
> of action and enterprise to protect and admire him. Or does the Negro lady
> of the races need, more precisely, a man of chivalry? . . . The lady of the races
> is certainly not capable of reforming himself. (*Manning* 244–45)

New Negro racial activism—whether political or cultural—took place
against this gendered backdrop. In asserting the masculine sufficiency of
the race, this activism often left the gendered hierarchies of the day largely
intact, as we have seen in artists from Du Bois to Hughes to Toomer to
Micheaux. In the argument I have been pursuing so far, the Christian faith is
"the lady" of the black race whose manifestation the masculine intellectual
may need to guard or protect but also which the masculine intellectual must
surely guard against lest the feminizing and pacifying qualities of Christian
faith infect and unman the race as a whole.

This structure assumes as well that women must stay in their place so
the masculine race as a whole can move into the public arena. Nella Larsen
examines and disputes this assumption, offering in her novel *Quicksand*
an unsettling portrait of not only Christianity but also the larger project of
racial uplift through masculine achievement. While Larsen herself has little
use for the particulars of Christian faith, what is surprising in the development of her novel is not the degree to which Christian faith is presented

as uniquely patriarchal or destructive of women but the ways in which educational aspiration, at least as it is embodied within the discourses of racial uplift, is continuous with and built upon Christian faith rather than in opposition to it. In developing this connection, Larsen implicitly critiques the forms of racial uplift that predominated among both male and female leaders of the race and certainly within the intelligentsia that had staked its claim to racial leadership on the deliverances of education.

George Hutchinson notes Larsen's wide reading and the likely roots of her novel in classical and European predecessors, besides its roots in her own autobiography. Hutchinson notes that the novel invokes, but finally veers away from, the conventions of the tragic mulatto story that are enlisted in a good many popular novels by European and African Americans alike (Hutchinson, *Larsen* 225). Helga Crane, not unlike the heroes in of "Of The Coming of John" and "Father and Son," travels in the wider world, receiving an education rooted in both school and experience. Her "return" to the people even bears the marks of the educated person's burden to return to the folk of the South that one finds in these two stories, in Toomer's "Kabnis," and in films like Micheaux's *Within Our Gates*. But as Hutchinson notes, this results in neither successful racial uplift or even messianic sacrifice but in Helga's total collapse and essential reabsorption into the forms of impoverished and uneducated existence she had imagined changing (Hutchinson, *Larsen* 235). The novel also invokes but ultimately refuses the conventions of the romance. As with Sylvia in *Within Our Gates*, Helga is courted by four suitors who represent different versions of masculinity: James Vayle, a conventional exemplar of the educated middle class, easily shocked and disapproving of the unconventional Helga; Robert Anderson, a more interesting and more liberal member of the still-conventional established class devoted to racial uplift; the Danish artist Axel Olsen; and the country preacher, Pleasant Green.[5]

That it is the preacher, Pleasant Green, who finally wins the pleasures of Helga's body if not the pleasures of her affections has been a source of deep consternation to many critics, who see her collapse into religious belief as powerfully rendered in and of itself but as an unexpected conclusion to the novel. The novel focuses on a character with deep self-possession, extensive education, and excessive caution who nonetheless throws away her individuality to be identified with a group. What is clear is that Helga's conversion and its aftermath, however powerfully rendered, is a disaster for her and is clearly intended to critique the received Christian faith of many African Americans in ways even more pointed than those of some writers and artists we have examined thus far. Nevertheless, in the novel, Christian faith merely symbolizes a larger treacherous path for educated women in early twentieth-century America, one in which education is continuous with rather than in opposition to the primary forms of patriarchal control exhibited in the Christian faith of the community.

Throughout the novel, Helga Crane fruitlessly seeks a place where her intellectual and aesthetic ambitions can flourish. The "quicksands" of Larsen's novel are many but are collected and symbolized ultimately at the end of the novel in the engulfing presence of the Christianity of the folk, especially in the expectations this Christian world has of both women and the life of the mind. In the last quarter of the novel, at a moment of material and psychic deprivation, Helga enters a Harlem church where a revival meeting is in full swing. At the meeting, an orgiastic space filled primarily with women is orchestrated and directed by a dominating male presence, and Helga's capacity for rational reflection is gradually overcome by the rising tide of religious emotion. The scene surely recalls other such scenes that we have examined so far: the shrieking and shouting women in "Of The Faith of the Fathers," the eerie and unsettling shouting of women across the valley in "Kabnis," even the comical denigration of such scenes in Micheaux. The crowd is "shouting and groaning" for her salvation; it is characterized by "writhings and weepings of the feminine portion," a portion with "frenzied women" who "gesticulated, screamed, wept, and tottered to the praying of the preacher." The event takes on a "Bacchic vehemence."

> And as Helga watched and listened, gradually a curious influence penetrated her; she felt an echo of the weird orgy resound in her own heart; she felt herself possessed by the same madness; she too felt a brutal desire to shout and to sling herself about. . . .
>
> Maddened, she grasped at the railing, and with no previous intention began to yell like one insane, drowning every other clamor, while torrents of tears streamed down her face. She was unconscious of the words she uttered, or their meaning: "Oh God, mercy, mercy. Have mercy on me!" but she repeated them over and over.
>
> From those about her came a thunder-clap of joy. Arms were stretched toward her with savage frenzy. The women dragged themselves upon their knees or crawled over the floor like reptiles, sobbing and pulling their hair and tearing off their clothing. Those who succeeded in getting near to her leaned forward to encourage the unfortunate sister, dropping hot tears and beads of sweat upon her bare arms and neck. (113–14)

With the exception of the conversion sequence in James Baldwin's *Go Tell It on the Mountain*, this is, to my mind, the single most powerful rendition of a revivalist conversion in African American literature, and like that novel it imaginatively and powerfully renders the close connections between erotic and spiritual ecstasy, a connection regularly explored in Western art. However, unlike Baldwin's work, which retains a residue of mysterious and ambiguous respect for John Grimes's prostration before the Lord, Helga Crane's conversion is riddled with disgust and despair at the antihumanism evident in this kind of religious manipulation.[6] Critics have struggled with the scene, even from the point of early readers at the publisher who asked for revisions. In what is otherwise a generally appreciative and powerful reading, George Hutchinson agrees with the novel's critics in focusing on its implausibility. For Hutchinson, Larsen

> wrenched her narrative out of its generally realistic development, for the reader has difficulty accepting Helga's sudden transformation in the revival scene, an episode seemingly imported from expressionist drama. Some of the most astute and admiring reviewers would balk at this aspect of the novel, feeling that a woman as modern and intelligent as Helga Crane would find some other way out of her predicament. (239)

Joanna Wagner attempts to see the scene, and the entire conclusion of the novel, as more continuous with the narrative as a whole in focusing on what she sees as the novel's resistance to heteronormativity. For Wagner, the revival scene is "emphatically lesboerotic" and continuous with repressed homoerotic desire that is evident throughout the novel (148). Yet even Wagner struggles with what seems to be a disappointing collapse into the most anti-intellectual and anticultural versions of Christian community imaginable and believes that Crane is "queering" our expectations of the romantic novel by focusing on Christianity as the root of heteronormativity to which the larger community has been pressing Helga throughout the narrative (151).

Although I think there are compelling rationales for both Hutchinson's and Wagner's readings, I am unsettled by both as they raise as many questions as they answer. Regarding Wagner's reading, it is unclear to me why Larsen would revert to Christianity at the end of the novel when Christianity has already been thoroughly critiqued elsewhere and when the press of heteronormativity is found everywhere. She could just as easily have collapsed into heteronormative relations with any number of men in the novel, so why this man, why this faith, and why now? I am less concerned with Hutchinson's reading but question it partially on old-fashioned aesthetic grounds: I see the ending as more consistent with the plot and with Helga's position in this social world than do Hutchinson and others. Though the conversion happens quickly, it does not feel like a *deus ex machina* resolution to the conflict. The shock of the scene is that, in the return to "primal" origins at the scene of folk Christian faith, the faith itself appears imperturbable and unaffected by the intellect and education of those who would seek to make it something other than it is. This kind of scene of return does, of course, show the heteronormative character of Christian communities. But what it does more emphatically is call into question the possibility of the educated man (or woman) serving as a savior of the race, as had been regularly envisioned in the literature of the African Americans since the nineteenth century. Ultimately, in Larsen's novel, the forms of education imagined in racial uplift and the forms of common Christian faith shared root and stem a variety of preoccupations—conformity to community and the subordination of women being chief among those forms. For Larsen, the educated establishment and the cultural avant-garde cannot deliver African Americans benighted by religion because they operate on a fundamentally similar premise. African American men exist to reproduce the race through cultural, political, and intellectual work; African American women exist to reproduce the race through having children.

The links between Christianity and education are found in both the beginning and ending of the novel. In the first pages of the novel, Helga recalls with repugnance the white preacher she's been forced to sit and listen to early in the day after having been "herded into the sun-baked chapel" (2). The preacher's blandishments are some of the usual racist fare concerning the need for the Negro race to keep to its place and be satisfied with the lot that God had given it. But the preacher also explicitly links his religious encouragement to the educational goals of Naxos, an institution modeled on Tuskegee, but perhaps also to some degree on Larsen's brief experience at Fisk. The preacher encourages them to take pride in Naxos, noting that he dared "any Northerner to come south and after looking upon this great institution to say that the Southerner mistreated the Negro. And he had said that if all Negroes would only take a leaf out of the book of Naxos and conduct themselves in the manner of the Naxos products, there would be no race problem, because Naxos Negroes knew what was expected of them" (2–3).

Helga responds with disgust and judgment: "The South, Naxos. Negro education. Suddenly she hated them all. Strange, too, for this was the thing which she had ardently desired to share in, to be a part of this monument to one man's genius and vision" (3). Interestingly, Helga does not respond with a racial judgment, despite the racial self-hatred that some critics detect in her. Her focus is on regional and institutional relations that she perceives working in concert toward conformity rather than toward the possibility

of individuality, of "one man's genius and vision." Naxos gives us products
rather than men and women, and especially products that know how to
stay in their place. This view of industrialized education is reemphasized
the next morning when Helga, conspicuously "out of place" by being in her
room rather than marching to breakfast, looks down on the quadrangle of
the campus

> at the multitude of students streaming from the six big dormitories which,
> two each, flanked three of its sides, and assembling into neat phalanxes
> preparatory to marching in military order to the sorry breakfast in Jones
> Hall on the fourth side. Here and there a male member of the faculty, im-
> portant and resplendent in the regalia of an army officer, would pause in his
> prancing or strutting, to jerk a negligent or offending student into the proper
> attitude or place. The masses phalanxes increased in size and number, blot-
> ting out pavements, bare earth, and grass. And about it all was a depressing
> silence, a sullenness almost, until with a horrible abruptness the waiting
> band blared into "The Star Spangled Banner." The goosesteps began. Left,
> right, left, right. Forward! March! The automatons moved. (12)

The critique of conformity is self-evident here, and while focused on "Negro
Education," it is worth saying that this industrial version of mass education
had become a common ideal in the United States by the turn of the century.
Moreover, Thompson notes that the ideal proto-fascist was an ex-soldier
(30), and remarks throughout his text on the fascination with militarism in a
wide variety of African American cultural institutions such as the rallies and
ceremonies of Marcus Garvey. The scene of military-style phalanxes at the
heart of the educational process in Larsen's novel emphasizes the centrality
of masculinism in the educational process and links it more broadly to the
white Christian emphasis on keeping Negroes in their proper place, whether
that place is understood in terms of bodily discipline, racial and class hierarchies, religious norms, educational norms, or gendered norms. The fact
that these "normalizing" forces are linked together so emphatically at the
opening of the book at least raises disquiet about the "one man's vision"
that an educational institution would serve as a model for the perfection
of the race and more broadly calls into question the masculine heroism
of the educated man in New Negro narratives, suggesting, in fact, that
masculine heroism may be a central part of the problem rather than a part
of the solution. Educational vision and heroism are not so distinct in this
setting from Christian vision and heroism, despite the presumptive educational purpose promoted by male intellectuals from Du Bois to Micheaux
of relieving the populace of the superstitions and religious ignorance that

besets them. Educational heroism, in this view, is another and different form of oppressive mysticism.

As Chapman points out, the most significant of these norms in Larsen's novel is the racial uplift ideology that focuses on the woman as the mother of the race, occupying her proper place in the bourgeois home (126ff). I will not elaborate or repeat Chapman's convincing arguments here except to note that later in the middle of the novel, again in the midst of educated and cultured friends and acquaintances, the desirability of a woman's intellect is reduced to the functionality of the woman's body. That is, education makes Helga a more desirable mate for an educated man, overcoming in part her lack of social pedigree. Reconnecting with the fiancé that she abandoned at Naxos, Helga engages him in conversation that turns on the question of marriage and children. Helga dismisses the idea, ironically foreshadowing her own demise by noting that "Marriage—that means children, to me. And why add more suffering to the world?" James Vayle recoils from what seems to be a betrayal of the racial good:

> James was aghast. He forgot to be embarrassed. "But Helga! Good heav-
> ens! Don't you see that if we—I mean people like us—don't have children,
> the others will still have. That's one of the things that's the matter with us.
> The race is sterile at the top. Few, very few Negroes of the better class have
> children, and each generation has to wrestle again with the obstacles of
> the preceding ones, lack of money, education, and background. I feel very
> strongly about this. We're the ones who must have the children if the race is
> going to get anywhere. (103)

The unnamed "others" who will still have children are, of course, the il-literate and laboring masses. Vayle invokes the notion that the educated man—as signified in part by his class station in racial life—is called upon to demonstrate his virility and fulfill his masculine responsibilities by im-pregnating women, reducing a woman's mind to the reproductive capacities of her body. While the rationale for the subordination of women to a race defined by male priorities is different from the rationales embedded within traditional Christian forms of patriarchy, the result for women is the same. Education, in this framework, cannot effectively liberate the race because it depends upon the subordination of women to the task of bearing, rearing, and educating children.

The inadequacy of education to the task of liberating women is revisited in the final sections of the book when it is opposed, fruitlessly, to the con-suming work of creating a Christian, and racial, community. Following her collapse into conversion, Helga plots and succeeds, for no apparently good

reason, to seduce a preacher who had been in the congregation into marriage. She then later acquiesces before his insatiable desire for children and
finally before the impenetrable resistance of the church community to her
desire to teach them. Ultimately Helga's mental world—and, by extension
the world of educated culture as a whole—founded on the efficacy of intellectual enlightenment runs aground against her church's view that Christ is
all sufficient. This form of anti-intellectualism—Cornel West's "insouciant"
community—suggests that the desires, questions, and doubts that characterize the life of the mind are impious or impractical. As she is recovering from
an illness after the birth of her fourth child, she grasps poignantly after a
vestige of her former possibilities. She asks that her nurse, Miss Hartley,
read to her from a story by Anatole France, "The Procurator of Judea":

> "'Laelius Lamia, born in Italy of illustrious parents,'" began the nurse in
> her slightly harsh voice.
> Helga drank it in.
> "'. . . For to this day the women bring down doves to the altar as their
> victims . . .'"
> Helga closed her eyes.
> "'. . . Africa and Asia have already enriched us with a considerable num-
> ber of gods . . .'"
> Miss Hartley looked up. Helga had slipped into slumber while the su-
> perbly ironic ending which she had so desired to hear was yet a long way
> off. A dull tale was Miss Hartley's opinion, as she curiously turned the pages
> to see how it turned out.
> "'Jesus? . . . Jesus—of Nazareth? I cannot call him to mind.'"
> "Huh!" she muttered, puzzled. "Silly." And closed the book. (132)

Helga's nurse lacks the imaginative and intellectual resources to even perceive the book as a challenge or an occasion for thought and imagination.
It is merely silly. Something to be closed, not longed after.

In many respects, Helga's plight reflects that of John the intellectual in
Du Bois's "Of the Coming of John," but without the possibility of resolution
through racial martyrdom since she is being destroyed by her own race. Toward the end of the novel, she is in conflict with various women who find her
aesthetic and intellectual interests odd if not pretentious. The novel makes
clear that the lives of these women are structured around male desire and
male priorities, especially as figured in her husband, the Reverend Pleasant
Green. Ultimately, Helga herself is entangled in these priorities despite her
fantasies of a return to a life characterized by books and art. In the final
lines of the novel, having recovered from her sickness and just begun to
imagine again the possibility of intellectual renewal, Helga is struck down by

her position as a woman: "AND HARDLY had she left her bed and become able to walk again without pain, hardly had the children returned from the homes of the neighbors, when she began to have her fifth child" (135).

Although not given a separate chapter heading, the typescript of the novel treats this paragraph in the same fashion as the beginning of every other chapter in the novel, with the lines in all caps, indicating that this is truly the final chapter of Helga's life. This is a kind of death, but one that denies this particular intellectual the meaning and closure of heroic martyrdom. Instead, we see Helga's grim future as she is absorbed by the ancient and uncaring priorities of others.

To some degree, Helga's problems are peculiarly individual; she cannot make good decisions about her own life and is thus responsible for her own disintegration. However, the expectation that the woman might be absorbed by the tasks of childrearing and motherhood, by the responsibilities of being a wife, was hardly limited to African American Christianity. The patriarchal assumptions of the vast majority of American modernists are well documented and suggest the degree to which writers and artists reflect their age as much as they lead it. Anecdotal evidence of the family lives of other African American leaders at the time suggests the same. In *The Big Sea*, Langston Hughes recalls his close friendship with Arna Bontemps and his wife, Alberta, who seemed to be always caring for children: "A year or two later there was another golden baby. And every time I went away to Haiti or Mexico or Europe and came back, there would be a new golden baby, each prettier than the last—so that was why the literati never saw Mrs. Bontemps" (192). This memory seems absent of malice and is couched in the ambiguously humorous but edged tone that Hughes deploys to both expose problems and hide direct statements about his readings of events. Nevertheless, read in conjunction with Larsen's novel, this brief glimpse at Alberta Johnson—referred to in Hughes's text only as "Mrs. Bontemps"—is unsettling. In significant ways, the patriarchal image of the man at work and the woman at home remained a Victorian ideal through which racial leaders imagined racial success for themselves and for those they sought to lead, this even when Du Bois and many others should be understood as feminist fellow travelers of their own period.

Throughout *Quicksand*, Helga Crane battles the kind of self-dissolution and absorption that is expected of women as a matter of course, a dissolution and absorption that anti-intellectual Southern Christianity does not cause but which it fulfills and symbolizes. At Naxos, she is appalled by the regimentation and conformity expected of the educated. A variety of potential suitors—several of them "good matches" by the conventions of middle class life—clearly imagine her as a wife to be possessed, as a satellite to their own priorities. This is true of the Swedish artist Axel Olsen, drawn to her by her exotic color, and who desires in her some sense of his own artistic immortality; of James Vayle, her former colleague at Naxos, who sees in marriage a plan for propagating the better classes of the race; even in Robert Anderson, a former principal of Naxos, who seems finally more concerned with retaining a form of social propriety than in acting upon what appears to be genuine desire for her. In each case, the woman is asked to submit to the higher male priority or to the priority of the group as expressed through the status of the educated male. Thus, late in the novel at the revival meeting, the congregation's singing of the lines from the old hymn, "Less of self and more of Thee / Less of self and more of Thee," signifies not so much the particular disaster of Christianity for Helga Crane—though it, indeed, represents that—but the general structure of cultural expectations of women as Helga has experienced them throughout the novel. In turn, this points to the ambiguities and the specific failures of the doctrine of education as a liberating force among African Americans.

"A POLISHED MAN OF STRENGTH AND POWER"

Race, Body, and Spirit in the Harlem Renaissance

For the heroes of Du Bois's "The Coming of John" or Hughes's "Fathers and Sons," education extends and amplifies masculine prowess. Moreover, this picture of the educated man is specifically deployed in contrast to the ministerial leadership that symbolized black life to those both within and without the culture. New Negro narrative regularly elevates education in comparison to religion, which is characterized by ignorance and superstition. Learning manifests and supports both virility and virtue. On the other hand, as my last two chapters have suggested, the figure of the educated hero is not without ambiguity and complication. Educated men and women are isolated or walk away or die, foreclosing the question of how exactly they might provide a form of enduring cultural leadership to a Christian people. While these deaths are sometimes redeemed through martyrdom, martyrdom inspires without answering the hard questions of everyday cultural and political life. This ambiguity is due not only to the ambiguous character of intellectual work in discourses about masculinity but also to other intense and legitimate practical questions forced by the dilemma of African Americans in American society. So far as the broader culture was concerned, an educated man was no less subject to lynching or the all-encompassing humiliations of Jim Crow than a man with no education at all. Perhaps more so in some respects, to the degree that his very education resisted the place to which he had been assigned. In the context of broad racial violence and economic misery, could intellectual life contribute to the success of the race? Were artists messiahs or only wishful thinkers? Bookerites were not the only African Americans who wondered.

The ambiguous status of intellectuals, however, also reflected a larger ongoing reorganization of traditional Western discourses concerning the relationship between the life of the body, life of the mind, and, I would argue, the life of the spirit. Drawing on arguments concerning American men and their fears of emasculation at the hands of a civilized, and apparently feminized, culture, Martin Summers points out the degree to which this anxiety provoked a gradual shift away from Victorian virtues as the content of masculinity and toward new attention to the body and physicality:

By the third quarter of the century, white middle-class men expressed anxiety over what they felt to be the overwhelming influence of female morality and its result, 'overcivilization.' The fear that men were becoming effete, either through the stifling moralizing of women or their own excessive intellectual pursuits, contributed to the growth of physical culture following the Civil War. Emphasis on building the body rather than the intellect gained much currency during this period. (79) If icons of European American masculinity have always oscillated between the extremes of Ichabod Crane and Brom Bones, it is not quite correct to say that Brom Bones was ascendant. However, one significant thread of the discourses of masculinity suggested that a robust masculinity depended on the thorough development of mind, body, and spirit alike and that if bourgeois and mostly Christian middle-class men of the late nineteenth and early twentieth century were lacking, they were certainly lacking in a fully developed physicality, in part because of the enervating effects of the increasingly white-collar and "intellectual" aspects of their public and private lives. The Physical Culture Movement, the advent of intercollegiate sports and especially football, the status of boxing as a national sport, as well as the increasing militarism of American society, spoke directly and indirectly to the "physical turn" and to the common intimation that physical, and especially erotic, vitality was sapped by books and reading. Men who lived by the mind emasculated themselves. The early twentieth century was, as Harold Segel demonstrates, a moment when the body was displayed, represented, analyzed, dissected, and even revered. Modern dance gave audiences the naked body staged in motion while freeze frame photography illuminated the musculature of sprinters in full stride. Professional sports, especially football, gradually became a national obsession, as did the modern Olympic movement. In the hands of Bernarr Macfadden, the Physical Culture Movement garnered followers who exhibited a near-religious devotion toward their own bodies and the bodies of others. Both art and athletics imagined the body not as fallen or corrupt but as infinitely malleable and improvable, and artists, entrepreneurs, and even ministers encouraged the elevation of athletes as national heroes and exemplars. The body itself became an object to shape, sculpt, and recreate in the image of human intention.

The racial dynamics of this change in masculinity were ideologically complicated. Among white people, whiteness stereotypically represented intelligence, education, literacy, and civilization while blackness signified sex, emotionality, and—somewhat contradicting Park's image of the Negro as the "lady of the races"—muscular strength. Blackness was the body without a brain, but whiteness risked being a brain without a body. Wrestling with a contradiction that equated intellect with enervation, white American writers struggled between a pole that secured white power at the price of disembodied and sexless masculinity and a pole that promised an atavistic virility through a descent into primitivism.

Nationalist fears were widespread and were often rooted in anxieties about the body and especially the masculine character of the nation. Spengler's work on the decline of Western civilization is fraught with a masculinist vision of the declining male potency of the West giving way before the sexualized hordes of the colored world. In popular culture, white Americans not only fretted about black rapists on screen in films like *Birth of a Nation* but also policed black bodies to block what they took to be the rapacious desire of those bodies. They fretted about Jack Johnson and other black boxers, seeing a racial prophecy invoked in the beat downs of white opponents in the ring.[1] Editorialists and politicians worried about black athletic superiority. Geoffrey Ward notes that Charles Dana warned against the "growing menace" of black physical superiority: "The black man is rapidly forging to the front ranks in athletics, especially in the field of fisticuffs. We are in the midst of a black rise against white supremacy" (14–15). The black body triumphant signified the failing masculinity of the white nation.

Alternatively, some parts of European American culture looked to blackness as a source of renewal. As David Levering Lewis points out, sympathetic whites of the twenties romanticized the black male as a sexual and spiritual dynamo. T. S. Eliot looked for masculine renewal in the "strong brown" river god of "The Waste Land." Similarly, Hemingway looked for renewed potency among the primitivisms he imagined in the Spanish countryside and African veldt. Many apparently sympathetic white patrons of the Harlem Renaissance embraced the image of the Negro-as-body and found in it the sources and examples of white renewal. Lewis quotes Malcolm Cowley: "One heard it said . . . that the Negroes had retained a direct virility that the whites had lost through being overeducated" (91).[2] Nevertheless, this fantasy of masculine and even spiritual renewal was fraught with risk as descent into blackness posed the problem of return. Mark Whalan notes that while African Americans passing as white feared discovery, white afi-cionados of blackness sometimes feared forgetting their whiteness. Whalan describes this as a fear of "over identification—a fear not of being punished for transgressing into monoracial space but of being unable to escape it" (143). Whalan points out that an effort at passing for black in the South on a trip with Jean Toomer created deep anxiety for Waldo Frank, a leader of the Young America literary movement and an early advocate of Toomer's work. "Upon reaching the South, Frank reported that his 'place on earth had frighteningly shifted.' Later, 'Lying in dark sleep I would dream I was a Negro, would spring from sleep reaching for my clothes on the chair beside the bed, to finger them, to smell them . . . in proof I was white and myself'" (*Manhood* 143).[3] These racialized fears spoke to a general anxiety of disintegration and decay based on the influx of darker others into the consciousness and physical spaces of the European west, an anxiety from which even most aficionados of blackness were not immune, preferring to be sprinkled in the font blackness but not immersed lest one drowns. Whites visited cabarets and salons uptown but kept house downtown.

This conflicted dynamic was also present among African Americans, though in a different register. While African Americans grappled with whether immersion in education and the intellect removes a hero too far from the people that one hopes to lead, it was similarly unclear that embrac-ing black physicality was doing anything other than celebrating the stereo-type that white Americans had made of the black body. Summers points out that there was, in fact, a broad response among middle-class African American men—the educated elite—that took up this discourse of physical-ity and its cultural practices for its own purposes. Garveyite intellectuals, and Garvey himself, regularly celebrated the physical superiority of black men over white, praised athleticism as a masculine virtue, and identified black physical prowess as a source of moral strength. This physical superiority was underscored through the military display and pageantry that evoked a form of masculine nationalism in the rituals and rallies of the Universal Negro Improvement Association.[4] Most of the discourses and institutions devoted to masculinity and the male body among European Americans had African American counterparts. The first decades of the century saw the opening of African American YMCAs, participation in the Physical Culture Movement, and the development of social clubs for men and boys. If Teddy Roosevelt thought that the strenuous life saved body, soul, and nation, so too thought Frederick Asbury Cullen, who devoted a chapter of his spiritual autobiography to the moral and racial uplift that athletics could provide (F. A. Cullen 102–105).

Nevertheless, these institutions and practices often had a different or at least an extended significance in African American communities. If European American men were anxious about the debilitating effects of middle-class lifestyles, African American attention to the body was driven in significant part by literal and direct attacks on the black body throughout their history in the Americas. Discourses about the beauty, power, and importance of the black body counteracted pervasive discourses that contributed to racial shame, and attention to "physical culture" promulgated by the YMCA and other organizations served not simply to instill bourgeois values but also to address questions of health and well-being for those on the margins. Moreover, attacks upon black physicality were literal and direct, whether through rape, lynching, or other forms of organized brutality such as mass imprisonment and forced labor. If one tracks the history of European and American modernism from the 1890s through the 1940s, this same period traces a bell curve of white lynchings of black Americans in the post–Civil War Era, atrocities typified by white attacks on the black male body in acts of ritualized sexual violence. Lynching rituals that began after Reconstruction can, to some degree, be considered continuous with efforts to police sexuality in general. However, the horrific forms of pornographic violence associated with lynching—including, for instance, emasculation, burning the body alive, dismembering its parts for souvenirs—to say nothing of its frequency and public nature is clearly a threat different in kind and import from the psychological ennui of the European American middle and upper classes. The combination of black male self-assertion, economic insecurity attendant upon industrialization and massive immigration, and the racial psychology of many Southern whites proved a toxic brew. Of the 3,513 lynchings of African Americans in the years between 1882 and 1927, two-thirds occurred after 1903. Ninety-seven percent of these victims were men (Harris 7). Simultaneously there were innumerable rapes and acts of sexual violence against black women, a separate but contiguous attack on the safety and integrity of the black body, male or female. This says nothing of the various race riots, beatings, and other forms of humiliation attendant upon white mythologies of black masculinity and femininity. For African Americans in such circumstance, celebration of the body was about a great deal more than overcoming modernist angst and ennui, though it served such purposes as well. The triumphant black body was itself an act of resistance to the expectations of white supremacy.

The growing attention to physicality and the attendant concerns with intellectualism and enfeeblement prompted many artists and some intellectuals to locate the wellsprings of their work in the body itself, and especially in sexuality. This discourse evoked a masculinity rooted in the life of a sexually desirable and desiring body, finding in the image of masculine erotic power not something shameful but the root of cultural and artistic renewal. Many artists and writers, European and African American alike, decried the supposed "Puritanism" of official culture. While they had very different political valences, bohemian New Women and jazz-age flappers both spoke to a libidinal liberation that hoped for socioerotic equality between men and women. According to Diane Chisholm, Djuna Barnes was drawn to the Surrealist vision that erotic transgression provoked other forms of social revolution. Similarly, although bohemian artists and writers tended to assume the patriarchal prejudices of their predecessors, Stansell demonstrates that bohemians used sexual transgression to strike a blow for not only self-realization but also social transformation. As she puts it, "[The] noble claims of free love turned adultery into intellectually justified revolt against bourgeois life" (278). Governments in the United States and abroad undertook new efforts to define, police, and punish illicit sexual behavior. The trials of Oscar Wilde made their way into the popular imagination by the threat he seemed to pose to the order of things. Ironically, Wilde's trial seemed to confirm what bohemians imagined in their wildest dreams: that sex could undermine the state.

In the day-to-day working life of many artists, attention to the body and especially to male Eros was not about a political and social revolution and also not primarily a desire to find a shocking and revelatory subject matter. In many of the discourses of art, authentic creativity was imagined as deeply tied to the body and even more specifically to erotic experience. William Carlos Williams's assertion that there were "no ideas but in things" emphasized that real poetry came from sensual attachment to the physical world. In his ruminations on Vorticism, Pound seemed to imagine art itself as a kind of physical experience. Although women contributed to this kind of thinking and writing, it was often deeply masculinist in tone and concept. Pound warned writers away from the vague and "feminine" spiritualities of decadent Victorian and Edwardian poetry. In Britain, D. H. Lawrence probably went furthest in believing that creativity itself came from the same sources as masculine sexual power. According to Poplawski,

> [Lawrence] considered the sexual impulse to be one of the most powerful and irresistible issues from the "unknown" creative unconscious, and in its unrepressed, uninhibited expression it provided him with an ideal model of pure spontaneity. As such, it is very closely implicated with his concept of creativity. While he considered it to be supremely creative and fulfilling in its own right, he also considered the fullest and broadest possible sexual gratification to be the royal road to a more richly creative and fulfilling life in general."(29–30)

Poplawski notes that Lawrence also drew connections between sexual experience and revolutionary change, and in *Fantasia of the Unconscious* seems to point to "literal physiological connection between sexual and creative activity": "men, being themselves made new after the action of coition, wish to make the world new" (Poplawski 32; *Fantasia* 136). Other writers drew similar connections. Edward Carpenter, a popularizer of the notion that homosexual men and women were a hybrid sex known as "uranians," argued that homosexual persons were better artists because of their ability to traverse the entirety of male and female experience. Virginia Woolf made a similar point in less explicitly sexual terms when she argued that the truest art requires a balance between masculine and feminine impulses in the imagination (Ganter 89; Woolf Chapter 6). Thus, for many avant-gardists in Europe and Anglo America, Eros and the body were the avenues to art.

As with the attention to the body generally, this consideration of the relationship between Eros and art in the modernist avant-garde was both deeply racialized and marked by cultural anxieties over gender. White masculine obsessions with the posturing and possibilities of the body sprang in part from a racialized paranoia that the white male body was wanting, softened by the advent of modernity in its various guises. The signature poem of high modernism, Eliot's "Waste Land," is about masculine failure and the degradation of the body, as is one of the first great modern American novels, Hemingway's *The Sun Also Rises*. The careers of both Eliot and Hemingway, as well as many of their literary fellow travelers, elaborate upon the consequences and potential remedies for this failure and degradation. This was not merely the preoccupation of a few artists making up for their anxieties with masculine bravado. Although Ann Douglas's thesis about the feminization of American culture has been disputed, it does seem clear that such feminization was very real in the minds of white men, who believed that the culture was threatened with racial bastardization as well.

The racialization of American sexual obsessions had important consequences for how African American writers considered the relationship between Eros and art. In several respects, African American discourse about art and sex was continuous with discourses elsewhere in European and American culture. Though African American interest in the projects and peccadilloes of the European and Anglo-American avant-garde varied considerably, the testimony of letters, essays, and the art itself suggests a considerable degree of awareness and participation in these discourses, even when bringing a different accent to the conversation. Indeed, critics from George Hutchinson to Ann Douglas to Mark Whalan to Barbara Foley have recently done much to show that far from a hothouse plant nurtured by white sponsors, as David Levering Lewis and Nathan Huggins tend to assume, the New Negro cultural movement was in many different respects deeply engaged with the broader national and international cultural movements of the day. This was true whether thinking of the broad appeal of socialism to writers like Hughes, McKay, and even Du Bois, the project of the New Americans to Toomer, or the profound effect of the development of intellectual movements like sociology and anthropology on Du Bois, Hurston, and many others.[5] The same was true of the discourses of the body as the source of spiritual and cultural renewal that developed during the period. One might suspect that the depredations visited on the black body would reasonably lead African Americans to discourses of the masculine body's failure and decline, at least as much as T. S. Eliot's bank job or Hemingway's failed marriages. However, the degree to which African American discourses about the black male body envisioned its prowess and self-realization is remarkable. African American writers didn't shrink from depicting the consequences of racism on body and spirit. The depictions of lynching and other forms of violence we've already encountered suggest at least as much. But African American writers also regularly idealized the black male body as an image of virility and vitality, even as an image of salvation for the nation at large. In Hughes's "I, too, Sing America," the black body grows large in the kitchen, threatening to take hold of its place in the body politic by main strength if that place isn't afforded through common civility. Similarly, Hughes's seminal essay "The Negro Artist and the Racial Mountain," while not primarily about the black body, roots vibrant creativity and the future of African American art in the ability to overcome the strangulating fear of depicting the "strange unwhiteness of his own features" and embracing the fact that he is "a Negro—and beautiful" (*Essays* 35).

The masculine prowess of culture heroes like John Henry found different expression in fictional characters like Arna Bontemps's protagonist in *Black Thunder*, Gabriel, leader of a slave revolt who is described as a giant and imposing masculine figure, his physicality seeming to be both a sign and a source of a larger political and even spiritual strength that guides the revolt. King Barlo in Toomer's *Cane* is described as a "clean-muscled, magnificent, black-skinned Negro" who functions as an unofficial leader and spokesperson for working class blacks (22). Barlo is something of a prophetic mystic who announces the impending arrival of apocalyptic black deliverance. Barlo's prophetic vision juxtaposes physicality and transcendence in his story of a giant African man. While communing with God, an African demigod is brought down by Lilliputian "white-ant biddies," enslaved, and brought to America (23). Barlo mirrors this mythic forefather in the minds of the people:

> Barlo rises to his full height. He is immense. To the people he assumes the outlines of his visioned African. In a mighty voice he bellows:
> "Brothers an sisters, turn your faces t the sweet face of th morning light. Open your ears— "(23)

The black male body as a fulfillment of masculine beauty—one that was connected to a form of racial resurrection and transcendence—was explored as well in the art and sculpture of the period. As only one example, Richmond Barthes regularly sculpted figures of African American types such as male boxers and slaves who seemed at one and the same time realistic and idealized, embodying both spiritual longing and masculine realization. The cover art of the *Messenger* in May 1923 captured this linkage of masculine physicality and prowess with spiritual and intellectual acuity by creating a version of Rodin's "Thinker" entitled "The New Negro."[6] The male body in African American work of the period was often depicted as not only the site of individual spiritual regeneration and vitality but also the sign, symbol, and source of racial hope. According to Gerald Early, "This became the basic idea of the New Negro–the black who asserted his rights and his manhood, who wanted to best the white, who was 'reckless, independent, bold and superior in the face of whites'" (26).[7] When, in "The City of Refuge," Rudolph Fisher's protagonist gawks at a black policeman ordering about white motorists, he is looking wide-eyed into the dawning of a form of black male self-assertion not previously thought possible in the face of white racism.

Beyond general attention the black body ascendant, some writers of the Harlem Renaissance identified explicitly with the notion that art sprang from the body and even the Lawrentian idea that it sprang from sex. Some viewed the exploration of Eros in general and sex specifically as an aesthetic and moral imperative. Among the contributors to *Fire!!*, violation of sexual taboos was seen as part and parcel of a modern literary movement devoted to truth telling.[8] In his most famous statement of aesthetic principles, Langston Hughes locates the impulse for black art squarely in the body, and if he did not locate it in erotic experience per se, he clearly shared with many others of the younger generation a sense that the violation of erotic taboos in literature served an aesthetic purpose. Wallace Thurman, for one, expressed interest in the theories of Edward Carpenter, who associated homosexuality with artistic sensibility (Ganter 89). To some degree, this interest in sexuality was expressed not simply thematically but as a social force that supported and furthered artistic achievement. Similarly, Countee Cullen wrote an extended letter to Alain Locke, thanking him for recommending Carpenter's *Iolaues: An Anthology of Friendship*, a work devoted to gay themes and interests. The multitude of letters between Cullen, Locke, Harold Jackman, Thurman, Bruce Nugent, Langston Hughes, and others, such as Carl Van Vechten, suggest that even where there were not specific or elaborated allegiances to any particular view of aesthetic inspiration, the social networks that sprang from erotic interest were mutually sustaining.[9]

To note all of this attention to the body is not, of course, to suggest that this attention was universally welcomed, endorsed, or supported, and with specific reference to the ways in which discourses of the body and sex intersected with the life of the church, things could obviously be fraught. It would be easy to divide the world between Puritanical church-going traditionalists and avant-garde libertarians, and many New Negro writers did just that. Nevertheless, the discourses were inconsistent and often quite nuanced. The African American public at large was divided on the relationship of the body's sex to the advancement of the race, to say nothing of the production of a racial art, a division that also found its way into the artistic community. The divisions concerning sex and literature between the older generation of Harlem writers like Du Bois or Jessie Fauset and the younger generation are well-documented and don't need to be completely rehearsed here. However, that story of bourgeois and bohemian aesthetic disagreements needs to be supplemented with three observations: First, whatever their disagreements about aesthetics, writers of both generations understood they operated within a discursive context in which the body generally, and sex specifically, was racialized. Second, for some writers, the body and its sex represented not just provocative subject matter, but were significantly related to the life of literature. Finally, the disagreements between the two groups of writers were not merely intraliterary squabbles but had a public life in that prescriptions on sex in literary and personal life were reinforced by the church, often working in concert with police to enforce various kinds of sexual and moral hygiene.

Despite the truism that Du Bois and other elders were uptight moralists while the bohemians were letting it all hang out, the picture of literary production in the period is much more complex. For instance, Du Bois's relative innocence and outrage at bohemian sexual practices is fairly clear: he was apparently stunned when a colleague was arrested for a homosexual liaison in a public facility, and his letters to Countee Cullen regarding the dissolution of Cullen's marriage to Yolande suggest blindness to the real sexual issues in the marriage. Yet, Du Bois's novel *Dark Princess* is frankly erotic in tone at times. If that eroticism is ultimately contained within the bounds of an appropriate marriage, the novel does suggest that Du Bois's concern with the novels of McKay or Van Vechten had to do with more than the frank exploration of sex per se. Moreover, the younger generation seemed acutely aware of the sexualization of race and viewed it with a jaundiced eye. The romanticization of black virility was only a small step from still-regnant cultural stereotypes. Seeing the black man as a hypersexualized dynamo may have titillated the adoring whites making their way uptown, but such adoration was continuous with a tradition that saw black men as all brawn and no brain. While Langston Hughes could celebrate the black body, he cast a cold eye on the propensity of white Americans to see in black men sex or sexual renewal and little else, as his stories "Rejuvenation Through Joy" and "Slave on the Block" attest. James Weldon Johnson and some others believed that the sexual license that afflicted African American culture in the cities of the North was primarily a viral infection from white Americans who carried their own twisted sexual obsessions with them into the clubs, speakeasies, and brothels of the black ghettos (Schwarz 21). Even Claude McKay, a man who in his own words was remarkably free from "Puritan" constraints about sex, tended to view white Americans as diseased and twisted in their views of and participation in sexual acts. Although utterly different and in many respects antagonistic, both McKay and Du Bois sought in the depiction of black male erotic desire a healthy sexuality that opposed the degraded white sexuality they saw or experienced in Harlem and elsewhere.

Sharp divisions regarding appropriate and inappropriate sexual practices were contested not merely on the grounds of concrete moral choices but also in the context of social approval and constraint. Christa Schwarz shows that antivice crusades peaked in the twenties and thirties and that efforts to police sexual behavior extended not only to prostitution and homosexuality but also to art and literature as well. McKay, Thurman, and others complained when publishers shied away from their work or requested revisions not on the basis of race but in an effort to tone down some passages to avoid violating censorship codes or just to circumvent general public disapproval. Even artists far from the bohemian scene worked within these prescriptions. Oscar Micheaux's work was censored because of its perceived violation of public decency standards and especially because it appeared to denigrate Christian ministers.

The traditional moral view of the black bourgeoisie was reinforced by the official line and program of the most important Christian churches as well as in the broader tradition of Christian morality. To be sure, African Americans were well aware of how far Christian reality was from the professed ideal. Preacher jokes regularly invoked the sexual peccadilloes of men of the cloth as a cause for knowing laughter, a tradition that Micheaux drew on to vitiating effect in portraying the minister in *Body and Soul* as not just sexually adventurous but sexually vicious. The sexual proclivities of men such as the evangelist Julius Becton or of Father Divine were readily recognized and remarked on as one source of their appeal. And the ambiguous sexual identity of Frederick Asbury Cullen and his perhaps questionable relationship to his adopted son, Countee, was the source of more than one rude joke in Harlem. The antihomosexual campaigns launched by Adam Clayton Powell in the late twenties were first and foremost directed at Christian ministers (Powell 56–58). Nevertheless, the shortcomings of particular Christian spokesmen did little to blunt the power of a Christian moral rhetoric to shape attitudes toward sex if not control the actual practice of sex. The line between a bourgeois sexual morality devoted to racial uplift and a traditional Christian ethic advocating sexual purity in the name of Jesus was impossible to draw. In practice these moralities were mutually reinforcing and drew readily on racial and theological rhetoric, both of which appealed broadly to the African American masses devoted in various degrees to Christian faith.

Antivice campaigns targeting homosexuality and prostitution along with gambling and alcohol were initiated by leading ministers of large urban congregations and were largely supported by the black press. Christa Schwarz points out that the black press regularly complained about lax enforcement of vice laws in black districts as evidence of white racial discrimination, part and parcel of a general white attempt to corrupt the black race through white immorality (9, 21). Similarly, various ministers, most famously Adam Clayton Powell, Frederick Asbury Cullen, and the Reverend A. V. B. Hightower of Pittsburgh, led antivice campaigns from the pulpit and even worked with police on cleanup campaigns. In 1929, Powell delivered a sermon entitled "Lifting Up a Standard for the People," which was widely reported in the black press and widely praised by other leading ministers (Powell 209–15). Powell described his sermon as not being against

> natural sins among men and women, but abnormal sins. It was the sin that destroyed Sodom and Gomorrah, that buried Pompeii alive and wrecked the mighty Roman Empire, that I thundered against that morning. Why did I preach against homosexuality and all manner of sex perversions? Because, as every informed person knows, these sins are on the increase and are threatening to eat the vitals out of America. (215–16)

Similarly, Frederick Cullen focused on his success as an antivice campaigner in his autobiography, noting his early successes against bootleggers in Maryland. He also noted that the New York Branch of the NAACP, of which he served as president, made antivice activities a particular focus of their work in Harlem. In attempting to protect "my Sunday School boys," Cullen claims to have dressed incognito as a pimp to visit such establishments and establish the truth of their immorality for himself (*Barefoot* 57). The elder Cullen's apparently double sexual life makes his motivations dubious, but it does at least suggest the imaginative lengths to which ministers would go in their efforts to root out sexual and other forms of corruption. Cullen notes that he was deeply involved with police forces in such efforts:

> The New York Branch of the NAACP was a terror to evil doers in Harlem. Street soliciting, gambling houses, places of vice where children frequented, public gambling on street in the daytime, and flagrant, vicious, and immoral acts of all kinds abounded in Harlem at that time. We sustained close cooperation with the police department and very often the captain of the precinct would call at my house and advise with me about conditions in Harlem. We sought to break up as best we could that condition. (57)

This kind of insistence was a rare instance of mutual concern by traditional Christian ministers, the NAACP, and Garveyite nationalists. As Summers points out, Garveyites not only promoted fairly typical middle-class Christian family values but also explicitly decried and attacked homosexuality specifically and sexual license generally, seeing in them a form of racial degradation and even hints of a white conspiracy to erode the morals of the race (91). Christian ministers and laymen may sometimes have made distinctions between the depiction of vice in art and the practice of vice in the body, but on the whole the church seems to have followed the biblical prescription that believers should "shun the appearance of evil." Indeed,

Reverdy Ransom felt like a lonely figure in being the only minister he knew who made friends with and ministered to musicians and actors, his more conventionally pious colleagues pulling in the skirts of their robes a bit more tightly in the presence of traditionally unsavory characters (*Pilgrimage* 207). Adam Clayton Powell lamented that it was impossible to separate "Luther and Lucifer" in German art and complained of the debasement of German culture in terms of the art found in the Sans Souci Palace in Potsdam. "In the dining room of that palace one will see the 'Bath of Bath-sheba' and other obscene pictures, calculated to arouse the baser passions, side by side with those of angels and holy men, Christ and saint, military heroes and scenes of violence. They are mixed and mingled in such a way that no one can tell which have the more prominent place" (92–93).

To say this, however, is not to say that the black bourgeoisie and black ministers were particularly ashamed of the black body. Indeed, within certain boundaries, quite the opposite could be the case. Summers notes that African American ministers certainly participated in the "masculinization of Christ" that was common to the Social Gospel movement and broader popular Christian movements such as the Men and Religion Forward Movement (104–5). The centrality of the black male body to political and even spiritual deliverance was imagined in grand terms in 1923 by Bishop Reverdy Ransom. Ransom's poem "The New Negro" evokes the black male body not as something oppressed, abused, or under attack but as a focal point that gathers together all the creative powers of nature, a force that slavery and racism has not been able to overcome:

> HE IS NEW, he is old as the forests primeval.
> Stark in their nakedness of limb,
> His forebears roamed the jungle and led the chase.
> Crystalized by the heat of Oriental suns,
> God made him a rock of undecaying power,
> To become at last the nation's corner stone.
> Rough hewn from the jungle and the desert's sands,
> Slavery was the chisel that fashioned him to form,
> And gave him all the arts and sciences had won.
> The lyncher, mob, and stake have been his emery wheel.
> TO MAKE A POLISHED MAN of strength and power.

In this rendering, black men are not impervious to the attacks of racism, but the allegorical black man has absorbed and, in some sense, redeemed those attacks. His character, represented here as something to be shaped like a body being perfected, has transformed oppression into strength and even beauty. Ultimately, this gives forth in the "higher" gifts of intellect, art, and even democratic freedom, these spiritual blessings seeming to spring from a body perfected by both nature and history, leaving him superior to the fainting races

> both white and Asian—that surround him.
> In him, the latest birth of freedom,
> God hath again made all things new.
> Europe and Asia with ebbing tides recede,
> America's unfinished arch of freedom waits,
> Till he, the corner stone of strength,
> Is lifted into place and power.
> Behold him! dauntless and unafraid he stands.
> He comes with laden arms,
> Bearing rich gifts to science, religion, poetry and song.
> Labor and capital through him shall find
> The equal heritage of common brotherhood,
> And statesmanship shall keep the stewardship
> Of justice with equal rights and privileges for all.

In the final lines, Ransom returns to the centrality of body and blood in prophesying the Messianic role of black men, one that establishes black preeminence, but articulates that preeminence as a gift for all human beings:

> HE KNOWS HIS PLACE to keep it
> As a sacred trust and heritage for all.
> To wear God's image in the ranks of men
> And walk as princes of the royal blood divine,
> ON EQUAL FOOTING everywhere with all mankind.
> With everfading color on these shores,
> The Oriental sunshine in his blood
> Shall give the warming touch of brotherhood
> And love, to all the fused races in our land,
> He is the last reserve of God on earth,
> Who, in the godly fellowship of love,
> Will rule the world with peace. (*Making the Gospel* 229–30)

Ransom draws on a tradition of racial messianism to see the black man as the advent of a new Christ saving the American nation. The black man is scientist, saint, and artist, the best gift to the new and fusing race called Americans. These gifts are directly related to the body's physical prowess. Nature and history have sculpted the black male body and made it a "rock of undecaying power." Within the body itself, at least as shaped by that nature and that history, lie the clues to all the sciences and arts. Ransom saw this messianic figure embodied as early as 1910 in Jack Johnson. On the eve of Johnson's fight with Jim Jeffries, Ransom said, "What Jack Johnson seeks to do to Jeffries in the roped arena will be more the ambition of Negroes in every domain of human endeavor" (Early 26). Though Johnson was popularly known to the white public for the variety of his sexual liaisons and for some questionable business enterprises, not for conventional piety, Johnson was regularly invited to speak in black churches as a kind of masculine exemplar to the race. His interest in classical music and literature, his self-consciousness that he served as a racial representative, as well as his powerful body made him an exemplar of the New Negro Man. On a very different register, this same role was played by Paul Robeson, who combined magnificent physique and athletic prowess with sensitive cultural values displayed in singing and acting on stage and screen.

The younger generation of Harlem Renaissance writers was less concerned with this nuance about the body and was particularly concerned with—and sometimes mocking of—the explicit denunciations of sexuality that they heard coming from the older generation in general and Christian churches in particular. Somewhat like the tension between intellectualism and religious faith, the relationship among sexual experience, desire, and artistic accomplishment, on the one hand, and the traditions of church regarding sexuality on the other resulted in varying kinds of imaginative responses. Some, of course, ridiculed the traditions of the church, either directly or implicitly. Some other African American writers sought a frankly erotic Christian presence in art, either directly or implicitly. In the poetry of Countee Cullen and Langston Hughes, in the painting of Bruce Nugent, and in some of Zora Neale Hurston's fiction, spiritual and erotic longing are difficult to distinguish and imperfectly reconciled. While artists made aesthetic gestures toward such reconciliation, proper society at least was largely closed to anything that resembled a Christian erotic imagination. We have no written record, but one can well imagine what Powell and other leading churchmen must have thought of Richard Bruce Nugent's frank eroticization of Biblical stories in painting and in prose. While there is some evidence that Harlem churchmen took pride in the cultural achievements or the Harlem Renaissance, there is abundant evidence that the Renaissance left many African American Christians and churches ill at ease. Various artists describe run-ins with Christians over the content of their work. In response to *The Blacker the Berry*, Wallace Thurman claims "a delegation of church members . . . flocked in on me and prayed over me for almost an hour, beseeching the Almighty to turn my talents into the path of righteousness."[10] Similarly, at least one minister forbade Hughes from reading blues poetry in his pulpit. Rampersad suggests that as his popularity rose, Hughes increasingly toned down or skipped poetry that was intended for audiences who might be offended by an anti-Christian tone in philosophy or morality. In this light, Hughes's much criticized decision to remove some of his more provocative political poetry, including "Goodbye Christ," from his collected poems is probably best understood not simply as a response in fear of anticommunist crusaders—as it is unusually narrated—but also as an effort to retain and speak to his black and largely Christian audience.

The point here is not only that African American writers of the younger generation faced proscriptions on the content of their work when it came to sex and the body—though that challenge is important enough to recognize given the tendency in Renaissance criticism to focus on the prescriptive tendencies of a white audience and publishers. But beyond dealing with the delicate sensibilities of audience, which nearly every artist since Chaucer has had to face, the material issue that such antivice programs posed for black artists spoke more closely to the root of their being as artists and as citizens. Especially, though not exclusively, for writers who were gay, antivice campaigns threatened both physical imprisonment and social ostracism or isolation.

Thus, as with other issues in the development of various secularized African American masculinities, the portrayal of sexualized masculinities was fraught with a conflicted dynamic not characteristic of the erotic politics of other American writers. While Mencken and others railed against Puritanism and ridiculed the Christian populace in which they found themselves, African American writers did not rail quite so feverishly or with so much self-assurance, however much they may have agreed with or admired the sexual explicitness of a writer like Mencken or Lawrence or Whitman or Carpenter. To be sure, sex is often depicted explicitly, and ministers are sometimes depicted in ways that suggest they are either sexually repressed or sexually twisted. But the antivice campaigns and the immense wealth of Adam Clayton Powell invited no comparisons to Sinclair Lewis's famous fictional portrayal of the hypocritical preacher, Elmer Gantry—such was the general cultural respect still due to ministers even among the cultural elite. Gantry's name became a byword for dismissing scheming ministers out to make a dollar in the name of morality, but Powell spoke with genuine moral and even political authority every Sunday morning. The bravado of someone like Hughes in "The Negro Mountain" or of other writers in claiming they did not care what other people thought is no doubt sincere but was an ideal honored more in the breach than in reality. Arnold Rampersad points out that by 1930, Hughes was writing three different kinds of poetry for three different perceived audiences, muting the bohemian, anti-Christian, and communist elements that characterized some of his verse in order to appeal more readily and straightforwardly to the cultural and racial pride of the black Christian masses (221). The sexual aesthetics associated with Alain Locke and his acolytes was mostly sotto voce and indirect, with the singular and important exception of Richard Bruce Nugent, thus avoiding the necessary break an openly homoerotic position might have precipitated with a black public. The sexual explicitness and expression at the center of much modern literary production lived in tension with the African American writer's sense of cultural responsibility as well as with his desire to carve out an acceptable place of cultural leadership in African America. The next two chapters will look in depth at two efforts to negotiate this divide as Countee Cullen and Zora Neale Hurston both respond to the body consciousness and sexualization of cultural life in ways that find surprising resonances and difficult chasms among physicality, sexuality, and Christian faith.

"THE SINGING MAN WHO MUST BE RECKONED WITH"
Private Desire and Public Responsibility in the Poetry of Countee Cullen

> His lyric gift was incontestable and, indeed, exceptional. But
> his poetry has none of McKay's fiery virility, and the treasures
> it encloses are, rather, those of a soul that at times indulged in
> an excess of sensibility and preferred to express itself in the
> half-tones and nuances of a high scrupulousness.
>
> —Jean Wagner

> No other Negro writer of the 1920s was more anxious to use
> primitive and atavistic motifs than the poet Countee Cullen.
> It is a bit ironic, because none of the Harlem writers was more
> formally schooled, none more genteel in inclination and taste,
> none indeed more prissy than Cullen.
>
> —Nathan Huggins

> Also, I *like* to teach.
>
> —Countee Cullen, Interview with James Baldwin

Midway through an interview with James Baldwin, one of Countee Cullen's
students at DeWitt Clinton High School, Cullen responded to Baldwin's
shock that he had not been able to make a living as a poet and had chosen
to take up his position as a teacher because "writing poetry cannot be
considered a means of making a livelihood."[1] The young Baldwin responds

earnestly that he guessed a teaching job "comes in pretty handy, then"—to which the elder Cullen, in the role of mentor, famously responded, "Yes. Also, I *like* to teach" (Baldwin, "Rendezvous" 601). Whether the emphasis is Baldwin's or Cullen's, Cullen's emphatic "*like*" in this exchange seems to have the point of persuasive emphasis. "You may not believe this," Cullen seems to say "and your question does not seem to assume it, but . . . I *like* to teach." The exchange exemplifies the dilemma of masculinity for the writer in general as well as the peculiar bifurcations surrounding public responsibility and the poetic desire that shaped much of Cullen's career. On the one hand, poetry's manifest implausibility as a career path makes it an unlikely choice for manly men, while making a living by other means is popularly conceived as a betrayal of poetry itself, a different manifestation of masculine failure in embracing stable and domestic roles and not "following one's dream" through masculine devotion to art come what may. Cullen's quick asser-tion, "Also, I *like* to teach," points to the peculiar form of emasculation that teaching implies for male writers and artists especially and for men more generally. Those who can, do; those who can't, teach. Or so the old saw goes. Its derision is directed, I think, at men, though it is also misogynistic since the teaching profession has been long characterized as a woman's profession. Teaching jobs may pay the bills for most writers in America, but by virtue of that fact, they are beneath consideration as a manly form of vocation. The *real* work of poetry and literature is in a masculine domain apart. Cullen's emphatic statement of desire, "I *like* to teach," underscores his lifelong effort to embrace both the poetry of romantic desire and the pedestrian pleasures of public usefulness. His failure, finally, to reconcile the two speaks to the divided and anxious means of defining masculine success in the twentieth century. The publically responsible bourgeois male may do good, but he fails in the codes of masculine bravado because he has had to sacrifice his masculine desires to do it. Public good comes at the cost of individual loss, a loss that marks the emasculation that domestication popularly entails. But on the other hand, the poet who eschews public responsibility for the life of private pleasure does so at the cost of other, more public and more enduring forms of masculine self-definition.

Countee Cullen's "Also, I *like* to teach" spells out this conundrum for a very private and very public poet, and his failure to reconcile these different impulses has led to very public pronouncements on his failed masculinity as a writer. It's difficult to read very far into the history of scholarship on Countee Cullen without noticing a drumbeat of sotto voce criticism, often eloquently stated but, in the end, mainly sophisticated versions of schoolyard taunts at boys who never quite manage to throw a spiral, who make the mistake of giggling a bit too often. "My God!" the (usually male) critics seem to agree disparagingly, "He writes like a girl!" Most often this dismissal of the poetry coincides with a dismissal of the man. For Jean Wagner, Cullen lacks McKay's virility, and, for the editors of the Riverside Anthology, he has exhausted whatever virility he may have had and is simply effete—perhaps a more politically palatable term than "effeminate." For Darwin Turner, he is "childishly petulant" and given to "self-pitying despair" (74). Nathan Huggins thinks he's "prissy." For David Levering Lewis, the combination of Cullen's suspect masculinity and his overwhelming popularity among talented tenth Harlemites signifies the general failings of the Renaissance as a whole. Lewis grants literary Harlem some manly discernment by hoping speculatively that "Cullen must have set even Harlem's teeth on edge with *Crisis* throwaways lisping of a 'daisy-decked' Spring with her 'flute and silver lute'" (77). But Lewis's general dismay at the failures of the black bourgeoisie comes quickly to the fore, as he notes, "Harlem loved Langston Hughes, Cullen's only serious rival . . . but it revered Countee Cullen. With his high-pitched voice, nervous courtliness, and large Phi Beta Kappa key gleaming on the chain across a vested, roly-poly middle, he was the proper poet with proper credentials" (77).

Alas, poor Cullen. Fat, high-pitched and lisping, childish and effete.

To some degree, these gendered interpretations echo the masculine anxieties of an Ezra Pound or a T. S. Eliot decrying the effeminate line of the Amygists. In this argument, the soft feminine spirituality of decadent Romanticism had to be displaced by the hard body of a truly modern poetry to reflect modern times. Poetry in form and content had to exhibit the "terrible honesty" Ann Douglas delineates so well in her book of that name. Although it is the case that the barely disguised sexism and implicit homophobia that lurks in these kinds of criticisms has moderated somewhat in the past decade, Cullen seems to remain an uncomfortable conundrum. Despite a useful biography by Charles Molesworth, and despite the turn to gender and sexuality studies in the same period, there has been no new "Cullen moment" in the way that we have seen renewed interest in a variety of writers of the period who seem to offer fruitful study for the ambiguities of race, gender and sexuality. Such rediscoveries have included Nella Larsen, Claude McKay, and Jean Toomer, as well as the continued and ever-expanding efforts of the Hurston and Hughes literary industries. This is surely on one level a sign of the triumph of a certain conception of what a white resistant and masculine aesthetic ought to look like. African American modernists thought a New Negro required a new poetry, a new and manly literature that confronted the racial and sexual realities of the modern period. Since

Hughes's denigration of Cullen as a poet who wanted to be white, Cullen's traditional line has been the exemplar of bloodless bourgeois literary efforts, an image that has dominated Cullen's critical reception. Such work sought to imitate a decaying white tradition rather than to create a newer and blacker literary response to the times.

The critical attention to Cullen's supposedly flaccid masculinity reflects a crisis over the nature of black masculinity that Cullen's poetry everywhere embodies. What was an appropriately muscular response to the facts of living in a racist culture? This crisis surely turns fundamentally on the unresolved tensions that poetry displays over the relationship between blackness and homoeroticism. But it also turns uncomfortably on the relationship of these concepts to Christian faith and ethics, a discomfort within both Cullen himself and his critical reception. No studies have looked at length at the complicated nexus of these different discursive fields in Cullen's work. While Gerald Early correctly says of Cullen's poetry that "most of it is racial and . . . all of it is Christian or could only have been produced by a Christian consciousness" (57), he is able to discuss the divide between paganism and Christianity in Cullen's work without noting at all that paganism is an all-but-transparent stand-in for homoerotic desire. Similarly, although Rachel DuPlessis announces her book as an examination of genders and religious cultures, there is almost no discussion directly of the difficult link between homoerotic desire and Christianity—either its prohibition in the dominant Christian religious cultures or its link and overlap in Cullen's imagination. Finally, Molesworth's biography, in the end, seems to marginalize both Cullen's spirituality and his sexuality, not registering that his pervasive Christian spirituality, in fact, complicated and granted a different resonance to his sexuality when compared to any of his peers. This seems to me an important gap for a poet that is universally recognized, for better or for worse, as the most popular poet of his own time period, however much his reputation has declined since 1928. It is possible to hypothesize that Cullen's popularity grew not only from his dangling Phi Beta Kappa key, but also because the tensions and contradictions that drive his work embody those of his cultural context. For many African Americans of the time, Cullen's success both signified and contained the racial and sexual turbulence of the new period precisely because it explores the tricky terrain in which the achievement of manhood is an achievement of racial self-realization, and does so directly through a discourse of Christian faith and practice. Cullen's portrayals of masculinity are framed by Christianity, blackness and homoerotic desire simultaneously, a conceptual and imaginative tension that was, for a very important and influential while, productive of some enduring and important poetry, however much it may have fallen out of fashion in the ensuing decades.

Cullen earned the dilemma of his masculinity honestly. Adopted out of an impoverished childhood, and perhaps illegitimacy, into the upper reaches of Harlem society by a Methodist minister, pursuing a variety of male lovers while marrying Yolande Du Bois, Cullen embodied the contradictory social significance of varying masculine styles in his one body. He was aware of this on some level, as his oft-quoted statement that he could not resolve a Christian upbringing with a pagan inclination makes clear. Critics often note the conflict between Cullen's Africanist longings and his attachment to white traditions of poetic form, and they have similarly noted Cullen's assertion that he could not reconcile a "pagan inclination" with Christian faith. But the implications of these motifs in terms of the discourses of masculinity at the time have not been thoroughly charted. Not only was "Africa" viewed as a primordial homeland, but also it was a specifically masculine and heterosexual homeland. The "paganism" of Africa was not the same thing as the "paganism" of homosexual desire, even if both Africa and paganism came to signify a form of sexual desire that Cullen could not reconcile with his desire for not only social approval but also social impact.

Few note that in Cullen's work, "paganism" stands primarily, if allusively, as a marker for erotic desire.[2] But more than this, Cullen's "pagan inclination," though largely closeted, was closely linked to his public face, and not simply in the sense that polite society apparently maintained a "don't ask, don't tell" policy toward the sexual proclivities of their favorite literary son. Letters to and from Harold Jackman, Langston Hughes, and especially Alain Locke—his mentor in things both sexual and literary—suggest that Cullen depended openly on these friendships that had no name in order to pursue his literary career.[3] Thus the terrible irony of Cullen's position. His closeted desires in some sense keep him separate and apart even as he becomes an exemplar of the race by writing poetry. His poetry often evokes an eroticism associated with blackness, normatively heterosexual in the reading public's mind, which nevertheless charted same-sex desires for Cullen. These desires clearly did not fit available heroic black male images embodied by Jack Johnson and the soldiers of the 15th regiment or even of the Christian public servant embodied by his father and men like Reverdy Ransom or Adam Clayton Powell. Indeed, many of these cultural leaders, and especially the Christian ministers, made a point of attacking or at least disapproving of homosexuality in general, and sometimes in terms that associated it with race betrayal. Thus, in asserting blackness and maleness, Cullen implied same-sex desire, the frank revelation and indulgence of which could only have served to diminish Cullen's position as a New Negro poet laureate. "What is Africa to me?" Indeed.

This dynamic resituates the racial framework in which Cullen's work has been analyzed, a framework first articulated when Langston Hughes accused Cullen of wanting to be white. Cullen is not simply conflicted between allegiance to Africa, African Americans, and white cultural forms; rather, that cultural conflict is also a coded conflict between the public and private body. The public persona performs its own very real public longing for approval and male leadership through bodily displays. One thinks of the dangling Phi Beta Kappa key at which Lewis smirks, the rather uncomfortable-looking suits that Cullen always seems to be wearing in publicity photographs, and even the visual pageantry of the society marriage into Harlem's intellectual royalty. All of these contrast with the erotic performances of the body in love or lust. Agreeing with Houston Baker that the predominant motive of Cullen's romantic poetry is love, we can further say that his illicit desires are the occasion for the lyric poetry that made him a public man, that his illegitimate private self made his public and proper self-display possible (53). Cullen embraced a particular form of public "blackness" in his position as poet, but that public position which he eagerly wished to maintain conflicted with a very different form of "blackness" embodied in his private desires for black men. Out of this tension—at first creative and later debilitating—much of Cullen's poetry is born.

In evoking the idea of a split in Cullen between gay desire and public rectitude, there is some obvious, though I would say too easy, recourse to the discourses of authenticity and identity. The "real" Cullen was the interior Cullen who desired other—usually black—men but remained falsely in the closet in order to live out the security of a public existence with all its approbation. There is, surely, something to the notion that Cullen hoped to maintain a public position, and the more frank revelation of his sexual desire would have been, in his own view, too costly. Nevertheless, this view of the authentic interior self is complicated by the fact of Cullen's genuine and authentic Christian faith. Whatever else may be said, he seems to have genuinely been a believer, one of the few associated with the younger generation of artists in Harlem. The "split" consciousness of Cullen, then, was not simply that which ends in hypocrisy and moral judgment—as if we were to say that he could not be "who he was" so he chose to be something he was not. The conflict seems much more profound than that, and it is both internalized and externalized. Cullen genuinely desired to be a Christian and genuinely desired other men and genuinely desired to be of public service to the African American culture. The tendency, even in Cullen himself, is to read this split in terms of what Foucault calls the "repressive hypothesis." That is, Cullen's struggle with his sexuality is assumed to be a repression of his authentic self in order to preserve some form of more comfortable, but false, social persona. In this reading, he can't possibly like to teach because to get there he had to give up everything else that made him who he was. By this way of thinking, who he was, fundamentally, had to be determined by sexual desire. Therefore, any questioning of or struggle with that sexuality must necessarily be between a true and false self. If, however, we extend Foucault's questioning of the repressive hypothesis and suggest that there are many versions of desire, many pleasures, including the pleasures of positive social contribution, social celebrity, and so forth, then different forms of desire that represent different versions of the self must be reconciled. For Cullen, there were no public models for how such desires, such various selves, might be articulated together.

This divided or multiple identity in Cullen was perhaps inevitable since open assertions of same-sex desire were still relatively rare. While Richard Nugent may have written a short story that frankly displayed homosexual desire and behavior, and while Claude McKay may have included a homosexual character in *Home to Harlem*, these few drops of public literary homosexuality seem meager indeed when compared to the rivers of desire that flowed between many of the Harlem Renaissance literary masters.[4] Du Bois's scathing denunciations of literary works that depicted bohemian sexual practices—he reviewed or spoke negatively of McKay, Van Vechten's *Nigger Heaven*, and the anthology *Fire!!*, which contained Nugent's short story—suggest the degree to which the cultural leadership of the Renaissance subscribed to traditional bourgeois sexual mores, at least as a matter of public discourse. Such criticisms were consistent with Du Bois's firing of Augustus Granville Dill from work on *The Crisis* after Dill was arrested during a homosexual encounter in a public lavatory. Du Bois's later expressed regret at this decision, but he also later wrote of homosexuality as a "new and undreamed of aspect of sex" (Lewis, *Fight for Equality* 205), and it was certainly an aspect of sex that the editor of the most important African American journal of opinion felt bound to disavow. Dill's firing occurred in 1927, a year before Cullen's marriage to Yolande, and must have reinforced to Cullen the clear distinctions that had to be made between private desire and public responsibility. Thus, while some in Harlem were clearly aware of Cullen's sexual preferences and didn't run him out of town on a rail, Cullen apparently was concerned enough about the relationship of his sexual practices to his public image as to keep them well-hidden from cultural leaders like Du Bois, upon whom his position as a "poet laureate" partially depended.[5]

The split between public and private was all the more inevitable for Cullen given his adoptive Christian home. On the one hand, rumor had it that Frederick Asbury Cullen modeled this kind of split for his son, serving both as exemplary Christian leader of the race and as seducer of choir boys (Lewis, *Vogue* 76). To some degree, the scholarly snickering at Frederick Cullen's rumored sexuality misses the degree to which the elder Cullen provided a self-conscious and public model of manliness for many Harlemites, certainly more so than most of the younger generation of writers of the Renaissance. What was important about Reverend Cullen, both for Harlem generally and especially for his adopted son, is Reverend Cullen's model of responsible Christian masculinity, "responsibility" in this case turning on one's public activity on behalf of the race. Reverend Cullen's autobiography is replete with the values of Christian self-renunciation in service to God and others. The elder Cullen transformed Salem Methodist Episcopal from a tiny and struggling mission church to one of the most powerful African American churches of the twenties, with more than three thousand members, large property holdings, and a plethora of ministries to the tidal wave of immigrants from the South. While much has been made of the criticisms that Reverend Cullen made of the cabaret and club life, as well as of the prostitution and sexual peccadilloes that his adopted son found alluring, Frederick Cullen was far from a simpleminded moralist. Indeed, some of his most important work included public action on issues attendant to the assertion of black maleness in the world. He served as president of the local chapter of the NAACP and helped to organize a protest of the race riot in Brownsville, Texas. He played a role in sending W. E. B. Du Bois to the League of Nations, organizing the Silent Parade, and founding the Urban League. Among his most important ministries at Salem was a commitment to the YMCA, through which he hoped to rescue Harlem boys from gang activity in the streets (Ferguson 20–21; Sernett 134).[6] He presided at major Harlem cultural events such as his son's wedding and the funeral of James Weldon Johnson. Whatever the limitations of such activities and activism, it can hardly be said that Reverend Cullen's Christianity encouraged racial self-hatred or was irresponsibly otherworldly. In many ways, Reverend Cullen stood, at least publically, as an exemplar of that icon of racial leadership, the black preacher, noted by Du Bois as a man at "the centre of a group of men, now twenty, now a thousand in number" (Souls 199).

Countee Cullen sought to replicate his father's belief in the importance of public Christian leadership and proper public deportment. The younger Cullen's complaint against the lowlife depictions of some Harlem Renaissance work surely reflects his father's moralism. But the son's position is at least as complicated as the father's, suggesting that any dismissal of him as "prissy" is a travesty arrived at by cursory reading. While not entering the ministry, the young poet was drawn to positions of leadership within his own vocation, serving as editor of journals and anthologies from his days as a schoolboy until the days he ceased most professional activity as a writer. His ending his career as a teacher has very often been narrated as a failure of some sort, whereas if looked at in view of a desire to give to his community, Cullen's choice to sacrifice other personal desires for the greater good of the community is more complicated. It was, and is, a path followed by many significant African Americans at the time and since. Linking it to criticism of Cullen's failure as poet—perhaps because of his unwillingness to be a bohemian—seems mostly tendentious rather than insightful. Similarly, while Cullen has been critiqued for not following an editorial policy more clearly focused on folk traditions when he brought out his anthology, *Caroling Dusk*, he clearly conceived of the project as a form of racial promotion, a way of putting the best racial foot forward, as it were. Houston Baker has suggested that Cullen's poetic project was "celebrated by black people because he demonstrated authentic, poetical achievement to appreciative whites" (47). This formulation obscures that a good number of sophisticated African Americans read more poetic achievement in Cullen's traditional forms than in Hughes's experimentation and were not celebrating him simply because he got good notices from white people.

Cullen seemed aware that in his role as poet he served a public and quasi-political office. Commenting on his former classmate, Martin Russak notes that Cullen served as a significant intellectual leader even among some white Americans at NYU, something that in its own way represented the kind of political and cultural power to which many African Americans aspired in the Harlem Renaissance (Tuttleton 130–31). Little wonder then, that many saw in the marriage of a daughter of Du Bois and a son of Cullen the marriage of a new Adam and a new Eve, an image of a New Negro race to be. Even according to the editors of the *Norton Anthology of African American Literature*, Cullen "was probably the figure from the Harlem Renaissance who most closely corresponded to Alain Locke's idea of the New Negro" (1303). Locke seems to have affirmed this in private correspondence with the poet, saying, "You and one or two more very much represent the younger generation as far as my hopes and interests go" (letter to Countee Cullen).[7] In light of Cullen's general imperative to public service, it seems unlikely that he could have ever endorsed Langston Hughes's call for an individual artist who didn't care what the African American public thought of him or her. Cullen did care, and deeply, precisely because he believed he existed for their sake and not they for his.

Seen in this light, Cullen's plaintive longing to be taken as only a poet, not a Negro poet, seems less like self-alienation and racial self-hatred than an attempt to mitigate the consequences of being "THE New Negro," a particular mode of blackness that he felt called upon—and indeed wanted—to embrace. Such a calling, however, made his own long-standing and deeply personal embrace of men like Harold Jackman deeply complicated indeed.

Cullen also seemed aware of the significance of public approbation and the costs of public ridicule and that the public character of his poetry was of paramount importance. In a letter to Harold Jackman, he accuses himself of playing to the public too readily: "There is actually no excuse for enjoying the plaudits of the populace as I do. I fairly revel in public commendation. Perhaps I am the one living poet who will confess that he doesn't write for his own amusement, and that what others think of his work can affect him" (Shucard 10). Still, Cullen seems to have been torn by the public significance of his work. When Alain Locke argued that "racial heritage" is more important than "personal genius," Cullen wrote a disturbed rejoinder that argued for the importance of the personal (Shucard 20). Indeed, even Cullen's famous repudiation of the more bohemian school of Hughes and McKay, while clearly concerned with the reception of a white audience, is also riven with anxieties about hidden and private things becoming exposed:

> There is no more childish untruth than the axiom that the truth will set you free; in many cases it will merely free one from the concealment of facts which will later bind you hand and foot in ridicule and mockery. Let art portray things as they are no matter what the consequences, no matter who is hurt, is a blind bit of philosophy. There are some things, some truths of Negro life and thought, of Negro inhibitions, that all Negroes know, but take no pride in. ("Dark Tower" 171)

Here, Cullen reflects the aesthetic assumptions of someone like Du Bois. Cullen seems primarily to be arguing for a particular mode of blackness, a definition of what a Negro is or ought to be, as well as for the freedom not to revel in or reveal the sexuality that threatened his public face.[8] Rather than exhibiting racial self-hatred, Cullen fears falling short of what a Negro ought to be—at least in his own mind and in the mind of the black bourgeoisie. Self-policing becomes a mode of racial uplift. The quotation moves from a general statement of the imprisoning effects of social ridicule to a general sense that there are any number of things that Negroes know about but would rather not discuss in public. Only after this does Cullen move to an explicit statement that the receptiveness of white audiences should be taken into account. Cullen is fearful of the consequences of his desires being uncovered as a general principle, not simply out of a slavish devotion to the prerogatives of white people. All of which suggests that desire is never a purely personal matter, at least for the person desiring a public voice.

This bifurcation between public and private lives is evident in Cullen's juvenile poetry, setting the tone for mature work to come. A poem printed in his high school yearbook, "Icarian Wings," contrasts a hidden and fantastic life at night with the public light of day. At dusk the soul of the poetic persona "goes clad like Icarus / To genie lands of summer snow." By contrast, as daylight breaks, the lyricist puts aside soaring fantasy. It is his "lot to don the drab dull husk / You know" (David Dorsey 68). Icarus has traditionally played an important role in gay iconography. While it is difficult to know how much the sixteen-year-old Cullen may have known of that, we can at least say that this poem reflects the conflict between hidden self and public self that drives all of his mature work. What the reader, the author's public, knows is only a drab husk that cannot conjure wings to fly through art or pleading. By comparison, the Icarian man of night is a man of intellectual and artistic enlightenment as well as raw physical power. The man we know longs silently for the man we don't.

A similar structure links the imagination with hidden, erotic powers of the night in Cullen's most important mature poem, "Heritage." "Heritage" is consumed by the fear of hidden desire being discovered. "Heritage" is, of course, about the problematic status of Africa in Cullen's imagination and in the Harlem Renaissance in general and is also about the sense of split between a pagan self and a Christian or civilized self. However, the poem is most vividly and immediately about the conflicted desires of the poet's own body. The narrator of the poem lies meditating on his body while presumably alone in bed. In this body he feels

> the unremittant beat
> Made by cruel padded feet
> Walking through my body's street.
> Up and down they go, and back,
> Treading out a jungle track. (106)

Cullen separates "the beat," a figure for desire, from the body and presents it as something walking on the narrator cruelly, as if dominating and beating down his body in an all but unbearable manner. A similar linking of anguish and desire occupies the next lines, as the body is no longer simply trod upon by desire but writhes in response:

I can never rest at all
When the rain begins to fall;
Like a soul gone mad with pain
I must match its weird refrain;
Ever must I twist and squirm,
Writhing like a baited worm,
While its primal measures drip
Through my body, crying, "Strip!
Doff this new exuberance.
Come and dance the Lover's Dance!"
In an old remembered way
Rain works on me night and day. (106)

The evident anguish here replicates the anguish caused by the "cruel pad-
ded feet" of the earlier line. However, the poet's body responds by twisting,
squirming, and writhing, movements associated with sexual passion, but a
sexual passion characterized by entrapment. Sexual ecstasy does not lead
to self-fulfillment. Rather, the narrator is a baited worm, a body trapped
by desires beyond his ability to control, desires that are in fact imperious
and demanding, calling for the narrator to "strip" and to "dance," verbs
used in the imperative voice.[9] Desire calls the poet to reveal himself fully
and to cease lying—that is, to get up and act on his sexual desire but also
to give up his duplicitous double life and reveal himself for who he is: a
desiring being.

Of course, the Romantic literary tradition in which Cullen is rooted
regularly links erotic desire and enslavement. Given that Cullen feels acutely
not only his own desire but also the hopes and longings of others, this association takes on particular resonances. The poem is dedicated to Harold
Jackman, Cullen's male lover of longest standing. However, the opening
segments of the poem evoke images of sexuality that are clearly heterosexual
and/or reproductive in character. The "Strong bronzed men, or regal black /
Women from whose loins I sprang," and the "Jungle boys and girls in love"
are fairly commonplace images of Africa for the time. However, these strong
images of heterosexual racial pride are associated with an Africa toward
which the narrator has an ambivalent attitude, an identification he can
only make through a cerebral engagement with books. More important
is the drumbeat within his own blood, the desires that would call him to
"strip" and cast aside his bookish images of Africa in favor of the dance. For
Cullen, of course, such book learning was one of the most important sources
of his public authority. Moreover, the clothes he is called upon to leave
behind symbolize the public face of respectability, the outward symbol of

a civilized, educated, and clearly heterosexual Christian gentleman who, writhing on his bed at night, has desires for something other than the things such civilization prescribes. Thus the dream, or desire, is always deferred. As a black gay man expected to perform in a number of publicly prescribed ways, the narrator here feels the necessity of keeping his desiring black body safely in the closet—or, in Cullen's case, safely encased within his ill-fitting suits and Phi Beta Kappa Key—unstripped, unrevealed, and writhing on his bed of lies.

That Cullen concludes the poem with an imagined prayer to Christ partially replicates this more general effort to protect the body. But at the end of "Heritage," Cullen is attempting desperately to reconcile his reasonable desire for safety with his longing to express his erotic desire for black men, and seeking to reconcile all of this with a desire to assert a black masculinity that will be taken as fully manly, even if it happens to be gay. Thus an angry and erotically compelling black Christ is a "dark god" that Cullen "fashions" so that he can have a black male with whom he can identify. This Christ has "Dark despairing features" that are "Crowned with dark rebellious hair," figures that suggest sexual vitality as well as Cullen's resentment at perpetually deferred sexual self-revelation. Nevertheless, even after fashioning such a Christ, Cullen withdraws from what he takes as an impetuous act of creation, begging forgiveness of the Lord because his "need" or desire "Sometimes shapes a human creed." In the poem's conclusion, the narrator follows not the imperative to "strip" as called for by his hot desire, but the imperative to self-renunciation.

> All day long and all night through,
> One thing only must I do:
> Quench my pride and cool my blood,
> Lest I perish in the flood.

Whereas his days and nights at the beginning and middle of the poem are wracked by desire and the necessity to act, even by the imperative to shape a black god who could fill his "need," the poem concludes with the need for self-protection.

The rejection of the Black Christ is peculiar on any number of scales. While much has been made of the embrace of a white Jesus throughout much of African American Christianity at the time, Cullen's longing that "he I served were black" is hardly novel to Cullen or to the Black Theology movement of the 1960s. As Kelly Brown Douglas suggests, among the educated and middle-class ministerial circles in which Cullen moved, assertions of a Black Christ were relatively common (9–34). Such images also had broad popular appeal in Harlem. In direct appeals to the masses, Garveyites incorporated the notion of a Black Christ, a Black God, and a Black Madonna into their quasi-religious ritualism, and the Cullen household had been known to take the Garveyites seriously.[10] Proclaiming a Black Christ was not a radical notion. Moreover, Edward Blum and Paul Harvey note that the general thrust toward physicality and embodied life that I have traced earlier in this book had its cognates in renewed concerns with depictions of the robust physicality of Christ. They note that this view was typified by men like religious writer Robert Warren Conant, who "was frustrated by the effeminacy and weakness he perceived in American men." They continue:

> Conant found little to praise in Christian art. He damned its Christ representations. "From lovely illuminated church windows and from Sunday school banners he looks down upon us," Conant complained, "meek and lowly," with an expression of sweetness and resignation, eyes often down-cast, soft hands gently folded, long curling hair brushed smoothly from a central parting—all feminine, passive, negative.
>
> What Americans needed was a tough and rough Jesus. They desired a savior more like Theodore Roosevelt and less like a teddy bear. They needed a Jesus with "a strong tonic of Virility." "The men of a strenuous age demand a strenuous Christ," Conant proclaimed. "If we want to win modern men" to the church," we must quit preaching the 'meek and lowly Jesus' and substitute the Fighting Christ. (164)[11]

It is surely the case that depictions of a virile and Fighting Christ had a lurking masculine erotic appeal. But it is often the case that erotic appeal in the American context has been deeply sublimated into the violence of fighting foes, secular or sacred. Thus, while the depictions of virile Christs had become more common, and while appeals to a black Christ were hardly uncommon at all, the depiction of highly eroticized and sexually appealing Christs was hardly seen. However heterodox the notion of a Black Christ might have been in some circles, what is truly unique and potentially disturbing to middle-class African American Christians or white readers is the depiction of an eroticized Christ whom the male narrator finds attractive. When the narrator wishes for a Black Christ so that his heart would not lack "Precedence of pain to guide it," the pain to be recalled within the poem itself is primarily that of the illicit and un-Christian sexual desire that pierces his body like a hook. Indeed, the narrator reinscribes the public/private split that frustrates Cullen's erotic desires when he wants the Black Christ to be able to feel his pain, "Let who would or might deride it" (107). The narrator longs for a publicly acceptable male object of desire, one who would release him from the pain of public censure, dismissing those who would deride him. One thinks here of the snickering nubile girls that Lewis evokes in his description of Cullen's social position in the Renaissance (76). In the predominantly Christian environs of Harlem, what could be more publicly acceptable than Christ himself? The problem, then, is not simply the blackness of Christ, but a Black Christ who can experience the pain of desire. While the former was well within the realm of acceptable speculative possibility, the latter could have been scandalous to many Christians, for whom Christ is marked primarily by his spirituality and "asexual" celibacy. Supportive readers may have indulged the sexual wandering of one of their leading lights, but could hardly have accepted his having looked or longed for those sexual wanderings in the Son of God.

So it is not surprising that, at the end of "Heritage," the narrator chooses survival. If his heart and head, his private longings, thoughts, and desires, have not yet realized they are civilized, he at least must guard against the destructive flood their publicity might entail. He seeks to cool his blood, an image of the death of his desire that avoids the social death that his stripping might occasion. Indeed, perhaps it is not accidental that in the collection *Color*, Cullen chose to follow "Heritage" with "For a Poet," wherein he imagines his dreams wrapped in a silken cloth and buried in a coffin-like box, a form of psychic death that purchases a form of public freedom.[12]

"Heritage" is sometimes taken as an exceptional poem in an otherwise mediocre literary career. However, in many ways "Heritage" foreshadows the obsessions of the rest of Cullen's career, particularly his need to sacrifice individual desire for some greater good, a sacrifice often but not exclusively associated with Christianity. In "Judas Iscariot," the clearly homosocial and suggestively homoerotic bond between Judas and Jesus is broken when Jesus asks Judas to betray him to fulfill God's work of salvation.

> Then Judas in his hot desire
>   Said, "Give me what you will."
> Christ spoke to him with words of fire,
>   "Then, Judas, you must kill
> One whom you love, One who loves you
>   As only God's son can:
> This is the work for you to do
>   To save the creature man." (*Soul's High Song* 126)

Here Cullen intriguingly follows the heterodoxy of the Gnostic traditions in reading Judas as a hero. In this reading, Judas is the most faithful disciple to his friend/lover Christ. He gives the "young Christ heart, soul, and limb/ and all the love he had" (128), but he gives that love precisely by giving up Jesus as the object of his "hot desire" for the higher purpose of the people's salvation. The poem also follows the basic narrative pattern of Richard Bruce Nugent's much more explicitly homoerotic story "Tree with Kerioth-Fruit," wherein Judas is seen as the closest of Jesus's disciples, comparing the deep love Jesus had for John to the superior love that Jesus had for Judas simply by noting, "But Judas, Jesus knew" (143). Jesus loves others as a father loves children, but Jesus loves Judas as a man and, in the biblical terms that Nugent evokes, in the way a man "knows" a lover sexually. As in Cullen's poem, Nugent's Judas eventually betrays Jesus in order to help Jesus fulfill his destiny as a savior of humankind. In Nugent's story, unlike Cullen's, it is quite clear that Judas kills himself not out of guilt at having betrayed Christ, but out of anguish at having lost him as a lover. Nugent was well known for developing fully eroticized depictions of biblical stories in both literary and visual art, and one of his paintings depicts Jesus and Judas, if not as lovers then at least as physically and erotically compelling, apparently touching one another, and in a spot secluded from the other disciples or Jesus's followers.

For both artists, the effort to find an overlay between desire and Christian faith, or at least the shadow of Christian faith, seemed paramount. Yet Cullen, far more than Nugent, seems to have been certain that such an overlay could only be flirted with and never explicitly announced or realized. Indeed, in his poem about Judas, Cullen suggests that Judas "bound / his throat as final fee," an almost eerie foreshadowing of the idea that public service required the renunciation of voice, a trajectory Cullen himself seemed to live out in ensuing decades. Such renunciation of desire for the greater good of others occurs repeatedly in Cullen's work, as does the more conventional loss of true love. In "The Ballad of the Brown Girl," the doubting "Lord Tom" gives up on the true object of his desire in order to marry a "nut-brown maid" with riches and social standing. Many of the poems that appear in *Copper Sun* and in *The Black Christ* deal with the problem of lost love, failed love, or the failure to love—too many to analyze individually. While some of this can be attached to his failing marriage with Yolande Du Bois, it also seems clear that Cullen is crestfallen at his decision to leave behind male lovers behind male lovers, men whom he cast in the role of poetic muses, for a publicly acceptable marriage. During this period, Cullen writes to Alain Locke, complaining not only of his sexual failures in marriage but also of his loss of social contact with male associates who have since been identified as gay (Reimonenq 150). Further, in the dedicatory poem for "The Black Christ," Harold Jackman and two others are described as three who have not bowed the knee to "grasp a lock / Of Mammon's hair."[13] Instead, they are those

Who have not bent
The idolatrous knee,
Nor worship lent to modern rites . . .
Three to whom Pan is no mere myth
But a singing Man
To be reckoned with (180)

Pan, as Early points out, is a mythological figure noted not only for his singing abilities but also for his sexual prowess, a predilection often directed
toward young males (180). For the poet, Jackman appreciates the powers
of a highly sexualized singing man. If Cullen's marriage to Yolande Du Bois
sealed his position in polite society, it seems that Cullen's lamentations of
the lost loves and desires of his youth have less to do with Yolande than
with the losses required to achieve social acceptance.

Ultimately, Cullen associates the loss of private desire with the loss of
poetry itself. The tensions and creative interactions between sexual desire,
creative production (or "singing"), and the temptations of social acceptance
form the central conflict of much of "The Black Christ." Its inability to
resolve these conflicts marks the dying fall of Cullen's poetic project. "The
Black Christ" makes explicit what remains lurking just beneath the surface
of "Heritage": that the realization of illicit forms of desire results in death,
a death Cullen is finally unwilling to undergo.

Whereas the drama of desire and self-renunciation in "Heritage" is figured as a split within the body of the narrator, in "The Black Christ" these
qualities are divided into various characters: the mother who becomes the
feminine figure of Christian patience and forbearance; the white mobs who
embody the threats that remain mostly felt but not seen in "Heritage"; the
rebellious brother Jim who represents both sexual desire and, to some degree, the inspiring spirit of lyric poetry; and, of course, the narrator, who in
the end represents nothing so much as the poetics of self-renunciation. The
poem, in fact, opens with the self-renunciation that concludes "Heritage," as
the narrator pleads with God for forgiveness, partially because he believed
God would not act of his behalf. The burden of his guilt is something that
the poet will carry with him to eternity, and his only response can be to
sing "For all men's healing." His poetry must serve a public social purpose
nobler than the failures of his individual soul, which is "of flaws/ Composed" (207).

Thus, we already know before things get started what the appropriate
mode of masculine behavior is to be: that of repentance and self-renunciation.
The combination of desires in "Heritage" at least makes the narrator
"writhe" with both ecstasy and indecision, creating a dramatic tension

that needs to be resolved; in "The Black Christ," the plea for forgiveness
and the enunciation of social purpose dissolve all dramatic tension from the
outset. Ironically, the poet goes on to ask a few lines later why no powerful
manifestations of masculine presence can be found in this historical moment:

> We cry for angels; yet wherefore,
> Who raise no Jacobs any more? . . .
> No men with eyes quick to perceive
> The Shining Thing, clutch at its sleeve,
> Against the strength of heaven try
> The valiant force of men who die;
> With heaving heart where courage sings
> Strive with a mist of Light and Wings,
> And wrestle all night long, though pressed
> Be rib to rib and back to breast,
> Till in the end the lofty guest
> Pant, "Conquering human, be thou blest." (208)

These lines interestingly render Jacob's wrestling with an angel as a figure
of masculine strength, creative power, and barely sublimated homoerotic
desire as these bodies "wrestle all night long, though pressed / Be rib to rib
and back to breast." However, the poem's opening lines have already offered
us a narrator less interested in such wrestling with gods or men than with
self-surrender. The necessary wrestling, the pressing close of bodies that produces poetry and masculine virtue, is largely associated with a mythic past.
Rather than wrestling blessings from angels, the narrator needs somehow
to wrestle a pardon from God that he will not receive until the last day.

   This effort to erase desire before it can ever really be articulated structures the entire poem. In the second stanza, the conflict is set between the
desiring Jim and his mother, whose voice emphasizes stasis, rootedness, and
acceptance over the writhing and dissatisfied activity of the desiring body:

> I count it little being barred
> From those who undervalue me.
> I have my own soul's ecstasy.
> Men may not bind the summer sea,
> Nor set a limit to the stars;
> The sun seeps through all iron bars;
> The moon is ever manifest.
> These things my heart always possessed.
> And more than this (and here's the crown)
> No man, my son, can batter down
> The star-flung ramparts of the mind.

So much for flesh; I am resigned,
Whom God has made shall He not guide? (211)

The mother's voice resists the very masculine striving that the narrator purports to long for in the figure of the athletic Jacob. Her feminine counsel to patience and forbearance implicitly opposes the longings of Jim's body, insisting that the beauty of creation amply compensates for the exclusion and imprisonment of the body. While awaiting a heavenly kingdom, she provisionally accepts the prison bars that immobilize and hide the body.

Ironically, besides being a sign of Christian pacification, the mother is clearly presented as an origin of black identity, whether linguistic or biological. The father is dead. The mother is presented in nearly mythical terms as an ur-mother, the black Southern woman at one with the earth, a figure of the Southern roots of what was taken to be authentic black culture. She conveys a form of black cultural heritage to her rebellious sons through "legends" of an enslaved people whom God saves after a long and arduous patience (212). In passing on these stories to her sons, she is the figure of intergenerational connection—indeed, the figure of generation, of blackness itself. She also seems to represent the fount of language, the mother tongue that makes it possible to articulate desire at all. While of a different class and geographical location, she symbolizes a mode of blackness with which Cullen would have been quite familiar, one marked by Christian longsuffering. But she is also the source of the Christian stories that framed much of black public and private discourse, stories that shaped a great deal of Cullen's poetry.

Thus, the mother provides the narrator with the languages necessary for poetry, but the contours of that language conflict with the realization of male desire. This is not to say that personal concerns and desire are necessarily opposed to racial solidarity, as Jim's anger at the world is often provoked by the death or humiliation of other black men. However, within the ideological framework of Cullen's perception of Christianity, Jim's desiring and desirable body, with its seemingly inexorable thrust toward sexual consummation, presents the central problem for Christian longsuffering. The body is in a conflicted relationship with the available language that can bring its desire to linguistic expression. Throughout the poem, the mother attempts to quell and quiet Jim's desire, seeing it as self-destructive.

Nevertheless, that body constantly threatens to break out beyond the mother's words that seek to control it through "sorely doubted litanies." Indeed, we first see Jim lying abed, not unlike the protagonist of "Heritage": "Jim with a puzzled, questioning air, / Would kick the covers back and stare."

Jim's language at this stage of the poem is primarily interrogative, a linguistic marker of his desire since the question moves toward its future answer rather than accepting the mother's hortatory litanies that refuse to assault the "ramparts" of God's mind and will. Jim kicks back the covers, exposing his body to the air, not unlike the writhing lover of "Heritage." His body contains an "Aetna" that seethes with passion and fury. His bones reveal themselves through the skin of his hands "like white scars" when he is enraged at the death of some other black man. He imagines himself speeding "one life-divesting blow/Into some granite face of snow." If the mother's words speak of spirit, Jim seems to be all body, naked and exposed. His physical expressions of rage are immediately "covered" by the mother's words.

> When such hot venom curled his lips
> And anger snapped like sudden whips
> Of lightning in his eyes, her words–
> Slow, gentle as the fall of birds
> That having strained to win aloft
> Spread out their wings and slowly waft
> Regretfully back to earth–
> Would challenge him to name the worth
> Contained in any seed of hate.
> Ever the same soft words would mate.
> Upon her lips: love, trust, and wait. (214)

Here, a disembodied language deflects and blunts desire, cooling the blood rather than inflaming it. Although Cullen attaches a sexual metaphor to the mother's words, the mating that occurs is of "soft words" and words that call for self-renunciation and passivity, for the deferral of desire: "Love, trust, and wait."

Jim's early but still restrained questioning and anger foreshadow his appearance as an erotically attractive male. As in "Heritage," the body of a young male is the only desiring and desirable body in the poem. A few lines after "hot venom" curls his lips, Jim is "handsome Jim" who, something of a cavalier, sets out to present his sexuality in the most overt and provocative ways possible.

> But Jim was not just one more fly,
> For he was handsome in a way
> Night is after a long, hot day.
> If blood flows on from heart to heart,
> and strong men leave their counterpart
> In vice and virtue in their seed,

Jim's bearing spoke his imperial breed.
I was an offshoot, crude, inclined
More to the earth; he was the kind
Whose every graceful movement said,
As blood must say, by turn of head,
By twist of wrist and glance of eye,
"Good blood flows here, and it runs high."
He had an ease of limb, a raw,
Clean hilly stride that women saw
With quickened throbbings of the breast.
There was a show of wings; the nest
Was too confined: Jim needed space
To loop and dip and interlace;
for he had passed the stripling stage,
And stood a man, ripe for the wage
A man extorts of life; his gage
Was down. (215)

The language here is clearly akin to that of "Heritage." Desire is figured in the blood, in this case "high" blood. Moreover, his high blood provokes restless movement as Jim has a "clean hilly stride." He "needed space/ To loop and dip"—language reminiscent of the command to dance the lover's dance in "Heritage."

Unlike the narrator in "Heritage," Jim doesn't hesitate to express desire. However, desire still throws him into conflict with the social world. While the narrator of "Heritage" struggles against the expression of desire, finally killing it to preserve the body, Jim expresses his desire openly and defiantly. Sexual expression becomes a means of challenge, of throwing down his "gage." He is lynched in short order.

The ritual of lynching centers on the white obsession with and fear of black male sexual desire. We might say that lynching is the public evocation of black male sexual desire on the part of white Americans, so that it might more securely be controlled or eliminated. It evokes black male sexuality to disallow it. On the one hand, that Cullen focuses on a lynching scene makes him part of a long literary tradition that includes Baldwin, Morrison, Wright, and others. Nevertheless, that this lynching takes place within a poem that is obsessed with and unnerved by black male desire leaves Cullen's rendering of the lynching and its aftermath deeply troublesome.

Just as the lynch mob erases Jim's body for his sexual and social transgressions against white Americans in the Jim Crow south, the narrator's language gradually erases Jim's physicality. After first attempting to hide the body away in a closet, the narrator turns to discover Jim miraculously reappearing before the mob itself, as if offering himself in sacrifice for the life of his family.

> Each with bewilderment unfeigned
> Stared hard to see against the wall
> The hunted boy stand slim and tall;
> Dream-born, it seemed, with just a trace
> Of weariness upon his face,
> He stood as if evolved from air;
> As if always he had stood there . . . .
> What blew the torches' feeble flare
> To such a soaring fury now
> Each hand went up to fend each brow,
> Save his; he and the light were one,
> A man by night clad with the sun. (227)

This is the first of two subtle but important transformations in Jim's body. The language here gradually removes the threatening sexuality that characterized Jim only a few lines earlier in the poem. Earlier "a man" in full bloom whose "gage" is down, here he is a "hunted boy" who is "slim and tall." Earlier characterized by movement, here he simply stands "As if always he had stood there," the desire signified by movement apparently drained from the now-undesiring body. He is "evolved from air" and "Dream born" rather than being the product of the sexual relations of the mother and the absent father, who is elsewhere in the poem described as a "dandy." Finally, of course, he is described as a "night clad with the sun," a phrase which echoes an earlier description of the mother as a sun lightening a dark sky. If we understand the mother as an unmoving and desexualized bearer of Christian light to her angry children, then whatever Jim was before the moment of the lynching, he is now gradually being covered or "clad" by the mother's vision—static, patient, and deferring every personal desire.

Gerald Early and James Smylie both suggest that the resurrection actually inverts the traditional Christian emphases on self-renunciation by having God approve of and embrace the life of the rebellious Jim, just as the resurrection in the Christian gospels is taken to be the seal of God's approval on the perfect obedience of Jesus. On this accounting, Jim would become the fully realized, rebellious, and desiring Black Christ that is desperately longed for at the end of "Heritage." However, this analysis fails to recognize the dramatic shift in Jim's persona at the resurrection scene. Just as "Heritage" concludes with an imperative to self-renunciation that rejects all that makes that poem most interesting, Cullen resurrects a Jim divested of all that makes him a desirable and powerful character in the first place.

While the lynching is occurring, the narrator laments his brother as "My Lycidas . . . My Jonathan, my Patrocles," saying, "For with his death there perished these" (232–33). The three references are common figures of homo-erotic desire, with Lycidas linked to the production of poetry and Patrocles to warfare against the enemies of Greece. If these figures died with Jim, one might have thought they would be resurrected with Jim as well, but this is clearly not the case. Although the narrator insists that Jim's "vital self" has been resurrected, that the vision is of the "Live body of the dead," we in fact get the barest glimpse of that body. The narrator approaches his resur-rected brother like a doubting Thomas and, for the briefest moment, passes his fingers "down his slim/ Sides, down his breathing length of limb" (233). This all-too-brief moment of physical intimacy may be manifesting Cullen's homoeroticism, but the narrator immediately withdraws and says, "No more," I cried, "this is too much/ For one mad brain to stagger through." This repudiation is strikingly similar to the repudiation of the sexualized black Christ at the end of "Heritage."

Jim's resurrection has an ironic effect on the narrator; rather than confirm-ing Jim's life and the image of sexual desire and rebellion that he embodied, the resurrection provokes the narrator to confirm the mother's vision that men should not assault the ramparts of God's mind. Indeed, despite Jim's reappearance, it is as if even his physical presence is too much for the poem itself, and he disappears without explanation. In the last 100 lines of the poem, the narrator moves away from touching Jim's resurrected body to strong assertions of Christian orthodoxy. This shift dissolves the disturb-ing and exciting aspects of the poem that the tension between the mother's language and Jim's body had provoked. The anger and desire to which Jim had given voice are trumped by his mother's disembodied patience, as there is now

> No sound then in the sacred gloom
> That blessed the shrine that was our room
> Except the steady rise of praise
> To Him who shapes all nights and days
> Into one final burst of sun" (234).

Given the association of the mother's Christianity with a sun that blots out the blackness of Jim's night, and with soft words that quiet Jim's angry, questioning desire, these lines suggest that Jim's resurrection has eradicated the possibility of a poetry of individual desire and love, a poetry that Cullen at one time sought to preserve. Such private desire is replaced with the publicly accessible music of hymn and prayer. There are no sounds, no individual voices, only the collective sounds of Christian hymns repeating the longing for heaven that the mother's earlier legends and litanies evoked. Romance, eroticism, human love, the stuff of lyric poetry associated with a figure like Lycidas are as effectively dead now as they were at the culmination of the lynching and indeed as they have been from the very beginning of the poem—perhaps more securely so because the narrator has interpreted Jim's death and resurrection not as a compelling call to follow in the footsteps of Jim's rebellion but as a call to erase his desire in accepting the public responsibilities of Christian behavior. As the poem concludes, in fact, Jim disappears entirely, and we see the narrator united in the stasis with which the poem began, united not with Jim or anything that looks like him, but with his mother in self-renunciation:

> While I who mouthed my blasphemies,
> Recalling now His agonies,
> Am found forever on my knees,
> Ever to praise her Christ with her,
> Knowing He can at will confer
> Magic on miracle to prove
> And try me when I doubt His love. (235)

At this juncture, the narrator praises "her Christ with her" rather than singing to "my Christ" or to "our Christ," which suggests the same poetics of renunciation that Cullen invoked at the end of "Heritage." In the latter poem, Cullen sought to write poetry that negates desire from the beginning, affirming instead a publicly acceptable masculinity that urges him to repeat inherited legends and litanies of the people of Israel. "The Black Christ" makes clearer that Cullen is not simplistically denying a readily given "blackness" in favor of white approval. Rather, he accedes to a particular mode of blackness by becoming the public face of the New Negro. In doing so, he gives up the poetry of private desire. Such desire could only be exposed at the expense of a social death Cullen was not willing to endure.

To return briefly to my comparison of Cullen's and Nugent's treatment of the relationship between Eros and Christianity, Cullen falls ultimately on the side of separation and distinction, however much he strove to find commerce between the two. The erotic black Jesus, a figure of desire, must die to be resurrected as the transcendent but invisible and, finally, voiceless Christ. Like Judas of that earlier poem, Cullen's gives up his throat, his voice, as a final fee for Christian fealty, not believing that desire and duty could comingle except in death. To some degree, Cullen's quandary reflects the quandary of any African American man of the Harlem Renaissance who felt he must put aside, or at least hide, personal desires in the name of racial leadership and responsibility. Certainly Du Bois reflected this split in different ways, maintaining the facade of a happy marriage while pursuing a variety of love affairs (Lewis, *Fight for Equality* 267). Langston Hughes kept his sexuality under such tight wraps that, as late as the 1980s, Arnold Rampersad refused to say definitively that Hughes had homosexual lovers. The encompassing realities of racism exacerbated the kinds of splits required of such public leaders, but it would seem that Hughes and Du Bois managed this tension with more energy and aplomb than Cullen could muster—perhaps in part because neither Hughes nor Du Bois took the specifics of Christian belief with such seriousness. The irony of Cullen's position is that in giving up on his desires in the name of a publicly acceptable poetry, he seemed to give up on poetry altogether, which is not to say that he gave up writing. Significantly, Cullen turned to prose works for children and, interestingly, to the publicly responsible position of teaching, living out a life that was socially productive in spaces and roles wherein erotic expressiveness is normatively forbidden.

In choosing the poetry of Christian ethics, Cullen gradually gave up being the sexualized Pan who is the "singing Man to be reckoned with." Nevertheless, such a sacrifice complicates the reading that declares him a failure. Indeed, what is clearest is that Cullen tried to sacrifice his private desires in order to be the public "Voice of the Harlem Renaissance." Rather than abandoning race, "The Black Christ" suggests that he abandons desire and embraces a particular Christianized notion of race. Almost alone among major figures of the Harlem Renaissance, Cullen continued to assert that it was Christianity that was at the center of racial formation rather than poetry or political activism—or, for that matter, even education. The racialized figure of the mother as an artist who tells the legends and litanies of the people is a figure of heterosexual reproduction that Cullen tried briefly to embody in his marriage to Yolande Du Bois. The mother is a figure of generational passage and biological inheritance upon which notions of race must in some fundamental sense rely. In embracing his role as "THE New Negro," Cullen tried, in the complicated and sometimes noble tradition of Christian self-renunciation, to sacrifice desire and art for what he perceived to be a higher purpose of religious racial uplift. It is perhaps a price expected more of saints than artists, but for Cullen it seems a price he felt destined, and ultimately willing, to pay.

"GODS OF PHYSICAL VIOLENCE, STOPPING AT NOTHING"
Masculinity, Physicality, and Creativity in Zora Neale Hurston

> There is nothing so exhilarating as watching well-matched
> opponents go into action. The entire world likes action . . . .
> Hence prize-fighters become millionaires.
>
> —Zora Neale Hurston, *The Sanctified Church*

> Writing is fighting.
>
> —Muhammad Ali

The broad attention to physicality, creativity, and human identity during the early decades of the twentieth century was in many respects an extension of other material critiques, or at least investigations, of the practical impact of Christian faith or the lack thereof.[1] When Du Bois and Hughes portray Christianity as ineffectual, they focus especially on its material ineffectiveness rather than dwelling on questions of philosophical or rational coherence, though, of course, for Du Bois this is at issue as well. Without saying so directly, associating Christianity with old men, fearful men, children, and women essentially reinforced a Nietzschean view that Christianity is a religion of the weak, of slaves, and of women. The superiority of the intelligentsia was most firmly secured in strength and found a symbolic analogue in physical strength. Thus figures like Jack Johnson and Paul Robeson could become both physical and cultural icons heralding the advent of the New

Negro, heralded for both their bodily strength and their physique while also being admired and looked to for their cultural and artistic impact. On the other hand, as I have suggested, this kind of discourse didn't preclude a virile Christ or a militant Christianity but in fact seemed to call for it. The image of the Black Christ could and did work in a similarly iconic fashion among many African Americans. Garvey's call for a Black God and a Black Christ was continuous with the militaristic and masculine pageantry that characterized his rallies. In an analogous but very different fashion, both Countee Cullen and Richard Bruce Nugent sought to create Christs who were not only virile and muscular but quite plainly sexualized—their erotic attractiveness a measure of both their spirituality and their power.

The work of Zora Neale Hurston usefully extends and complements this discourse about Christianity, masculinity, and the body, but it also provides an important contrast. This book has focused closely on the specific contest between men for a form of masculine supremacy among African Americans. However, as my discussion of Nella Larsen has pointed out, the negative consequences of masculinism in the prosecution of a New Negro cultural movement suggest the potentially devastating consequences of such cultural forms for women, a suggestion that may imply New Negro Men are not that dramatically different from Old Negro Men. Moreover, this study has emphasized that men establish masculine identities not simply by contrasting themselves positively with women as a negative referent but also by contrasting themselves with other men. The work of writers like Larsen and Zora Neale Hurston points out that masculine definition is not something that men arrive at on their own. Through a variety of social practices—including their significant role in education, their growing roles in social service agencies, their pervasive presence as the backbone if not the head of the church, as well as their writing and intellectual work—women deeply affected conceptions of appropriate and inappropriate masculine identities and styles. In concluding this book with close attention to Zora Neale Hurston, I hope to suggest not only her unique angle on the discourses of masculinity in relationship to Christianity but also more broadly the ways in which women appropriated such discourses for their own creative and intellectual empowerment.

Of all the writers of the period, Hurston had, perhaps, the closest view of the migration and its religious pulses. In many respects, she embodies the history of the migration and values of the New Negro, scrambling her way by imagination, main strength, and force of will from a modest Florida home to a graduate degree in anthropology and eventual recognition as a major American writer. She was, in fact, the only major writer of the younger generation of the New Negro Renaissance to be raised in the rural landscape of the Deep South. As the most significant woman writing during the Renaissance—and arguably the most influential writer on later writers' views of gender and community—Hurston's suspicions that the Christianity of her youth was a weak and even unmanly response to the problems facing modern African Americans clarifies the degree to which masculinity was a central issue in the discourse on gender, race, and religion during the period.

Crucial to her developing sense of gender and religion were Hurston's years growing up in the home of a Christian minister. Early in her auto-biography, *Dust Tracks on the Road,* Hurston defines her struggles with gender expectations by insisting that her body matches blow for blow and stride for stride the boys with whom she travels as an equal companion. The ability to dish it out and take it lifts her above the common run of girls:

> I discovered that I was extra strong by playing with other girls near my age. I had no way of judging the force of my playful blows, and so I was always hurting somebody. Then they would say I meant to hurt and go home and leave me. Everything was all right, however, when I played with boys. It was a shameful thing to admit being hurt among them. Furthermore, they could dish it out themselves, and I was acceptable to them because I was the one girl who could take a good pummeling without running home to tell. (39)

Hurston palpably admires the masculine culture of the playground. Among boys, Hurston discovers her body as a weapon, and she knows it as extra strong primarily because the girls complain and run "home to tell." Hurston apparently hurts the boys as well, but "It was a shameful thing to admit being hurt among them." Boys display an incipient self-reliance by being able to "dish it out themselves," whereas girls rely on powerful adult others for solace. Being a girl here means looking to others to defend or secure your place in the game of the world. Being a boy means refusing to recognize pain in order to remain part of the pack. Hurston asserts her status as an individual by her ability to sustain herself in a masculine culture on its own terms. In short, Hurston first discovers herself as a person not by doing the things required of the little girls in her childhood culture but by following the path of self-reliance—an often treacherous and oppressive path but one that is ideologically required of little boys.

These lessons of the playground are reinforced by the lessons learned in her intellectual and spiritual development. Describing the gendered fea-tures of what she calls her "inside search," Hurston everywhere refuses the stereotypical behavior of little girls. She can't play with dolls like all the other girls. She can't please her father by acting in a demure and ladylike manner, nor can she quell her ambitious imagination even in the face of her father's threats that she was acting "too white." While Hurston remembers her father's disgust at having two daughters, what stands out most in these memories is Hurston's unwillingness to play the role of the little girl that her father assigned her (*Dust Tracks* 38–40).

George Chauncey and Judith Halberstam both suggest that the early decades of the twentieth century were a time of upheaval in which the rigid limits of conventional gender categories became increasingly permeable. Thus, by the time Hurston publishes her autobiography in 1942, she can be seen as participating in a tradition of literary assault on gender conventions, one that includes writers as varied as Carson McCullers, John Radclyffe Hall, George Strand, and Gertrude Stein, or raucous musicians such as Bessie Smith. However, while the rigid limits of conventional gender categories had become increasingly permeable by 1942, in the childhood she records, community standards enforced gender conventions along familiar lines of nineteenth-century, middle-class propriety. As Martin Summers points out, even early black women's organizations that promoted the freedom and dignity of women in the late nineteenth and early twentieth centuries tended to reinforce the general idea of separate spheres of influence based on notions of inherent gendered differences (112–15). Hurston's resistance to entrenched gender roles inevitably clashed with the conservative religion that shaped the community into which she was born. Hurston grew up in a middle-class household of a respectable and influential small-town minister, a household that valued the gender ideals of the late nineteenth-century middle class, ideals of feminine virtue reinforced by their Christian faith. Remembering her childhood gender trouble, Hurston recalls the role of religion and mythology in her awakening literary imagination. Breaking past the feminine virtue expected of a young Christian girl in her household, young Zora is drawn not to the Christian God of her community nor even to the goddesses of antiquity. She rejoices instead in the seductive power of the male gods and demigods of the pagan religions:

> Why did the Norse tales strike so deeply into my soul? I do not know, but they did. I seemed to remember seeing Thor swing his mighty short-handled hammer as he sped across the sky in rumbling thunder, lightning flashing from the tread of his steeds and the wheels of his chariot. The great and good Odin, who went down to the well of knowledge to drink, and was told that the price of a drink from that fountain was an eye. Odin drank deeply, then plucked out one eye without a murmur and handed it to the grizzly keeper, and walked away. That held majesty for me. (*Dust Tracks* 53)

Of all the gods and goddesses, Hurston resolved to be like Hercules, who makes his future mostly by main strength and force of will. The "tricks and turns" of all the others "left [her] cold" (54). Leaving her cold too are the fictional female models promoted in Christian books that her parents gave her to read: "Thin books about this and that sweet and gentle little girl who gave up her heart to Christ and good works. Almost always they died from it, preaching as they passed. I was utterly indifferent to their deaths . . . . I didn't care how soon they rolled up their big, soulful, blue eyes and kicked the bucket. They had no meat on their bones." (54). The picture Hurston gives of Christian women here is in deep contrast to the powerful and even overwhelming women that are depicted in the childhood churches of Langston Hughes or James Weldon Johnson, or even in a slightly later autobiography of Richard Wright. Churchwomen in these contexts exercise extensive control over the men in their lives, at least within the boundaries of the life of church and home. Hurston seems to be invoking the girl heroines of nineteenth-century sentimental romance, female Christs whom Harriet Beecher Stowe idealizes in Little Eva of Uncle Tom's Cabin and whom Mark Twain skewers in his rendering of Emmeline Grangerford in The Adventures of Huckleberry Finn. Gloria Cronin suggests that Hurston constructs a feminocentric spirituality to combat the overbearing patriarchy of her youthful Christianity. However, in her autobiography, at least, she characterizes Christianity not with overbearing men but with weak women, or more precisely, "girls" who have "no meat on their bones." Here one catches a whiff of Hurston's suspicion that the Christianity of her childhood was too girlish to do her good, and she is evoking the general cultural notion at the time that Christianity was, perhaps, effete and weak, if not definitively "feminized" in a pejorative use of that term.

Of course, "girlish" behavior and patriarchy are hardly incompatible. Indeed, one means of establishing patriarchal control is to insist on the demure and disembodied spiritualism of women, just as, in another vein, asserting that the black race was the "lady of the races" served the purposes not so much of racial uplift but of white supremacy. However, for Hurston, not only are thin girls' books thin gruel for the spirit, but Christianity as such shows all too little force of spirit, all too little meat on the bones to do much good. Describing her earliest reading of the Bible she idealizes a virile masculinity that she suspects the Christianity around her has lost, or perhaps never even possessed.

> I happened to open to the place where David was doing some mighty smiting, and I got interested. David went here and he went there, and no matter

where he went, he smote 'em hip and thigh. Then he sung songs to his harp awhile, and went out and smote some more. Not one time did David stop and preach about sins and things. All David wanted to know from God was who to kill and when. He took care of other details himself. Never a quiet moment. I liked him a lot. So I read a great deal more in the Bible, hunting for some more active people like David. Except for the beautiful language of Luke and Paul, the New Testament still plays a poor second to the Old Testament for me. The Jews had a God who laid about Him when they needed Him. I could see no use waiting till Judgment Day to see a man who was just crying for a good killing, to be told to go and roast. My idea was to give him a good killing first, and then if he got roasted later on, so much the better. (54–55)

For Hurston, the Jewish God is a "real man" who gets things done, as are the people who follow him, like David. The ambiguity of the last sentences in this passage is especially telling. On the one hand, of course, Hurston imagines some unjust man getting what is coming to him, by her first and by God later. On the other hand, the man Christians wait to see on judgment day is Christ himself: ironically, a man who has, in the Christian narratives, had a "good killing." Within the categories of the conservative Southern Protestantism into which she was born, he is also the man who will quite likely tell her "to go and roast" on judgment day. However, Hurston has little use for the intricacies of salvation and damnation. She plainly admires the main strength of David and David's God, men who set their face toward the world and act, men who make a difference here and now, which may mean, indeed, making a difference in blood.

The complexities of Hurston's attitudes toward Christianity reflect and engage with exceedingly complex, and I would say surprising, conceptions of gender in general and masculinity in particular. Critics have written frequently on Hurston's understanding of gender, sometimes focusing on the androgynous appeal, and threat, of characters such as Janie Crawford in Hurston's best-known novel, *Their Eyes Were Watching God*. In characters like Janie, Hurston demonstrates her fierce belief in an absolute individualism and consequent self-reliance. Deborah Plant and others underscore how this individualism informs Janie's understanding of gender and race alike, believing that every tub—white or black, male or female— "must sit on its own bottom." Such a philosophy did not bode well for rigid definitions of gender identity. Robert Hemenway suggests that, even in her youth, Hurston's behavior collided with gender expectations in her community: "Her parents urged her to play with her Christmas dolls, but dolls caught the devil around Zora: 'They got into fights and leaked sawdust before New

Year's.' She was an unreconstructed tomboy who spied noble, grew like a gourd vine, and yelled bass like a gator" (14).

While recognizing Hurston's rejection of feminine stereotypes, Hurston criticism has done less to examine the complexity of her attitudes toward masculinity, underscoring instead Hurston's self-description as the "eternal feminine" and emphasizing the role of her heroic women in resisting patriarchy. Men, and the way men behave, tend to be seen as antagonists that women must resist and refuse. At the extreme, Susan Meisenhelder sees a Manichaean division between men and women in Hurston's work, with black men as insidious surrogates of white power. Enclosed in her role as an exemplary literary ancestor, Hurston's pugnacious defiance of the gender categories tends to disappear meekly behind the gender divide of contemporary criticism.

Taking Hurston's appeal to equality, individualism, and androgyny seriously, it seems clear that men and what it means to "be a man" play a more complicated and important role in Hurston's imagination than is generally recognized. Above all, men possess and display power—whether sexual, geographic, literary, or religious—that Hurston desires for herself. Males, then, are regularly oppressive, but their "masculinity" is also desirable. Indeed, careful examination of Hurston's work suggests that far from simply trying to lay men low, Hurston idealizes many "masculine" cultural styles as she saw them embodied in her home community of Eatonville and elsewhere. I use the term "masculine" in quotations to indicate the difficult and ambiguous terrain that this term invokes. Indeed, one consequence of my argument in this chapter is that Hurston contributes to a project in which notions of masculinity are decomposed, a project that announces the end of the binary "masculine"/"feminine" opposition that has served patriarchy so well. Judith Halberstam, especially, has pointed out that women have contributed to the formation of masculinity in ways that demonstrate masculinity should not simply be equated with "male behavior." I agree with Halberstam on this point and see Hurston participating in an effort to dislodge "masculinities" from their enclosure in a privileged male domain.

Nevertheless, it seems crucial to recognize that while "masculinities" may bear no essential relationship to maleness, they do bear a deeply imbedded historical relationship to maleness, perhaps nowhere more clearly than in small, rural, and deeply religious Southern towns such as the one in which Hurston grew up. Indeed, even Halberstam's analyses depend on the fact of this connection between maleness and masculinity as she describes female masculinities that negotiate that historical relationship through imitation, parody, appropriation, identification, or repudiation. Thus, in this chapter,

I remain critically interested in how masculine styles influence Hurston's understanding of herself as a thinker and an artist. While never shrinking from the chance to criticize the abusiveness of men, especially in their effort to secure masculinity as a privileged male preserve, Hurston finds certain "masculinities" crucial to her own developing aesthetic and religious vision, so much so that she champions women such as Janie and Big Sweet who break out of their assigned "feminine" roles to seize the "masculine" for themselves. Recognizing such gender-crossing in Hurston's work reveals the human complexity of her male characters and also suggests that masculine cultures provided an important resource for Hurston's sense of herself as an artist.[2]

Hurston constructs the relationship between Christianity and masculinity in ways that reflect this nuance and complexity throughout her nonfiction and not only in her mature autobiography, suggesting that her experiences and perceptions on the playground were the seed of her adult philosophy, near the root of her hard-edged individualism that matured during the Harlem Renaissance. These lessons echo in her derision of the "sobbing school of Negrohood," and suggest an early aesthetic distaste for fastidious and subtle introspection.[3] Hurston's attack on Wright and others who accused her of being insufficiently oriented toward protest in her literature replicates the values of the playground in nearly every instance. "Even in the helter-skelter skirmish that is my life, I have seen that the world is to the strong regardless of a little pigmentation more or less. No, I do not weep at the world—I am too busy sharpening my oyster knife" (*I Love Myself* 153). She refuses to waste time on emotional regret; she views life as a battle and believes respect is most due to those able to not only survive but also attack in the great "skirmish" of life.

This general attitude toward life, and specifically the role of Christian religion in life, contributed not only to her self-perception but also to her understanding of African American culture. Eight years prior to *Dust Tracks,* Hurston indicated that embodiment and successful physical action are the first and most necessary characteristics of African American culture heroes. She lists Peter the Apostle as a culture hero third in importance behind Jack and the Devil, explaining her ranking as follows:

> The Negro is not a Christian really. The primitive gods are not deities of too subtle inner reflection; they are hard-working bodies who serve their devotees just as laboriously as the suppliant serves them. Gods of physical violence, stopping at nothing to serve their followers. Now of all the apostles, Peter is the most active. When the other ten fell back trembling

in the garden, Peter wielded the blade on the posse. Peter first and foremost in all action. The gods of no peoples have been philosophic until the people themselves have approached that state. (*Sanctified* 56–57)

Hurston determines the validity of God or the gods not through the refinements of theological insight or the consolations of philosophy but through the exercise of material power as represented in a particular form of masculinity. To some degree, of course, this speaks to the idea voiced by C. Eric Lincoln that African Americans seek a practical God. But whereas Lincoln is speaking broadly of the nature of black Christianity as a practical religion more than anything, for Hurston Christianity as such is not practical or pragmatic in that it cannot get things done.

This need for forceful and physical action partially explains Hurston's championing of conjure men and women and her appreciation of the entire mythology and practice of voodoo. Critical to Hurston's conception of voodoo and African American folk religions is not that it is feminocentric and only partially that it is egalitarian. Rather, for Hurston, the spiritualism of such men and women delivers the goods. In one of the most dramatic of the folktales Hurston records, Uncle Monday, a conjure man, takes terrifying revenge on a conjure woman, Aunt Judy Bickerstaff, who had tried to usurp his power. Using his power as a conjure man, Uncle Monday leaves her in a gator-filled swamp unable to walk or even speak to cry out for help. Unlike "Sweat," in which a story of an abusive husband elicits our sympathy for the victimized wife, this tale recalls Hurston's belief that if she wanted to dish it out, she had to be prepared to take it as well, and her belief that prizes in life go to the strong. Similarly, in *Tell My Horse,* Hurston favorably evaluates the primarily male pantheon of gods in Haitian Voodoo, again basing this evaluation on the practical benefit of the voodoo religion.[4] Indeed, Mark Thompson, following on Paul Gilroy, argues that Hurston's fascination with masculine military figures in Haitian life amounts to a fascist fantasy, which is congruent with her views on voodoo in her work (121). I admit this reading seems too extreme, but it does suggest that critics like Cronin and Meisenhelder overread Hurston's usefulness for contemporary forms of feminism. Gloria Cronin emphasizes the feminocentric aspects of Hurston's worldview, and Meisenhelder emphasizes the ways in which voodoo is egalitarian. Both seem to base their notions in part on Hurston's positive representation of voodoo and, in Meisenhelder's case, of the voodoo goddess Erzulie, whom Hurston calls the goddess of "the love bed." However, while Hurston clearly values voodoo for being less sexually repressed than Christianity, she recognizes that it hasn't resulted in the emancipation of women, as evidenced by life in Haiti and Jamaica. Indeed, Erzulie seems to function primarily in relationship to men and leaves women sad and bereft. This fact speaks simultaneously against the notion that she easily assimilated voodoo to empowerment for women but also against Thompson's notion that she is guilty of a fascist or quasi-fascist fantasy in this work.

Nonetheless, Hurston clearly evokes traditional masculinist metaphors to get at the human qualities that she believes lie at the root of empowerment, and she finds the Christian faith sorely lacking that masculinist ethic. Late in *Dust Tracks,* as Hurston summarizes her thoughts about the progress of organized religion and especially of Christianity, she paints it as a crutch for those too weak to face life on their own:

> People need religion because the great masses fear life and its consequences. Its responsibilities weigh heavy. Feeling a weakness in the face of great forces, men seek an alliance with omnipotence to bolster up their feeling of weakness, even though the omnipotence they rely upon is a creature of their own minds. It gives them a feeling of security. Strong, self-determining men are notorious for their lack of reverence. Constantine, having converted millions to Christianity by the sword, himself refused the consolation of Christ until his last hour. Some say not even then . . . . Prayer is for those who need it. Prayer seems to me a cry of weakness, and an attempt to avoid, by trickery, the rules of the game as laid down. I do not choose to admit weakness. I accept the challenge of responsibility. Life, as it is, does not frighten me. (277–78)

Hurston aligns herself with men like Constantine, whom she perceives as strong and self-determining. Indeed, earlier in the chapter, she suggests that without Constantine's willingness to use the sword, Christianity would have died an early death. While she clearly appreciates the drama of the rural church of her childhood, she cannot follow the humble example of the men and women who fall on their knees and pray. For her, they are too much like the weaker gods who get things done by trickery, too much like the girls of her childhood who run home to their mothers when the game turns against them.

The practical power exemplified by the masculine gods lies close to the nub of not only Hurston's understanding of religion but also her artistic creativity. Insipid girls' books and their tearful Christianity are not simply bad in terms of their ideology; they are bad artistically, failing to hold Hurston's aesthetic interest when compared to the works of Thor and Odin. Similarly, David moves fluidly from singing to slaying, from swinging the sword to singing his songs. She leaves David's sometimes-questionable morality unmentioned; indeed, she reconstructs him as a man unconcerned with ethics in a way that seems critical to his character as artist and soldier: he doesn't waste time preaching about "sins and things." While Paul and Luke have beautiful language, they have no drama and thus little that holds the reader's interest. Indeed, Hurston sees the dramatic battlers as exemplary of life as it ought to be lived combat between equals being a kind of art form in itself. Conflict, well played, gives Hurston aesthetic satisfaction:

> Discord is more natural than accord. If we accept the doctrine of the survival of the fittest, there are more fighting honors than there are honors for other achievements. Humanity places premiums on all things necessary to its well-being, and a valiant and good fighter is valuable in any community. So why hide the light under a bushel? Moreover, intimidation is a recognized part of warfare the world over, and threats certainly must be listed under that head. So that a great threatener must certainly be considered an aid to the fighting machine. So then if a man or a woman is a facile hurler of threats, why should he or she not show their wares to the community? Hence, the holding of all quarrels and fights in the open. One relieves one's pent-up anger and at the same time earns laurels in intimidation. Besides, one does the community a service. There is nothing so exhilarating as watching well-matched opponents go into action. The entire world likes action, for that matter. Hence prize-fighters become millionaires. (*Sanctified Church* 60–61)

Like conjure men, prizefighters deliver the goods. Such men change the world, the fundamental premise of creativity. The creative artist finds her best models in these men of action. Significantly, Hurston sees language as one important area in which men and women readily participate on an equal creative basis. While men dominate the practices of signifying and tall-tale-telling or "lying" in Hurston's work, women such as Big Sweet readily participate. Noting Big Sweet's facility with language, Hurston describes playing the dozens:

> If you are sufficiently armed—enough to stand off a panzer division—and know what to do with your weapons after you get 'em, it is all right to go to the house of your enemy, put one foot up on his steps, rest one elbow on your knee and play in the family. . . . But if you have no faith in your personal courage and confidence in your arsenal, don't try it. It is a risky pleasure. (*Dust Tracks* 187)

People who use language well are creative battlers, every bit as important to the community as the warrior. They exist, in Hurston's mind, at the opposite extreme of the praying faithful, who were often taken as the best symbols of African American spiritual and cultural power.

As Hurston's work repeatedly shows, she imagined herself as a creative battler with words, evincing personal courage and confidence in her linguistic arsenal. Most accounts of her life by contemporaries suggest that she was herself a "valiant and good fighter" with both her tongue and her pen and thus much admired and valuable to her intellectual community. But the degree to which Hurston lived out her ideals shouldn't mask the tensions she often felt with her status as a participant observer in the communities she wrote about and in some sense longed for. Indeed, her autobiography suggests that she felt this distance with her own community in ways that linked her to a community of writers far outside of the world of Eatonville. Somewhat like the stories of Du Bois and Hughes examined earlier in this book, Hurston felt her own intellectuality and imaginative capabilities left her at some distance from her home community. When she remarks on visionary experiences she had as a child—experiences she links to her reading and educational accomplishments—she emphasizes her isolation from others who lived conventional lives in her community:

> I never told anyone around me about these strange things. It was too different. They would laugh me off as a story-teller. Besides, I had a feeling of difference from my fellow men, and I did not want it to be found out. Oh, how I cried out to be just as everybody else! But the voice said No. I must go where I was sent. . . .
> I consider that my real childhood ended with the coming of the pronouncements. True, I played fought and studied with other children, but always I stood apart within. Often I was in some lonesome wilderness, suffering strange things and agonies while other children in the same yard played without a care. I asked myself why me? Why? Why? A cosmic loneliness was my shadow. Nothing and nobody around me really touched me. (*Dust Tracks* 59–60)

Hurston's statement that she is "apart within" signifies both spiritual apartness and physical location. She is isolated within the community even as she is surrounded by it. The passage draws, of course, especially on the story of Samuel who hears God's voice calling him in the night. But it also vibrates sympathetically with the tones of African American testimonial narratives that recount time spent on the mourners' bench seeking God. In the traditional conversion narrative, the seeker is apart from others and in travail before God, isolated and distant from others; this isolation results ultimately in a fuller belonging to the community through conversion. However, Hurston's experience of "divine" voices and visions is all but purely individual and isolating. It marks her difference from the immediate community around her and is an experience shared by very few. Interestingly, her sense of connection with others comes not through any kind of religious experience but through the office of reading many years later, when she connected to "a sentence or a paragraph now and then in the columns of O. O. McIntyre" and with the writings of Rudyard Kipling. In these writers and others, she "took comfort in knowing that they were fellow pilgrims on my strange road" (59–60). Though it's impossible to know which paragraphs of McIntyre Hurston may be referring to, McIntyre was well known for writing about the glamour and excitement of city life from a small-towner's point of view. Kipling's significant 1888 collection, *Plain Tales from the Hills,* begins with "Lispeth," a story of a young Indian girl who is a convert to Christianity but then is betrayed in love by English adherents to the faith. The story, among other things, raises issues of miscegenation, assimilation, education, and religious conversion and hypocrisy. The first lines of the headnote call into question the efficacy of Christianity for the indigenous peoples of India,

> Look, you have cast out Love! What Gods are these
> You bid me please?
> The Three in One, the One in Three? Not so!
> To my own Gods I go.
> It may be they shall give me greater ease
> Than your cold Christ and tangled Trinities.

Tame, Kiplingesque stuff, perhaps, but stuff Hurston would have run into if she read much Kipling at all. A theme she would have not found much supported in her Christian home and community, and a theme applied to African Americans through *Dust Tracks* generally. Despite her long and well-chronicled identification with Eatonville, Hurston finds her deepest sense of community with literary works rather than with the Christian communion available in her hometown. Somewhat like Janie at the end of *Their Eyes Were Watching God,* who has traveled far and returns changed to a community that talks about her more than it talks with her, Hurston's work suggests an intimate distance, a sense of standing apart even while being within the community as a whole. How else to account for her fullest sense of community with men of letters very far from the dusty roads and front porches of Eatonville? Her sense of being apart within no doubt sprang from many personal and social sources, but one important source was the distance she felt from the religion of her youth, a spirituality she felt blunted her ambition, dulled her verbal arsenal, and preferred the glories of the hereafter to the glories Hurston felt and saw in the here and now.

Hurston's regard for the ideology of masculine self-sufficiency extends to her depiction of men in her fiction. On the whole, even generous readings of Hurston's men see them as robust and talented beings who are tragically flawed by virtue of being male. Most of Hurston's literary characters, however, are creative battlers with both their tongues and their fists, participating in the vitality that Hurston found so appealing in the male demigods of her childhood reading. While these men are often given to ridiculous or oppressive "tricks and turns," they also often possess the kind of spunk and main strength that Hurston finds attractive. They are keepers of a dangerous fire that Hurston, a female Prometheus, finds desirable.

John Pearson of *Jonah's Gourd Vine* is one case in point. Pearson rises from abused child to manual laborer and finally to an influential minister and local leader. Characterized by immense physical strength, sexual virility, and magnificent gifts as a speaker, John's rise to cultural leadership is complicated by his tendency to remain a "natural man." He expresses this "naturalness" in his multiple infidelities. By turns, critics see Pearson as "an irresponsible child" or a tragic character unable to control the "brute-beast" of his own sexuality (Hemenway 190; Meisenhelder 41). Others see him as a surrogate for Hurston's father, which allows Hurston to write "a female revenge story," while still others see "a broken man, defeated by his sexual license" (Brown, "'De Beast" 76–85; Cronin 54). Hurston's own judgment of John Pearson is quite different. Hurston wrote to James Weldon Johnson, complaining that critics had misread her accomplishment, and particularly that the critic did not seem to understand that "a Negro preacher could have so much poetry in him." She goes on to note that "being a good man is not enough to hold a Negro preacher in an important charge. He must also be an artist" (Hemenway 193–94). Pearson, as Hurston evaluates him, exemplifies the very folk culture from which her creativity springs. Pearson's moral failings are not his defining feature: "merely being a good man" is not enough. Rather, John's physical power and creative power are crucially related: he must be a poet and an actor, and he must cut an impressive physical image in both voice and figure. Hemenway and Brown emphasize the split between the "natural man" and the "man of God" within John Pearson, tending to see Pearson's "natural" sexual urges as uncontrollable and thereby destroying his abilities as a "man of God." However, Hurston's tendency to closely link physical and artistic prowess suggests that, in her view, Pearson's effort to be a "man of God" undermines and destroys him as a "natural man," that is, destroys—or, at least, compromises—the natural root that feeds his poetic leadership.

John Lowe rightly notes that, to the degree that this story is autobiographical, Hurston told her father's story, which "meant not only appropriating his voice, but becoming that voice" (93). Like Janie in a different context, Hurston crosses rigid gender divisions by becoming the masculine voice of her father. Further, Lowe makes clear that, in many respects, John Pearson's voice—the root of his preacherly authority—is a sexual instrument for provoking and fulfilling desire (95–97). Thus, the irony of *Jonah's Gourd Vine* lies not in John's fatal inability to control his sexual urges but in the contradictory requirements placed upon a preacher in a small southern town. The minister occupies a social position in which the community requires poetry that springs from the "natural man," even while the community contradictorily demands adherence to the strictest version of Christian morality, a morality with which Hurston is fundamentally impatient. Alan Brown comes closest to the crux of this argument when he suggests that "the contempt that was shown John Pearson—sexually potent bull—by the upright members of the community—the ravenous, cowardly wolves—was fueled by a lethal combination of fear and jealousy" (84). Extending his reading, we can suggest that in *Jonah's Gourd Vine* Hurston critiques not so much sexually adventurous men but a moralistic ethos that she believes will not allow for the virile poetry that the church community otherwise demands of its leaders.

Seen in this way, John Pearson recalls Hurston's David—a man who "smote 'em hip and thigh;" a man who plays on his harp before going out to smite some more; a man, too, who had little time for preaching about sin; a man, finally, whom Hurston sets in opposition to failed and fainting Christians in her autobiographical writings. Indeed, what seems to fit John for leadership is not his devotion to a Christian morality or doctrine but rather his physical strength, sexual energy, and creativity with language. Early in the novel, John establishes his essentially moral nature by protecting his mother from his stepfather's abuse. Similarly, in a logging camp, John establishes his leadership through his physical strength and willingness to pummel those who betray his friends. John's leadership in the community seems most "natural" when expressed in the Negro quarters and only becomes compromised and complicated as he begins to pursue leadership in the church, partially as a consequence of a marriage to Lucy.

At the end of the novel, after a long life of philandering and repentance—having fallen one last time into infidelity following a long period of faithfulness—John dies in an automobile wreck. However, John only dies after verbally abusing his paramour, saying, "Ah hope you rot in hell! Ah hope you never rise to judgment." Shoving her in a ditch, he desperately drives away toward home, accusing himself as "False pretender! Outside show to the world!" He further swears that he will now have "Faith and no questions asked" (199–200). Symbolically and literally, John gives himself over to the moralistic discourses of sin and damnation that Hurston elsewhere finds exasperating. The car crash happens not as John flees marriage and Christian convention but as he flees his status as a natural man for the more dubious embrace of some of the most basic conventions of a normative Christian morality. Given Hurston's judgment on the failed drama of such morality, we might wonder whether what has depleted John in Hurston's mind is his virile sexuality or his Christianity. Becoming the conventional Christian man, John holds no interest as a verbal artist. The *deus ex machina* ending of the train hitting John's car as he is speeding home to the arms of his loving wife signals not so much judgment on John's philandering ways as that John's Christianity has finally dissolved the fundament of poetry located in "the natural man." Like the girls of the Christian books Hurston read as a child, John has finally given up his life to "Christ and good works." Like them, he has "died from it," preaching as he passed.

Following this line of thought, we can see that most of Hurston's men fall into this dynamic wherein physical prowess—whether sexual, pugilistic, or something else—determines creative power. Moses, in *Moses, Man of the Mountain*, is both a warrior and a conjure man who can make nature obey him. While it is easy to shrink from Moses's killing of Aaron at the end of the novel, this act hews closely to what Hurston has valued elsewhere in her writing. Aaron is primarily a sniveling coward whom no one could count on to stand up and be trusted. His sycophancy and willingness to do anything out of fear have, in the context of the novel's discourses of power, made him a man in need of a good killing. Similarly, Jim Meserve's rape of Arvay in *Seraph on the Suwanee* is horrifying; however, viewed in the context of the culture that Hurston examines, what is vicious in the novel is not simply Jim's violence but Arvay's disembodied and repressed Christianity, a religion that Jim mocks readily and seems to tolerate only when and where he has to. While Jim has freed himself to experience his body and its powers, Arvay struggles with a religious world in which sex can only be understood as evil. Jim, by contrast, is a man who acts upon the world to change it.

This structure extends in some ways even to that great male hero of contemporary Hurston criticism, Teacake from *Their Eyes Were Watching God*. While contemporary criticism emphasizes Teacake and Janie's mutuality as if Teacake were a precursor to contemporary forms of postfeminist masculinity, Teacake also falls into any number of stereotypical masculine behaviors. Teacake is as willing to use violence as is Moses or John, he is a risk taker who makes his living by gambling, and he is a traveling man who feels restless if he stays in one place too long. If we must see Teacake as a man given to mutuality and the more stereotypically "feminine" traits of mutual conversation and nurture, we must surely also see him embodying everything stereotypically "masculine" that Hurston has given every indication she finds attractive. Teacake, on this score, is Janie's androgynous counterpart, embodying "masculine" and "feminine" in such a way that leaves these categories largely indeterminate.

Finally, this rereading of Hurston's literary men suggests the need for rethinking her literary women, and that rereading in turn requires a similar awareness of the ways Hurston's work decomposes the traditional under-standings in her own day of sharp divisions between appropriate behavior and spheres of action for men and women and in doing so makes a rigid divide between the masculine and feminine exceedingly permeable. Under-standing Hurston's appreciation for masculine creativity, we discover her delight in women who seize masculine preserves for themselves. Her favored strong woman throughout *Mules and Men* and *Dust Tracks* is Big Sweet, a well-armed and physically impressive woman who, after disputing with and dismissing a white sheriff, is described by a male partner as "uh whole woman and half uh man" (*Mules* 152). In *Seraph on the Suwanee*, Arvay's world so alienates women from their bodies that Arvay can barely experi-ence sexual pleasure. In this respect, Arvay embodies the passive female that Hurston consistently scorns and that she disparages in favor of the frankly erotic gods of Haiti. In her exaltation of the goddess Erzulie, one of the few female gods Hurston discusses in *Tell My Horse*, Hurston pointedly disputes the tendency to equate Erzulie with the Virgin Mary of Catholi-cism: "Erzulie is not the passive queen of heaven and mother of anybody. She is the ideal of the love bed. She is so perfect that all other women are a distortion as compared to her. The Virgin Mary and all of the female saints of the Church have been elevated, and celebrated for their abstinence. Erzulie is worshiped for her perfection in giving herself to mortal man" (*Tell My Horse* 121). Here, Hurston critiques the Virgin and exalts Erzulie's eroticism for the same reasons that, in her autobiographical writing, she dismisses Jesus and embraces David. For Hurston, the gods of Christianity are spiritual and passive in comparison to goddesses like Erzulie who have meat on their bones. Like the male gods of the pantheon, Erzulie feels free to exploit and achieve her desires ruthlessly. Unlike what Hurston views as the passive Christians idealized in the Virgin Mary, Erzulie vigorously seeks out her own will and desires.

Even Janie's apotheosis in *Their Eyes Were Watching God* depends partly on her wresting the sources of male creative and sexual power for herself. While many readings of the novel emphasize Janie's mutuality with her friend, Phoeby, as they sit talking together on the porch, this mutuality partly depends on Janie's willingness to cross the gender divide—evident in her return to the town. John Lowe has shown how the comedic impulse in *Their Eyes* depends upon Janie's ability to emulate and learn from the men around her (156–204). Janie's embodiment as a powerful and sexually assertive woman comes, in part, from her ability to appropriate masculine styles and thereby make the rigid spatial and behavioral divisions between men and women more permeable. The novel opens with Janie striding into town dressed in overalls, her refusal to occupy a settled gender type leading the townspeople on the porch to fear and deride her. In the course of the novel, she learns to play the dozens and disparages Joe Starks's masculinity, an event so traumatic that Joe Starks dies. She learns to play checkers from Teacake, which, as represented in the novel, is a game that enacts a ritual of masculine dominance from which the men had carefully excluded Janie. Teacake's teaching her the game is a representation of egalitarianism but also suggests that such egalitarianism expects Janie to compete as his equal in at least this part of the masculine world. In the end, Janie even takes up Teacake's gun to kill him when he has gone mad from a dog bite, having learned from him the willingness to use violence to protect herself. Janie faces and joins the masculine world as an equal. She has become the kind of woman that Hurston describes herself as being, a woman like David, standing "on the peaky mountain wrapped in rainbows, with a harp and a sword in [her] hands" (*Dust Tracks* 280).

As the contexts I have provided suggest, Hurston's constructions of the relationship between gender and religion are innovative, but they are hardly idiosyncratic. Rather, they participate much more broadly in what Harold Segel calls "the physical imperative," a discursive movement throughout Europe in the late nineteenth and early twentieth centuries, evident in writers as diverse as Nietzsche, Bergson, and Teddy Roosevelt. Jean Toomer's allegiance to the Physical Culture movement and even the physicality of Gurdjieffian mysticism can be seen as an extension of the same impulse. Segel demonstrates that this physical imperative issued in criticisms of organized religion. Christianity and Judaism, especially, were understood as effeminate or unmanly.[5] Hurston's construction of a Christianity emasculated when compared to the virility of Old Testament or pagan gods further reflects a much larger tide of discourse flowing into, through, and out of the New Negro Renaissance.

Hurston's work intrigues not simply because she is connected to these larger discourses but because her use of these discourses transforms them and breaks down traditional conceptions of gender roles and relations. As Gerald Early, Hazel Carby, and many others suggest, the political and cultural imperatives of the New Negro were imperatives to "manhood." Thus the projects and politics of the New Negro Renaissance were with very few exceptions a privileged male preserve. While Hurston clearly employs a dominant Renaissance discourse concerning religion and masculinity, she uses it to break down the masculine cultural preserve. One of the most significant ways in which men such as Jody Starks are destructive in Hurston's work is in their effort to preserve supposedly "masculine" cultural styles as an exclusively male domain. Janie Crawford, like all the most powerful and interesting women in Hurston's writing, crosses the boundary of gender that is so readily apparent in her community, and in Hurston's childhood. As a result, Hurston's work proclaims what Hurston sees as the end of "masculinity" as exclusively male, indeed, imagines an end to the masculine/feminine divide. Recognizing these blurred gender codes in Hurston's work allows also for a greater appreciation of Hurston's literary men and women, who are, ironically, made in the image of Zora Neale Hurston herself.

GOODBYE CHRIST?

Christianity and African American Literary History

In 2003, Henry Louis Gates wrote, produced, and was featured in *America Beyond the Color Line,* a documentary commemorating and updating W. E. B. Du Bois's signature work, *The Souls of Black Folk,* on the centenary of its publication. Focusing on icons of black achievement from Cornel West to Alicia Keyes, the documentary proclaims the continued relevance of Du Bois's work, calls attention to black progress in the intervening 100 years, and places Gates within a tradition of cosmopolitan African American intellectual work. At one point late in the documentary, Gates visits an African American church at worship in South Los Angeles, Bishop Noel Jones's Greater Bethany Community Church. The building is finely appointed and many worshippers are drawn from Hollywood's black elite; the scene both echoes and contrasts with Du Bois's ur-text, *The Souls of Black Folk,* especially Du Bois's formative pilgrimage to a rustic southern church in "Faith of the Fathers." Du Bois's text focuses the reader's imaginative gaze on the preacher. Similarly, Gates's camera closes in on Bishop Jones in full cry, surrounded by assistants and worshippers as his sermon—part song, part dance, part chant—drives the congregation toward a transcendence that the preacher both exemplifies and provokes. As the service reaches its ecstatic peak, the camera pans across the congregation before zooming in on Gates, who stands smiling, watching respectfully, clapping his hands occasionally. Gates, however, is clearly not driven toward the spiritual fervor of many of those around him. His head does not tilt, his hands do not rise, nor do his eyes close in reverence. Less ill-at-ease with the faithful than Du Bois in the country church, Gates remains a participant observer in the Duboisian tradition, and perhaps more observer than participant.

After the service, as the camera pans away to the streets of Los Angeles, Gates negotiates this tension between identification and distance. Directing his first words to the anonymous audience behind the camera, Gates says, "Bishop Jones' spell-binding sermon is so good that it almost makes me get the Holy Ghost." Gates's ironic and jocular tone is consistent with his public personality and with the tenor of the documentary as a whole. However, his words also signify a complicated positioning of many African American intellectuals in relation to African American Christianity. Gates's wry "almost" signals his apartness, his difference from the spectacle the documentary has just displayed. At the same time, his words, his tone, his relaxed posture all lay claim to both intimacy and authority, suggesting that he is familiar enough with the event to speak its language, to be its spokesperson. If he does not speak in the tongues of angels, he is an able translator. He is a translator of the spiritual otherness that he and his audience do not fully share with the congregation. Gates's light humor recalls Du Bois's fretting that the "Frenzy" of black worship too readily provokes laughter, which could potentially destabilize the grave self-presentation of serious intellectualism on which Du Bois's authority seemed to rest. At the same time, Gates is willing to laugh respectfully and joke about the possibility of over-identification, suggesting a degree of intellectual self-confidence buttressed by institutional imprimatur that was not readily available to an early twentieth-century black thinker, even one with so formidable an intellect and self-confidence as Du Bois. Gates's playfulness suggests that although he may not yet talk about the color line without talking about black religion, he has no worries that his identity as a black intellectual will be swallowed by the oversaturated image of black religiosity.

Gates's visual re-embodiment of Du Bois's trek to the site of Southern worship indicates significant continuity but also vast changes in the circumstance and situatedness of black intellectuals vis-à-vis the Christian church. The church itself, of course, is urban and modern—a far cry from the rural wooden sanctuary of Du Bois's youthful journey—its interior and exterior splendor recalling in symbol, if not in fact, the huge Gothic structures north of Central Park that men like Frederick Asbury Cullen or Adam Clayton Powell built almost from nothing. If Hollywood stars and public intellectuals in attendance at Greater Bethany suggest an America moving beyond the color line, it is hardly the case that that color line has disappeared, as recent events in Ferguson, Missouri, and elsewhere have so vividly reminded the American public at large. The church remains. And, indeed, the documentary itself is a visible reminder that the color line is nowhere more visible than in the segregation of America on Sunday morning. If it is no longer clearly the unquestioned center of black life, Gates's trek to South LA reminds us that it is impossible to grapple with black life in America without taking on the church. That intellectual and cultural figures no longer feel the need to locate themselves within the Christian tradition speaks to the work of men like Du Bois and others in establishing an intelligentsia that operated independently of dogma and ecclesiology. At the same time, vital and visible public intellectuals who are also Christian preachers or theologians on the order of Cornel West or Michael Eric Dyson are almost impossible to identify among other cultural groups in the United States, testifying to the enduring importance and relevance of the Christian religion in African American life to the present. If African American writers have said goodbye to Christ on more than one occasion since Langston Hughes in the 1930s, it is not clear that Christ has ever left the house of African American culture.

In her introduction to a collection of essays on James Baldwin's *Go Tell It on the Mountain*, Trudier Harris declares that the work of Baldwin and his contemporary Lorraine Hansberry were "Christianity's last stand" in African American literature (21). Although I have some doubts about the finality of that statement, the implied literary-historical narrative in Harris's evaluation broadly matches the general historical narrative that has motivated my readings of African American literature throughout this book. At the beginning of the twentieth century, the environing horizon for African American literature included an inevitable engagement with the dominance of the church and its primarily male leadership. The story of the twentieth century is of cultural diversification and a coextensive reordering and diversification of models of masculinity and black identity. This diversification birthed alternative versions of African America that say goodbye to Christ or at least welcome him primarily on their own terms. These changes included and facilitated a newly secularized intelligentsia with an elite group of men—and, gradually, women—at the center. Given that the creation and elaboration of such an intelligentsia was one of the dominant concerns of the New Negro Renaissance, this cultural history suggests that the traditional story of Harlem's "failure" as a literary movement needs at least some amendment. While scholars are right to point out that the notion of eradicating racism through writing poems and stories was largely a romantic fantasy, that fantasy was deeply motivated by the belief that Christian patience and virtue would not do away with racism—an argument that was itself part of a vision of a new and more secular black culture for the twentieth century. Leaving aside the contemporary debates in African American communities as to whether the decentering of the church has been a good or bad thing, it seems to me that there is little question whether the discourses and imaginative worlds developed by writers in the first half of the twentieth century justified and encouraged the cultural diversification that has occurred. Without making the simple-minded argument that these writers "caused" such cultural diversification, it's clear they made a difference. Writers that followed in the wake of the New Negro Renaissance elaborated upon the discursive world early twentieth-century writers envisioned even when later writers dismissed, in sometimes vicious terms, the writers of the Renaissance themselves. In this view, the Renaissance, whatever the failures of its aspirations, was clearly a success.

As my argument has illustrated, viewing the Renaissance as a hot house creation begun in 1923 prevents us from seeing its continuity with discourses concerning religion and art stretching as far back as 1903 and beyond. Similarly, declaring it definitively over with the advent of the stock market crash in 1929 prevents us from acknowledging the threads of Renaissance discourse that are woven through much of the twentieth century. But an examination of the discourse of religion, art, and gender of the period does suggest that a very different world existed by the beginning of World War II than before the advent of World War I. This is evident not only in younger writers who followed the Renaissance but also in the developing careers of those now-mature writers who first made their marks during the heyday of the Renaissance. Langston Hughes is by far the best example. Younger writers following the Renaissance tend to follow Hughes's lead with increasingly blunt assessments and criticisms of black Christian faith. These writers are less worried about their reception by the church, but even they continue to negotiate with the reality of the church in African American lives through the middle decades of the twentieth century. Richard Wright notoriously dismissed the writers of the Harlem Renaissance in masculinist terms but followed the general outlines of Renaissance discourse when he attempted to negotiate a settlement between the Christianity of African Americans and his own socialist convictions in the late thirties. Certainly the multitude of fatuous preachers and mindless Christians throughout Wright's work supports the thesis that Wright followed H. L. Mencken into atheism. Nevertheless, in his fiction of the late 1930s, Wright articulated a vision far more nuanced than anything we can imagine pouring from Mencken's pen. In "Fire and Cloud," a Christian minister is torn among desires to avoid confrontation with white folks, to keep the respect of his congregation, and to recognize the legitimate claims of the more radical socialist organizers in his community. Attempting to be all things to all people, he is paralyzed with indecisiveness. He is finally forced into decision after being beaten nearly to death by whites in the town. Nevertheless, this beating doesn't result in a wholesale rejection of Christianity but rather an effort to rearticulate Christianity in broadly socialist terms. In a similar vein, the Christian mother in "Bright and Morning Star" is led toward her son's socialist convictions, eventually abandoning the patience and longsuffering of traditional Christianity in favor of a straightforward attack on white racism when she shoots the man who has been leading a lynching party against her son. While she repudiates dominant aspects of her Christianity, her language throughout is couched in terms of the familiar rhetoric of Christian apocalypticism. Much as Du Bois sought to transform the language of Christianity into an acceptable form of enlightened thinking for the educated elite, Wright sought to apply the general Christian rhetoric of social transformation to the specifics of a socialist world view, imagining communism as a paradoxical fulfillment of Christian utopianism. Although Wright's later work is less accommodating to the specifics of Christianity, in the 1930s, at least, he continued to look for an ameliorative position that would allow for a seamless continuity between his secular vision of the future and the Christian realities of his past and present.

Whether Trudier Harris is correct that James Baldwin is the last writer for whom the black church was a necessary context, it is certainly the case that he continued down the road travelled by earlier writers. Even while rejecting Wright, Baldwin attempted to find an acceptable ground through which the highest Christian ideals might be realized in some other secular or spiritual incarnation. Especially, as I have argued elsewhere at length, he attempted to construct a version of African American masculinity that relied heavily on the principles of Christian confession and conversion even while he remained suspicious of the specifics of Christian theology.[1] Baldwin disparaged the grunting he-men of American popular culture who sought self-protection in their refusal to need others. Baldwin's men are perversely isolated in their attempts to guarantee their right to "belong" to a society. Therefore, Baldwin sees in confession the potential of an alternative community without fear, a vision he develops out of his experience of the holiness church, at least in its rhetorical ideals.

We could see Baldwin as Harris does: the last of a long line of writers who felt compelled to address the language of the Christian church in order to effect an imaginative transformation. Indeed, it does seem to me that Harris is right that this tradition becomes less central as African American literature entered the 1960s. Nevertheless, it is unclear that the tensions between the power and language of the church and the aspirations and imagination of artists and intellectuals disappear as definitively as Harris's dictum might suggest. For many African American artists and intellectuals coming of age in the 1960s and 1970s, repudiation of Christianity was a necessary prerequisite for full participation in the world as men. To be sure, many writers—male and female—associated with what is broadly called the Black Arts movement of the '60s and '70s have seen Christianity as an emasculating force to be rejected because of the damage it has done to black male self-realization. Sometimes this rejection of Christianity collapses into melodrama. For instance, in Jimmy Garrett's play "We own the Night, A Play of Blackness," the context is a revolutionary war being fought by young black men against white police officers somewhere in New York. The play turns primarily on the confrontation between Johnny, who is the leader of the rebels, and his Christian mother. In the play's final moments, as the hero is approaching death, the mother condemns him for his un-Christian behavior and friendships and makes a traditional American Christian connection between whiteness and goodness. Johnny responds: "Johnny (points the gun at her back): We're . . . new men, Mama . . . Not niggers. Black men. (He fires at her back. She stops still, then begins to turn. Johnny fires again and she stumbles forward and slumps to the stage. Johnny looks at her for a moment, then falls away. There is a loud explosion followed by gunfire.)" (Baraka, *Black Fire* 540). Being a new man has seemed consistently to entail a new effort to rid oneself of the whiteness of a received Christian faith, even at the expense here of the melodramatic (and frankly misogynistic) killing of his own mother. In some respects, Garrett's play burlesques subtler and more critically complex renditions of Black Nationalist anxieties about Christianity. In *The Autobiography of Malcolm X*, Malcolm Little's coming of age as Malcolm X requires him to escape a failed masculinity associated with his mother's Christianity. The *Autobiography* portrays Malcolm Little growing up under his mother's inadequate Christian tutelage, contrary to some of the historical evidence unearthed about Malcolm X's life. While Malcolm X portrays his mother as a fundamentalist bent on squashing his freedom, it seems clear that his mother actually attempted to expose the young Malcolm Little to a variety of religious traditions so that he could think and choose for himself. By comparison, his father was a somewhat inconsistent and haphazard Garveyite (DeCaro 61–81). Elsewhere in the book, Malcolm X tentatively embraces his memories of the masculinist and misogynist world of Harlem street hustlers because it saved him from being a "Christian Negro." This formula carried over into Malcolm X's critical ridicule of Martin Luther King, Jr.'s policy of nonviolence when he describes participants in the Civil Rights movement as "Uncle Toms" (DeCaro 179–80). Other works and authors mine a similar vein. In *Soul on Ice*, Eldridge Cleaver associates King's Christian nonviolence with James Baldwin's homosexuality, seeing both as degrading and suicidal (97–111). Claude Brown opens his autobiography, *Manchild in the Promised Land*, by having his mother and other women praying over his lost soul in a hospital, telling him that it was God's grace that he had been shot by a white policeman. His home is a feminine, Christian world he constantly seeks to escape by embracing the all-male world of a boyhood gang (10ff).

In recent decades, these harsh critiques have somewhat given way to more complicated views of the Christian inheritance in African American culture, but tension remains. Spike Lee, an inheritor and revisionist of the Black Arts sensibility, views Christianity with a skeptical eye while returning hesitantly to the ambiguities of an earlier era of African American cultural discourse. In *Jungle Fever*, Ossie Davis portrays a worn out preacher whose religion sounds like the raving of a lunatic, a character who must be supported by his long-suffering wife. Near the beginning of Lee's film, *Malcolm X*, Christianity is associated with Malcolm Little's first girlfriend. Out of respect for her Christian grandmother, she will not sleep with Little. This same woman later becomes a prostitute performing fellatio on a drunken white man. She thus symbolically conflates the Black Nationalist critique of Christianity as prudish with the critique that it degrades the morals of black women while also reasserting the vision of Garrett's play in which black Christian women are dominated by corrupt white males. In the course of the film, Malcolm X demonstrates the superiority of the Nation of Islam by rhetorically defeating an older white preacher who insists that God is white. The final scenes of the film are introduced when Malcolm X steps from his car to be engaged in a conversation by an older, black, Christian woman. This woman says that she is praying to the Lord to protect Malcolm X and that he should just keep on doing what he is doing. The ineffectiveness of the Christian God in protecting Malcolm X is quickly demonstrated when he is gunned down in the Audubon ballroom, a distant echo of Langston Hughes's critique that Jesus was not a real guy who could be counted on to get things done.

Lee offers a somewhat more positive portrayal of Christianity in *Get On the Bus*, his most extended and direct—and perhaps overly didactic— reflection on black manhood. Here, Ossie Davis portrays an older, avuncular man who offers the wisdom of the ages to a busload of men headed for the Million Man March. Davis leads the group in a Christian prayer before they set out; nevertheless, he reveals that he wasn't courageous enough to get out and march with Martin Luther King, Jr. as a younger man. At the end of the film, he dies of a heart attack, symbolizing that new black men may think of Christianity affectionately but that it is to be located firmly in the past. Thus, a good bit of contemporary cultural work by men accepts a dichotomy between active, forceful "masculine" qualities and passive, resigned "feminine" qualities that are associated with the Christian religion. To the degree that these writers see Christianity encouraging passivity, they see Christianity undermining the masculinity necessary to racial strength. Thus Christianity is in collusion with a white world that has sought to metaphorically or literally emasculate the race by emasculating its men.

However, this critique is also at times balanced by a vision that seeks not so much to abandon Christianity as to re-envision it and its masculine potential. In *Do the Right Thing* Spike Lee's linking Malcolm X and Martin Luther King, Jr. is one example of this ambiguity. Similarly, whatever his limitations, Ossie Davis's character in *Get on the Bus* is clearly meant to be sympathetic, even if the future seems to be elsewhere. Finally, in more recent work, Lee has returned directly and indirectly to sympathetic investigations of Christianity. In *4 Little Girls*, his documentary on the bombing of 16th Street Baptist in Birmingham, Lee demonstrates the resourcefulness and resilience of the black Christian folk involved in the Civil Rights Movement. And in *He Got Game*, Denzel Washington portrays a character concerned that his son may be growing up without any recognizable connection to Christianity.

More crucially, while Black Arts literature repressed the ambiguous status of Christianity in its surface content, this ambiguity is often woven into its form. For instance, De Caro and others point out the ways in which *The Autobiography of Malcolm X* follows the form of what is essentially a Christian narrative of conversion, and through this form, Malcolm X is able to connect with the deeply felt Christian imagination of African Americans even while rejecting the overt manifestations of Christian belief (92–93). In David Garrett's play that I discussed earlier, the new black man destroys the feminine and Christian past only to fall to the floor to the sound of a loud explosion and a darkened stage, not unlike the clap of thunder and darkened sky at the death of Christ. This reminds the viewer that putting off the old man and putting on the new man is a basic Christian narrative. The conclusion of Garrett's play suggests that if the Christian past is destroyed, the era of the New Black Man cannot be fully articulated. The lights dim with Old Christian Woman and New Black Man dead together on the floor. Similarly, Ossie Davis's heart attack in Spike Lee's *Get on the Bus* prevents the men from reaching their destination. At the conclusion of Lee's *Malcolm X*, Malcolm X's isolated and protestant integrity is gunned down only to be resurrected in the voices of a multitude of black hosts discovering their authenticity by proclaiming a unique relationship to this source of being: "I am Malcolm X! I am Malcolm X! I am Malcolm X!" Similarly, in Ossie Davis's eulogy for Malcolm X, which is included in the film, Davis proclaims Malcolm X the embodiment of black manhood, "our living black manhood!" and does so in terms that bear a strong residue of Christian rhetoric concerning Jesus:

> Did you ever talk to Brother Malcolm? Did you ever touch him, or have him smile at you? Did you ever really listen to him? . . . And if you knew him you would know why we must honor him. Malcolm was our manhood, our living, black manhood! This was his meaning to his people. And, in honoring him, we honor the best in ourselves. . . .
>
> However, we may have differed with him or with each other about him and his value as a man let his going from us serve only to bring us together, now. Consigning these mortal remains to earth, the common mother of all, secure in the knowledge that what we place in the ground is no more now a man but a seed which, after the winter of our discontent, will come forth again to meet us. And we will know him then for what he was and is a Prince, our own black shining Prince! who didn't hesitate to die, because he loved us so. (Ellis 29)

This is one of the most moving and powerful moments of American prose. It is no denigration of its beauty to note that it is also deeply ironic. In it, Malcolm X—whose life was characterized by a thorough and consistent critique of Christian thought and practice—is haunted by, even possessed by, a rhetoric of Christian manhood. Malcolm X in this passage is, in fact, the Black Christ envisioned by Reverdy Ransom, Countee Cullen, and many others. Transcending the mother to whom he has been consigned, wherein he is not a man but a seed, he will be resurrected from the womb/tomb of the earth as a shining prince to save by his love.

Whether this particular form of rhetorical and imaginative engagement will be sustained remains to be seen and no doubt depends upon the tensions and developments within African America itself. It is remarkable that perhaps the most significant of a younger generation of writers, Ta-Nehisi

Coates, casts himself as a direct inheritor of James Baldwin but is at the same time vastly different from Baldwin in his engagement with the church and its rhetoric. In *Between the World and Me*, Coates seems to have a studied indifference to the church and its claims, especially when compared to Baldwin's anguished judgment on the church on the basis of its own ideals. The rhetorical power of Baldwin, or of Ossie Davis, or of many others before them rested on a productive tension between Christianity and various versions of blackness and masculinity rather than on a resolution of those tensions. However changed the political and culture discourse of the later twentieth century, we can still feel in these lines of inheritance the intimate distance that seems to be required of many African American writers as they negotiate a relationship with the Christianity that remains a significant cultural element of African American life. In this broader context of African American literature in the twentieth century and the first two decades of the twenty-first, we can recognize the persistence and power of the imaginative work set in motion by the writers of the New Negro Renaissance. While these writers did not realize the dream that cultural work would transform African American socio-political realities, they did develop a discursive frame that continues to inform African American writing and its engagement with Christian belief in African American culture. The persistence of this framework, more than an artist's ability to cure the racial ills of our society, is the surest sign of the continuing importance we should assign to the writers of the Renaissance.

Introduction

1. See also the related *Digital Harlem Blog* for mapping analysis of a wide range of issues in Harlem from 1915–1930.

2. For a good overview of the allure of romantic racialism that posits the innate religious or spiritual superiority of African Americans, see Curtis J. Evans, *The Burden of Black Religion*. The concept is discussed throughout the book to different degrees, with chapters five and six, pages 177–222, being particularly pertinent to the time period focused on in *Goodbye Christ?*

3. Said Ransom on the eve of Johnson's fight with Jim Jeffries, "What Jack Johnson seeks to do to Jeffries in the roped arena will be more the ambition of Negroes in every domain of human endeavor" (cited in Early, 26).

4. The historical material related to religion in the next several pages is drawn from the several articles I completed for *The Encyclopedia of the Great Migration*, ed. Steven A. Reich and for *The Encyclopedia of the Harlem Renaissance*, ed. Cary Wintz and Paul Finkelman.

5. For a general discussion of the growth and development of the ministries of Abyssinian Baptist Church and of Salem Methodist Episcopal, see the autobiographies of Adam Clayton Powell and Frederick Asbury Cullen.

6. For the best study of the origins of the social gospel in late nineteenth- and early twentieth-century African America, see Dorrien, *The New Abolition*.

Chapter 1

1. See, for instance, Russ Leo's edited volume *Cities of Men, Cities of God: Augustine and Late Secularism* for a variety of postmodern takes on this subject rooted in Christianity's Augustinian inheritance.

2. Herbert Aptheker argues against the notion of Du Bois's "irreligiousness" on the basis of Du Bois's deployment of God language. However, using "religious" language is different from participating in the specifics of Christian faith and dogma, as did most African Americans at the time to varying degrees. Du Bois's understanding of religion and his relationship to black churches fall within the general parameters of the modernist/fundamentalist debates that exercised Christianity as a whole during the time. At the time, fundamentalists lamented the influence of German scholarship upon the true faith. By contrast, many intellectuals looked to Germany as a model for intellectual work in America. Thus, it seems fair to say that Du Bois's religiousness had more in common with the developing intellectual class than with the dogmatic or enthusiastic expressions of Christian faith found among most African Americans.

3. As many commentators have pointed out, early African American claims to full participation in American democracy were seen to rest on the ability to speak and write fluently in the English language. Du Bois inherited this tradition and supplemented

it with images of manhood he learned at Harvard, images that also relied on the ability to speak and write well. Most recently Du Bois's ideas about manhood have been explored by Eric Sundquist, Hazel Carby, and Kim Townsend. One could also look at Byerman's psychoanalytic study of Du Bois and Moses's study of messianism. My own work builds on the insights of these important studies and, I hope, adds to them to the degree that none looks explicitly at the problem of religion and masculinity as a motivating feature of Du Bois's intellectual life.

4. The following is a standard description of the seizure that was Delphi: "The traditional view is that the priestess, the Pythia, entered the small inner sanctuary of the Temple of Apollo, in which were located a golden statue of Apollo, the Omphalos, the supposed tomb of Dionysus, and a deep chasm surmounted by a tripod on which she seated herself. After drinking water from a sacred spring, chewing laurel leaves, and shaking a laurel branch, she fell into a trance induced by vapors arising from the chasm. Then, writhing on the tripod, with hair disheveled and lips foaming, in prophetic frenzy she uttered hysterical words that the priests recorded" (Fine 1).

5. The most obvious reference here is Ann Douglas's *Feminization of American Culture*. However disputed her interpretation about its larger significance for American culture, the fact of women dominating the pews in American religion goes undisputed.

6. The music here and in following pages is produced via the musical notation program *Finale*. Thus the image does not appear as a facsimile from an edition of *The Souls of Black Folk*.

7. There's a small peculiarity in Du Bois's rendering of the time signature. Although listed as 4/4 time—a common meter in Western classical and popular music—the first and third measures contain only 3 and a half beats. This could be a mistake on Du Bois's part—he does claim to have no technical expertise in music (157)—though the fact that the "error" is repeated makes me suspect not. Although I have nothing more than textual evidence for the surmise, Du Bois may have been attempting to represent an African rhythm that cannot fit within the conventions of Western musical notations. I have found nothing to explain this particular discrepancy, but if I'm correct it provides an interesting glimpse at Du Bois's efforts to articulate an African reality within a Western context, one that I think comports with my general argument that Du Bois's rhetoric locates authentic blackness in something African that bypasses the degradation of black experiences of Christianity. By having access to this African music, Du Bois has access to a truer racial lineage than his male counterparts in the Christian churches.

8. In the text itself, these lines are included with musical notation. I have removed the notation for convenience because it wasn't pertinent to my argument at this point in the chapter.

Chapter 2

1. As my chapter on Hurston will suggest, I think that Hurston isn't really an exception to this general rule and instead associates the folk with what Judith Halberstam calls "female masculinities" as a means of distinguishing their "virile" difference from the fainting femininity of white and Christian culture.

2. Scott Caspar points out that in the American context, biographers and auto-biographers resisted the romantic turn to the inner and private manner in favor of a model of republican biography that stressed the public character of individual lives. Indeed, early in the nineteenth century, collective biographies were often more popular than biographies of individuals, since the proper role of the individual life was to be seen in its public and collective context (39–40). Thus, autobiographers of the eighteenth and nineteenth centuries bore a residue of the Christian conversion narrative and its calling of the individual believer to a specific communal vocation.

Chapter 3

1. Posnock's references are from Alexander Crummell, *Destiny and Race: Selected Writings, 1840–1898*, edited by Wilson Moses. Amherst: U of Massachusetts P, 1992; and David Walker, *Appeal* (1829). New York: Hill and Wang, 1995.

2. See also Lawrence Burnley's *Cost of Unity*, especially chapter 3 (p. 55 and following). Although more narrowly focused on African American education within the Disciples of Christ, Burnley charts not only the zeal for education broadly speaking but also the location of literacy campaigns within the churches themselves through formal school arrangements, Sunday Schools, and the like.

3. Arguably, of course, this attitude remains true to the present. More than one commentator has recognized the transformation of the American university into training centers for careers. As of 2004, less than one percent of American colleges and universities could be identified as liberal arts colleges wherein fewer than 20% of the student body were in career-oriented majors such as business, engineering, nursing, and the like. Although these careers are a far distance from the training for manual labor that Booker T. Washington undertook at Tuskegee, it is arguable that in the course of American educational history, W. E. B. Du Bois won the ideological battle with Washington but lost the educational war in American higher education as a whole.

4. Hofstadter cites R. R. Bowker (*Nation*, Vol. XXXI [July 1, 1880]: 10), who was himself referencing a letter to *The New York Times* dated June 17, 1880.

5. Hofstadter cites *The Congressional Record*, 19th Congress, 1st session, (March 26, 1886), 2786.

6. See especially Bryant's *Born in a Mighty Bad Land* and Scott Reynolds Nelson's study of the legend of John Henry, *Steel Drivin' Man*.

7. Posnock cites Booker T. Washington, *Up from Slavery*, 92.

8. Posnock cites David Levering Lewis, *W.E.B. Du Bois: Biography of a Race, 1868–1919*, 301.

9. Posnock cites Booker T. Washington, *My Larger Education: Being Chapters from My Experience*.

10. Hofstadter quotes from William G. McLoughlin, *Billy Sunday Was His Real Name*. 132, 138.

11. For superior discussions of the relationship of African American intellectual discourse to Darwinism, see especially Jeffery Moran and Eric D. Anderson.

12. Other than Hofstadter, an excellent discussion of the anti-intellectual tendencies of American evangelicalism may be found in Mark Noll's *The Scandal of the Evangelical Mind.*

13. I should note here that I have made a similar though somewhat different argument in my study of the literature written by contemporary ethnic women. In *Recalling Religions,* I argue that one commonality in the work of many different ethnic women writers is the use and reimagination of dominant ethnic religious traditions in order to address contemporary political problems—whether focused on race or gender. Thus, Alice Walker reimagines certain aspects of African American Christianity, Leslie Silko draws on Native American spiritualities, and Cynthia Ozick's work is deeply embedded in textual and ethical traditions springing from Judaism, and so forth. This process of reimagining is similar to Du Bois's and Johnson's aestheticizing of African American Christian discourse. However, Johnson certainly is primarily interested in turning religion into art, and Du Bois's religious impulses are so hard to trace, it is far more difficult to argue that he is positing spirituality as a means of addressing contemporary issues than it is to note that he uses religious language as a motivating factor in addressing racism. Even less is it the case that writers like Langston Hughes or Wallace Thurman or Richard Bruce Nugent seem primarily interested in expanding or redeploying our understanding of Christian spirituality, though the distinctions here are fine and I don't want to make more of them than is justified.

Chapter 4

1. I will note here that this conflict is to some degree inherent within the educational process, and especially so for students with vocations to be intellectuals. It is not an uncommon experience for intellectuals from the working class, from various white and nonwhite ethnic traditions, or from white religious cultures to experience immersion in educational culture as a kind of conversion that alienates them from their home cultures. Well-known narratives of this process include Anzia Yezierska's *The Promised Land,* Richard Rodriguez's *Hunger of Memory,* and the plethora of recent memoirs based on what might be called postreligious conversion narratives. In such narratives, writers describe leaving religion behind for various versions of unbelief. Readers may see for their own interest my introduction to *Recalling Religions* for the ways in which books, reading, and the intellectual life can draw one into conflict with one's home culture. Having said this, I do not want to downplay the fact that different cultures experience this differently, and many white ethnic and religious cultures do not experience the expectation that they are incapable of intellectual work due to race, however much they may experience the prejudgment that their religious culture actually is incapable of or has no intellectual life.

2. Toomer also shared the modernist disdain for "Puritanism" evinced by H. L. Mencken, Randolph Bourne, and others. For Toomer, Puritanism was characterized by its mechanical qualities, splitting the mind and body. In a critique of Paul Rosenfeld, he endorsed Van Wyck Brooks's analysis of "Puritan dividedness" in favor of a program for wholeness and integrity. "Practically this [program] said: touch the soil, America, one's own body, and begin with them. Mr. Rosenfeld could not engage in such a practice. For to him, the local soil was dirt, America hideous, and his body as raw as

any that has been subjected to the modern grinding" (*Selected Essays* 38). In this and similar passages, spiritual and material failures are interwoven; the failures of modern art are due to its inability to overcome the fracturing tendencies of the modern world.

Chapter 5

1. I should note here that I do not believe I am at odds with Bowser and Spence on this specific score. Throughout their book, they reference Micheaux's interest in portraying the leadership potential of the educated elite. Chapman makes a similar argument. See especially pages 39 through 47 in *Prove It On Me* for the ways in which Micheaux used depictions of educated African Americans to counter stereotypes of ignorance. Certainly what I am doing here builds on such arguments. As I hope my reading will show, I am less convinced that this critique does not extend to religion as such; indeed, I am far more convinced that Micheaux's argument is ideologically focused on Christianity per se as destructive to the race rather than simply inconsequential to racial advancement.

2. New York State Motion Picture Commission to Micheaux Film Corporation, 9 November 1925 (New York State Archives). Cited in Regester, "Oscar Micheaux on the Cutting Edge."

3. For examples from popular culture, see Michelle Wallace, "The Celluloid Cabin."

4. The insertions specifying effeminacy and manliness are Bhabha's interpretive additions.

5. I have no specific knowledge that Larsen watched Micheaux's film or was influenced by it. I find Hutchinson's interpretation of Larsen's influences in writing *Quicksand* quite compelling, and so it is most likely that any similarities to be drawn are simply in the conventions of the literary and cultural air that Micheaux and Larsen drew upon. See Hutchinson, *In Search of Nella Larsen*, 224–39.

6. For my reading of Baldwin's novel, see "The Treacherous Body." In my view, Baldwin's rendering not only leaves open the possibility of some kind of genuine spiritual transcendence, however problematic and multilayered it may be, but the conversion is also a source of personal power that John Grimes is able to leverage against his father, a positive source for moral and social development that can't be imagined in Larsen's novel.

Chapter 6

1. For the best study of Johnson's symbolic role in the period, see Geoffrey C. Ward's *Unforgiveable Blackness*.

2. This fascination with the supposedly superior virility of the African American male is, of course, not restricted to the Harlem Renaissance. Writers as various as James Baldwin and Amiri Baraka have analyzed it, and white writers like Norman Podhoretz in "My Negro Problem—And Ours" and Norman Mailer in "The White Negro" were stating this fascination bluntly in the 1960s. For a brief survey of the place that black men occupy in the minds and imaginations of white men, see bell hooks, 74–75.

3. Whalan is citing Waldo Frank's *Memoirs*, 105.

4. See Summers Chapter on Garveyism, "A Spirit of Manliness" (66–110). As I have noted, Thompson makes similar claims about Garvey's appropriation of fascist ideas emanating from Germany.

5. For discussions of the appeal of socialism, see especially the work of Barbara Foley and William Maxwell. For the significant role of the discourses of anthropology and especially ethnography, see Daphne Lamothe. Whalan's study on this subject, *Race, Manhood and Modernism,* does an excellent job of tracing the effect of the New Americans movement on Toomer and more broadly among African American cultural figures.

6. See Courbold, 53–56, for an excellent discussion of the ways in which visual culture contributed to the development of a sense of African heritage that was deeply masculine, if not masculinist, in its orientation.

7. The link among athleticism, spirituality, and racial deliverance has a long history worthy of a paper of its own, only one important instance being Muhammad Ali's relationship with Malcolm X and the Nation of Islam. See Wilson Moses, 155–82, for the most significant investigation of this relationship to date.

8. See A. B. Christa Schwarz. For an extensive discussion of the significance of truth telling to aesthetic movements in Manhattan, see Ann Douglas, *Mongrel Manhattan.*

9. This point is elaborated by Schwarz, Eric Garber, and Alden Reimonenq.

10. From a letter to William Rapp, n.d., cited in Christa A. B. Schwarz, 37

Chapter 7

1. Significant portions of this chapter were previously published under the same title in *African American Review* 34, no. 4: 661–78.

2. See D. H. Mader on the prevalence of pagan motifs among "Uranian" poets beginning in the 1890s. Although I sometimes in the ensuing pages use the terms "gay" and "homosexual," I am more concerned with the question of same-sex desire than the question of sexual identity. While I agree with Reimonenq that readings of Cullen and other African American writers have been damaged in their eliding the question of sexuality, I'm more hesitant than is he to ascribe a positive gay identity anachronistically to Cullen since the idea of having a positive gay "identity" is a relatively recent phenomenon. Cullen's sexual desires seemed to range usually to men but sometimes to women. And despite the failure of his first marriage to Yolande Du Bois, his second marriage managed decently enough by contemporary standards. Letters to Ida Mae Roberson suggest genuine affection at least as much as his letters to men regularly suggest same-sex desire. For a good reading of the complications surrounding homosexual narrative, see Dennis W. Allen. For a thorough biographical description of the various sexual relationships that Cullen developed with men throughout his life, see Reimonenq.

3. Letters suggesting the nature of Cullen's relationships with his wife and different male companions such as Harold Jackman can be found in the Countee Cullen collection at the Amistad Research Center, Tulane University, New Orleans. I don't take a position here on Rampersad's much-disputed thesis in the standard biography regarding the nature of Langston Hughes's sexual identity or experience. At least some letters suggest that whether these desires were acted upon, they were expressed. On February 12,

1923, Hughes sent Cullen some short lyrics with a dedicatory note "To a fellow poet." The poems included such lines as "Just because I love you / That's the reason why / My heart is a fluttering, aspen leaf / When you pass by," and "I found [Joy] driving the butcher's cart / In the arms of the butcher boy!" Such lines suggest that Rampersad's effort to remove all sexual desire from Hughes's impulses is a bit strained. It may be that Hughes's "asexuality," as Rampersad prefers to define it, is an even more thoroughgoing and rigorous form of the public/private split than I am analyzing here with Cullen—the significant difference being that Cullen articulated this split through a discourse of religion.

4. There are by now many different studies of the gay and lesbian life and themes in Harlem, including Gary Holcomb's *Claude McKay Code Name Sasha*, Shane Vogel's *Scene of the Harlem Cabaret*, and Isaac Julien's documentary "Looking for Langston." I continue to think that Eric Garber's "A Spectacle in Color" remains the best succinct overview description of the gay and lesbian subculture in Harlem.

5. The degree to which homosexuality was accepted within the African American community prior to the 1960s has been a matter of some debate. Marlon Ross makes the persuasive argument that homosexuality was far more visible and acceptable within the African American community than the white community at least up until the 1970s. Nevertheless, even Ross seems to suggest that the tolerance of homosexuality was a matter of degree that fell somewhat short of endorsement. As he puts it, "How could the white homosexual understand that black society's embracing of their homosexual sons was not the same as black society's embracing of homosexuality itself" (201).

6. For a short biography of Frederick Cullen in relation to the Harlem Renaissance, see my entry in the *Encyclopedia of the Harlem Renaissance*. See also Cullen's autobiography, *From Barefoot Town to Jerusalem*. Charles Molesworth provides an excellent overview of the sometimes overwhelming and energetic presence of Frederick Cullen in his foster son's life early on. See Molesworth, 7–37.

7. For the symbolic characteristics of the Cullen-Du Bois wedding, see Huggins, 306. For a description of Cullen as a public representative of the Harlem Renaissance, see Shucard, 118–20.

8. See Baker, 61–63 for a description of Cullen's commitments to artistic freedom for African Americans over and against the prescriptions of a white audience or what he took to be somewhat faddish indulgence in low-life Harlem among other poets of the moment.

9. My colleague Samuel Smith has suggested that the worm upon the hook is a medieval image of the Christian doctrine of the atonement, wherein the worm is the physical body of Jesus designed to lure Satan into a trap set for him by God. Whether Cullen had this image in mind is impossible to say, but to trace out the analogy, the divine action of God in the medieval image becomes the sexual passion of the hook in Cullen's poem. The possibility is intriguing here given that Cullen goes on in the poem to portray a highly sexualized Christ and to long for that sexualized Christ so that he can identify with Cullen's suffering. The link is also suggestive in that Christ's suffering is typically referred to as his "passion." But from what I have been able to discover thus far, such a reading would have to remain within the realm of speculation.

10. From Rev. Cullen's autobiography: "While sight seeing we met Mr. and Mrs. Marcus Garvey, my old friend, who had been forced out of the United States for his aggressive race loving spirit"(90).

11. Blum and Harvey cite Conant's book, *The Virility of Christ*, 12–13, 118–20.

12. I'm indebted to Amitai F. Avi-Ram's study of Cullen, though Avi-Ram is far more he is far more interested in the specifics of poetic form than am I. Avi-Ram reads the coffin/box of "For a Poet" as the homosexual closet in which Cullen hides his sexual identity.

13. British poets and writers from Spencer to Milton to Carlisle have depicted Mammon as an evil god or fallen angel, an embodiment of the Christian mortal sin of greed.

Chapter 8

1. Substantial portions of this chapter were published in *Religion and American Culture* 12, no. 2: 229–47, 2002. The original title was "Gods of Physical Violence, Stopping at Nothing: Masculinity, Religion, and Art in The Work of Zora Neale Hurston."

2. See especially Judith Halberstam, *Female Masculinity*, 1–43.

3. Hurston's distaste for personal revelation and the difficulties it created for her in writing her autobiography are found in a letter to Hamilton Holt, 1 February 1943, Hamilton Holt Papers, quoted in Darwin Turner, *In a Minor Chord*, 89.

4. For Hurston's evaluation of Haitian voodoo, see *Tell My Horse*, especially 57–62, 113ff.

5. This link between physicality and opposition to organized religion often issued in a vicious antisemitism that characterized the work of many modernist writers and intellectuals, the political consequences of which were most horrifically evident in the developments of German nationalism after World War I. By the evidence of her work, Hurston seems to have avoided this violent extreme, if anything, tending toward the opposite extreme of philo-semitism evident in her evaluation of the God and heroes of the Hebrew Bible. See Segel, 219–41 for a discussion of the physical imperative and religion.

Conclusion

1. See my essay "The Treacherous Body: Isolation, Confession, and Community in James Baldwin."

WORKS CITED

African Methodist Episcopal House of Bishops. "Address on the Great Migration." *African American Religious History*, edited by Milton C. Sernett, Duke UP, 1999, pp. 360–63.

Allen, Dennis W. "Homosexuality and Narrative." *Modern Fiction Studies*, vol. 115, no. 3–4, 1995, pp. 609–34. doi:10.1353/mfs.1995.0112.

Anderson, Eric D. "Black Responses to Darwinism, 1859-1915." *Disseminating Darwinism: The Role of Place, Race, Religion, and Gender*, edited by Ronald L. Numbers and John Stenhouse, Cambridge UP, 1999, pp. 247–66.

Anderson, Jervis. *This Was Harlem: A Cultural Portrait, 1900-1950*. Farrar, Straus and Giroux, 1982.

Anderson, Paul A. *Deep River: Music and Memory in Harlem Renaissance Thought*. Duke UP, 2001.

Anderson, Victor. *Beyond Ontological Blackness: An Essay on African American Religious and Cultural Criticism*. Continuum, 1995.

Aptheker, Herbert. "W.E.B. Du Bois and Religion: A Brief Reassessment." *Journal of Religious Thought*, vol. 39, Spring/Summer 1982, pp. 5–11.

Arbour, Robert. "Figuring and Reconfiguring the Folk: Women and Metaphor in Part 1 Of Jean Toomer's *Cane*." *Texas Studies in Literature & Language*, vol. 55, no. 3, 2013, pp. 307–27.

Asad, Talal. *Formations of the Secular: Christianity, Islam, Modernity*, Stanford UP, 2003.

Avi-Ram, Amitai F. "The Unreadable Black Body: 'Conventional' Poetic Form in the Harlem Renaissance." *Genders*, vol. 7, 1990, pp. 32–46.

Baer, Hans A., and Merrill Singer. *African-American Religion in the Twentieth Century: Varieties of Protest and Accommodation*. U of Tennessee P, 1992.

Baker, Houston A. *Afro-American Poetics: Revisions of Harlem and the Black Aesthetic*. U of Wisconsin P, 1996.

———. *Blues, Ideology, and Afro-American Literature: A Vernacular Theory*. U of Chicago P, 1987.

Baldwin, James. *Go Tell It On the Mountain*. Modern Library, 1995.

———. "Rendezvous with Life: An Interview with Countee Cullen." *My Soul's High Song: The Collected Writings of Countee Cullen, Voice of the Harlem Renaissance*, edited by Gerald Early, Doubleday, 1991, pp. 601-02.

Banks, William. *Black Intellectuals: Race and Responsibility in American Life*. W.W. Norton & Co, 1996.

Baraka, Amiri, and Larry Neal, editors. *Black Fire: An Anthology of Afro-American Writing*. Morrow, 1968.

Becker, William H. "The Black Church: Manhood and Mission." *African-American Religion: Interpretive Essays in History and Culture*, edited by Timothy E. Fulop and Albert J. Raboteau, Routledge, 1997, pp. 177–200.

Bederman, Gail. *Manliness and Civilization,* U of Chicago P, 1995.

Bell, Bernard. *The Afro-American Novel and its Tradition.* U of Massachusetts P, 1987.

Berman, Russel A. "Du Bois and Wagner: Race, Nation, and Culture Between the United States and Germany." *The German Quarterly,* vol. 70, Spring 1997, pp. 123–35. http://www.jstor.org/stable/407548.

Bhabha, Homi K. "Are You a Man or a Mouse?" *Constructing Masculinity,* edited by Maurice Berger, Brian Wallis, and Simon Watson, Routledge, 1995, pp. 57–68.

The Birth of a Nation. Directed by D. W. Griffith. Kino on Video, 2002.

Blond, Phillip, editor. *Post-Secular Philosophy: Between Philosophy and Theology.* Routledge, 1998.

Bloom, Harold. *The Anxiety of Influence: A Theory of Poetry.* Oxford UP, 1973.

Bloom, Harold, editor. *Langston Hughes.* Chelsea House Publishers, 1989.

Blum, Edward J., and Paul Harvey. *The Color of Christ: The Son of God & the Saga of Race in America.* U of North Carolina P, 2012.

Bontemps, Arna. *Black Thunder.* Beacon, 2003.

Bowser, Pearl, and Louise Spence. *Writing Himself into History: Oscar Micheaux, His Silent Films, and His Audiences.* Rutgers UP, 2000.

Braxton, Joanne. *Black Women Writing Autobiography: A Tradition within a Tradition.* Temple UP, 1990.

Brown, Alan. "'De Beast' Within: The Role of Nature in Jonah's Gourd Vine." *Zora in Florida,* edited by Steven Glassman and Kathryn Lee Seidel, U of Central Florida P, 1991, pp. 76–85.

Brown, Claude. *Manchild in the Promised Land.* Macmillan, 1965.

Bryant, Jerry H. *"Born in A Mighty Bad Land": The Violent Man in African American Folklore and Fiction.* Indiana UP, 2003.

Burma, John H. "Humor as a Technique in Race Conflict." *Mother Wit From the Laughing Barrel,* edited by Alan Dundes, Prentice Hall, 1973, pp. 620–27.

Burnley, Lawrence A. Q. *The Cost of Unity: African American Agency and Education in the Christian Church, 1865–1914.* Mercer UP, 2008.

Burroughs, Nannie H. "Report of the Work of Baptist Women." *African American Religious History,* edited by Milton C. Sernett. Duke UP, pp. 376–02.

Butler, Judith. *Gender Trouble: Feminism and the Subversion of Identity.* Routledge, 1990.

Byerman, Keith E. *Seizing the Word: History, Art, and Self in the Work of W. E. B. Du Bois.* U of Georgia P, 1994.

Calhoun, Craig J., Mark Juergensmeyer, and Jonathan VanAntwerpen. 2011."Introduction." *Rethinking Secularism,* edited by Craig J.Calhoun, Mark Juergensmeyer, and Jonathan VanAntwerpen, Oxford UP, pp. 3-30.

Carby, Hazel V. *Race Men.* Harvard UP, 1998.

The Carnegie Foundation for the Advancement of Teaching. "Undergraduate Instructional Program Tables." www.carnegiefoundation.org/classifications/index.asp?key=800.

Carpenter, Edward. *Ioläus, an Anthology of Friendship.* Pagan Press, 1982.

Caspar, Scott E. *Constructing American Lives: Biography and Culture in Nineteenth-Century America.* U of North Carolina P, 1999.

Chapman, Erin D. *Prove It on Me: New Negroes, Sex, and Popular Culture in the 1920s.* Oxford UP, 2012.

Chauncey, George. *Gay New York: Gender, Urban Culture, and the Making of the Gay Male World, 1890-1940.* HarperCollins-Basic Books, 1994.

Chin, Frank. "This is not an Autobiography." *Genre,* vol. 18, no. 2, 1985, pp. 109–30.

Chisholm, Dianne. "Obscene Modernism: Eros Noir and the Profane Illumination of Djuna Barnes." *American Literature,* vol. 69, no. 1, 1997, pp. 167–206.

Cleaver, Eldridge. *Soul on Ice.* McGraw-Hill, 1967.

Coates, Ta-Nehisi. *Between the World and Me.* Spiegel & Grau, 2015.

Conant, Robert W. *The Virility of Christ: A New View.* N.p., 1915.

Cooper, Wayne. *Claude McKay: Rebel Sojourner in the Harlem Renaissance.* Louisiana State UP, 1987.

Corbould, Clare. *Becoming African Americans: Black Public Life in Harlem, 1919–1939.* Harvard UP, 2009.

Cripps, Thomas. *Slow Fade to Black: The Negro in American Film, 1900–1942.* Oxford UP, 1977.

Cronin, Gloria, editor. *Critical Essays on Zora Neale Hurston.* G. K. Hall, 1998.

———. "Going to the Far Horizon: Zora Neale Hurston and Christianity." *Literature and Belief,* vol. 15, 1995, pp. 48–71.

Crummell, Alexander. *Destiny and Race: Selected Writings, 1840-1898,* edited by Wilson Moses. U of Massachusetts P, 1992.

Cruse, Harold. *The Crisis of the Negro Intellectual: A Historical Analysis of the Failure of Black Leadership.* Morrow, 1967.

Cullen, Countee. *Caroling Dusk: An Anthology of Verse by Negro Poets.* Harper & Bros., 1927.

———. *Color.* New York: Harper & Bros., 1925.

———. "The Dark Tower." *Black Writers Interpret the Harlem Renaissance,* edited by Cary D. Wintz, Garland, 1996, pp. 139-60.

———. *My Soul's High Song: The Collected Writings of Countee Cullen, Voice of the Harlem Renaissance,* edited by Gerald Early. Doubleday, 1991.

Cullen, Rev. Frederick Asbury. *From Barefoot Town to Jerusalem.* N.p., 1924.

Dace, Tish, editor. *Langston Hughes: The Contemporary Reviews.* Cambridge UP, 1997.

Davis, Ossie. 1965. "Eulogy for Malcolm X." *Say it Loud: Great Speeches on Civil Rights and African American Identity,* edited by Catherine Ellis and Stephen Smith, New Press, 2010, pp. 25-9.

De Jongh, James. *Vicious Modernism: Black Harlem and the Literary Imagination.* Cambridge UP, 1990.

DeCaro, Louis A. *Malcolm and the Cross: The Nation of Islam, Malcolm X, and Christianity.* New York UP, 1998.

Digital Harlem Blog. Sydney: U of Sydney, 2009. www.digitalharlemblog.wordpress.com.

Digital Harlem: Everyday Life 1915-1930. Sydney: U of Sydney, 2007. www.digital harlem.org.

Dorrien, Gary J. *The New Abolition: W.E.B. Du Bois and the Black Social Gospel.* Yale UP, 2015.

Dorsey, David F. "Countee Cullen's Use of Greek Mythology." *College Language Association Journal,* vol. 13, 1969, pp. 68–77.

Dorsey, Peter A. *Sacred Estrangement: The Rhetoric of Conversion in Modern American Autobiography.* Pennsylvania State UP, 1993.

Douglas, Ann. *The Feminization of American Culture.* Knopf, 1977.

———. *Terrible Honesty: Mongrel Manhattan in the 1920s.* Farrar, Straus and Giroux—Noonday, 1995.

Douglas, Kelly Brown. *The Black Christ.* Orbis, 1994.

Du Bois, W. E. B. *Dark Princess: A Romance,* edited by Claudia Tate. UP of Mississippi, 1995.

———*Darkwater: Voices from Within the Veil,* edited by Henry L. Gates and Evelyn B. Higginbotham. Oxford UP, 2014.

———. *Dusk of Dawn: An Essay Toward an Autobiography of a Race Concept.* Schocken, 2007.

———. *The Negro Church.* Altamira, 2003.

———. *The Oxford W.E.B. Du Bois Reader,* edited by Eric J. Sundquist. Oxford UP, 1996.

———. *The Souls of Black Folk: Authoritative Text, Contexts, Criticism,* edited by Henry L. Gates, and Terri H. Oliver. W.W. Norton, 1999.

———. *W.E.B. Dubois: The Crisis Writings,* edited by Daniel Walden. Fawcett Publications, 1972.

Dundes, Alan, editor. *Mother Wit from the Laughing Barrel: Readings in the Interpretation of Afro-American Folklore.* Prentice-Hall, 1972.

DuPlessis, Rachel B. *Genders, Races, and Religious Cultures in Modern American Poetries, 1908-1934.* Cambridge UP, 2001.

Early, Gerald. "Introduction." *My Soul's High Song: The Collected Writings of Countee Cullen, Voice of the Harlem Renaissance.* Anchor, 1991, pp. 1–73.

Evans, Curtis J. *The Burden of Black Religion.* Oxford UP, 2008.

Fauset, Arthur Huff. *Black Gods of the Metropolis: Negro Religious Cults of the Urban North.* U of Pennsylvania P, 1944.

Favor, J. Martin. *Authentic Blackness: The Folk in The New Negro Renaissance.* Duke UP, 1999.

Ferguson, Blanche E. *Countee Cullen and the Negro Renaissance.* Dodd, 1966.

Fichte, Johann G, Reginald F. Jones, and George H. Turnbull. *Addresses to the German Nation.* Open Court Publishing, 1923.

Fine, John V. A. "Delphi." *Encyclopedia Americana Online.* ea.grolier.com/cgibin /buildpage?artbaseid=012349000.

Fisher, Rudolph. *The City of Refuge: The Collected Stories of Rudolph Fisher,* edited by John McCluskey. U of Missouri P, 1987.

Fisher, Rudolph. *Walls of Jericho.* U of Michigan P, 1994.

Foley, Barbara. *Jean Toomer: Race, Repression and Revolution.* U of Illinois P, 2014.

Foucault, Michel. *The History of Sexuality.* Pantheon Books, 1978.

Frank, Waldo D. *Memoirs of Waldo Frank.* U of Massachusetts P, 1973.

Fredrickson, George M. "Chapter Four: Uncle Tom and The Anglo-Saxons: Romantic Racialism in The North." *Black Image in the White Mind: Debate on Afro-American Character & Destiny, 1817-1914.* Wesleyan UP, 1987, pp. 97–129. ezproxy.messiah .edu/login?url=http://search.ebscohost.com/login.aspx?direct=true&db=sih&AN =37357687&site=ehost-live.

Fulop, Timothy E., and Albert J., editors. *African-American Religion: Interpretive Essays in History and Culture.* Routledge, 1997.

Gaines, Jane. "Fire and Desire: Race, Melodrama, and Oscar Micheaux." *Black American Cinema,* edited by Diawara Manthia. Routledge, 1993, pp. 49–70.

Ganter, Granville. "Decadence, Sexuality, and the Bohemian Vision of Wallace Thurman." *MELUS: The Journal of the Society for The Study of the Multi-Ethnic Literature of the United States,* vol. 28, no. 2, 2003, pp. 83–104.

Garber, Eric. "A Spectacle in Color: The Lesbian and Gay Subculture of Jazz Age Harlem." *Hidden from History: Reclaiming the Gay and Lesbian Past,* edited by Martin Bauml Duberman, Martha Civinus, and George Chauncey, Jr. Penguin–NAL, 1989, pp. 318–31.

Gates, Henry Louis, Jr. "Blacklash?" *New Yorker,* May 17, 1993, p. 42.

———. "The Trope of a New Negro and the Reconstruction of the Image of the Black." *Representations. Special Issue: America Reconstructed, 1840-1940,* vol. 24, Autumn 1988, pp. 129–55. doi:10.2307/2928478.

———. *The Signifying Monkey: A Theory of African American Literary Criticism.* Oxford UP, 2014.

Gates, Henry Louis, Jr., and Dan Percival et al. *America Beyond the Color Line.* PBS Home Video, 2003.

Gates, Henry Louis, Jr., and K. A. Appiah, editors. *Langston Hughes: Critical Perspectives Past and Present.* Amistad, 1993.

Gates, Henry Louis, and Nellie Y. McKay, editors. *The Norton Anthology of African American Literature.* Norton, 1997.

Genovese, Eugene D. *Roll, Jordan, Roll: The World the Slaves Made.* Random House— Vintage, 1976.

Gilroy, Paul. *Against Race: Imagining Political Culture Beyond the Color Line.* Belknap Press of Harvard UP, 2000.

Gordon, Taylor. *Born to Be.* U of Washington P, 1975.

Green, J. Ronald. *Straight Lick: The Cinema of Oscar Micheaux.* Indiana UP, 2000.

Halberstam, Judith. *Female Masculinity.* Duke UP, 1998.

Haraway, Donna. "A Manifesto for Cyborgs: Science, Technology, and Socialist Feminism in the 1980s." *Norton Anthology of Theory and Criticism,* edited by Vincent B. Leitch. W.W. Norton, 2001, pp. 2269–99.

Harris, Trudier. *Exorcising Blackness: Historical and Literary Lynching and Burning Rituals.* Indiana UP, 1984.

———. *New Essays on Go Tell It on the Mountain.* Cambridge UP, 1996.

Hegeman, Susan. *Patterns for America: Modernism and the Concept of Culture.* Princeton UP, 1999.

Hemenway, Robert. *Zora Neale Hurston: A Literary Biography*. U of Illinois P, 1977.

Heyward, DuBose. Review of *Fine Clothes to the Jew*, by Langston Hughes. *Langston Hughes: Critical Perspectives Past and Present*, edited by Henry Louis Gates, Jr. and K. A. Appiah. Amistad, 1993, pp. 8–10.

Hill, Patricia Liggins et al., editors. *Call and Response: The Riverside Anthology of the African American Literary Tradition*. Houghton Mifflin, 1998. Hofstadter, Richard. *Anti-Intellectualism in American Life*. Knopf, 1964.

Holcomb, Gary Edward. *Claude McKay, Code Name Sasha: Queer Black Marxism and The Harlem Renaissance*. UP of Florida, 2007.

hooks, bell. "Micheaux: Celebrating Blackness." *Black American Literature Forum*, vol. 25, no. 2, Summer, 1991, pp. 335–50.

———. "Reconstructing Black Masculinity." *The Masculine Masquerade: Masculinity and Representation*, edited by Andrew Perchuk and Helaine Posner. MIT UP, 1995, pp. 69–88.

Huggins, Nathan. *Harlem Renaissance*. Oxford UP, 1971.

———. *Voices from the Harlem Renaissance*. Oxford UP, 1976.

Hughes, Langston. *The Collected Poems of Langston Hughes*, edited by Arnold Rampersad and David Roessel. Random House-Vintage, 1995.

———. *The Collected Works of Langston Hughes: Autobiography The Big Sea*, edited by Joseph McLaren. U of Missouri P, 2002.

———. *The Collected Works of Langston Hughes: The Early Simple Stories*, edited by Donna S. Harper. U of Missouri P, 2001.

———. *The Collected Works of Langston Hughes: Essays on Art, Race, Politics, and World Affairs*, edited by C. C. De Santis. U of Missouri P, 2002.

———. *The Collected Works of Langston Hughes: The Plays to 1942, Mulatto to The Sun Do Move*, edited by Leslie Catherine Sanders. U of Missouri P, 2002.

———. *The Collected Works of Langston Hughes: The Short Stories*, edited by R. Baxter Miller. U of Missouri P, 2002.

———. Letter to Countee Cullen. 12 February 1923. *Countee Cullen Papers, 1921–1969*. Amistad Research Center, 1992.

Hughes, Langston, and Carl Van Vechten. *Remember Me to Harlem: The Letters of Langston Hughes and Carl Van Vechten*, edited by Emily Bernard. Random House-Vintage, 2002.

Hull, Gloria T., et al. *All the Women Are White, All the Blacks Are Men, But Some of Us Are Brave: Black Women's Studies*. Feminist P, 1982.

Hurston, Zora Neale. *Dust Tracks on a Road: An Autobiography*. U of Illinois P, 1984.

———. *I Love Myself When I am Laughing . . . and Then Again When I am Looking Mean and Impressive*, edited by Alice Walker. Feminist P, 1979.

———. *Jonah's Gourd Vine*. Perennial Library, 1990.

———. Letter to James Weldon Johnson, 8 May 1934, James Weldon Johnson Papers, Yale U Library.

———. *Mules and Men*. Perennial Library, 1990.

———. *The Sanctified Church: The Folklore Writing of Zora Neale Hurston*. Turtle Island Foundation, 1981.

———. *Tell My Horse: Voodoo and Life in Haiti and Jamaica*. Harper and Row, Perennial Library, 1990.

———. *Their Eyes Were Watching God*. U of Illinois P, 1978.

Hutchinson, George. *The Harlem Renaissance in Black and White*. Belknap Press of Harvard UP, 1996.

———. *In Search of Nella Larsen: A Biography of the Color Line*. Belknap Press of Harvard UP, 2006.

Johnson, Charles S. "Black Workers and the City." *Survey Graphic* Harlem Number. March 1925, pp. 641–43, 718–21. etext.virginia.edu/harlem/JohWorkF.html.

Johnson, James Weldon. *Along this Way: The Autobiography of James Weldon Johnson*. Viking, 1968.

———. *The Autobiography of an Ex-Colored Man*. Sherman, French, 1912.

———. *God's Trombones: Seven Negro Sermons in Verse*. Viking, 1927.

Julien, Isaac. *Looking for Langston*. Film. Sankofa Film and Video, 2007.

Kelly, John D. "Seeing Red: Mao Fetishism, Pax Americana, and the Moral Economy of War." *Anthropology and Global Counterinsurgency*, edited by John D. Kelly, Beatrice Jauregui, Sean T. Mitchell, and Jeremy Walton. U of Chicago P, 2010, pp. 67–83.

Kent, George E. "Hughes and the Afro-American Folk and Cultural Tradition." *Langston Hughes*, edited by Harold Bloom. Chelsea House, 1989, pp. 17–36.

Kimmel, Michael. *Manhood in America: A Cultural History*. The Free Press, 1996.

Kipling, Rudyard. *Plain Tales from the Hills*, Project Gutenberg, 1990. www.gutenberg.org/files/1858/1858-h/1858-h.htm.

Lackey, Michael. *African American Atheists and Political Liberation: A Study of the Sociocultural Dynamics of Faith*. U of Florida P, 2007.

Lamothe, Daphne M. *Inventing the New Negro: Narrative, Culture, and Ethnography*. U of Pennsylvania P, 2008.

Larkin, Margaret. "Review of Fine Clothes to the Jew, by Langston Hughes." *Langston Hughes: Critical Perspectives Past and Present*, edited by Henry Louis Gates, Jr. and K. A. Appiah. Amistad, 1993, pp. 10–12.

Larsen, Nella. *Quicksand; And, Passing*, edited by Deborah McDowell. New Rutgers UP, 1986.

Lawrence, D. H. *Psychoanalysis and the Unconscious: And, Fantasia of the Unconscious*, edited by Bruce Steele. Cambridge UP, 2004.

Lee, Spike, dir. *4 Little Girls*. Film. HBO Home Entertainment, 2001.

———. *Do the Right Thing*. Film. Universal City Studios, 2009.

———. *Get on the Bus*. Film. Columbia TriStar Home Video, 2000.

———. *He Got Game*. Film. Touchstone Home Entertainment, 1998.

———. *Jungle Fever*. Film. Universal Home Video, 1998.

———. *Malcolm X*. Film. Warner Home Video, 2000.

Leo, Russ, editor. *Cities of Men, Cities of God: Augustine and Late Secularism*. Duke UP, 2008.

Lewis, David Levering, editor. *The Portable Harlem Renaissance Reader*. Penguin, 1994.

———. *W.E.B. Du Bois: Biography of a Race, 1868-1919*. Henry Holt, 1993.

------. *W.E.B. Du Bois: The Fight for Equality and The American Century, 1919–1963*. Henry Holt, 2000.

------. *When Harlem was in Vogue*. Oxford UP, 1981.

Lincoln, C. Eric. *The Black Church Since Frazier*. Schocken, 1974.

Lincoln, C. E., and Lawrence H. Mamiya. *The Black Church in the African-American Experience*. Duke UP, 1990.

Locke, Alain. "Common Clay and Poetry." *Langston Hughes: The Contemporary Reviews*, edited by Tish Dace. Cambridge UP, 1997, pp. 115–16.

------. "Enter the New Negro." *Survey Graphic. Harlem Number*, March 1925, pp. 631–34.

------. Letter to Countee Cullen, 16 November 1922. *Alain LeRoy Locke Papers, 1841–1954*. Moorland Spingarn Research Center, Howard University. Box 164–22, Folder 35.

------. "The New Negro." *The Portable Harlem Renaissance Reader*, edited by David Levering Lewis. Penguin, 1994, pp. 46–51.

------. editor. *Survey Graphic: Harlem Mecca of the New Negro*. Black Classic, 1980.

Lowe, John. *Jump at the Sun: Zora Neale Hurston's Cosmic Comedy*. U of Illinois P, 1995.

Mader, D. H. "The Greek Mirror: The Uranians and Their Use of Greece." *Journal of Homosexuality*, vol. 49, no. 3–4, 2005, pp. 377–520.

Malden, Graham Ward, editor. *The Postmodern God: A Theological Reader*. Blackwell Publishers, 1997.

Manganaro, Marc. *Culture, 1922: The Emergence of a Concept*. Princeton UP, 2002.

Marable, Manning. "The Black Faith of W.E.B. Du Bois: Sociocultural and Political Dimensions of Black Religion." *Southern Quarterly: A Journal of the Arts in the South*, vol. 23, no. 3, 1985, pp. 15–33.

------. *W. E. B. DuBois: Black Radical Democrat*. Twayne, 1986.

Maxwell, William J. *New Negro, Old Left: African-American Writing and Communism between the Wars*. Columbia UP, 1999.

Mays, Benjamin E. *The Negro's God, As Reflected in His Literature*. Russell & Russell, 1968.

Mays, Benamin E., and Joseph W. Nicholson. "The Genius of the Negro Church." *African American Religious History*, edited by Milton C. Sernett, Duke UP, 1999, pp. 423–34.

McKay, Claude. *Banjo: A Story Without a Plot*. Harcourt, Brace, Jovanovich, 1970.

------. *Home to Harlem*. Northeastern UP, 1987.

------. *A Long Way from Home: An Autobiography*. Pluto Press, 1985.

McKay, Nellie. "Jean Toomer." *Afro-American Writers from the Harlem Renaissance to 1940*, edited by Trudier Harris-Lopez and Thadious M. Davis. Gale, 1987, pp. 274–88.

McLoughlin, William G. *Billy Sunday Was His Real Name*. U of Chicago P, 1955.

Meer, Sarah. *Uncle Tom Mania: Slavery, Minstrelsy, And Transatlantic Culture in The 1850s*. U of Georgia P, 2005.

Meisenhelder, Susan Edwards. *Hitting a Straight Lick with a Crooked Stick: Race and Gender in the Work of Zora Neale Hurston*. U of Alabama P, 1999.

Men and Religion Forward Movement. *Messages of the Men and religion movement, including the revised reports of the commissions presented at the congress of the Men and religion forward movement, April, 1912, together with the principle addresses delivered at the congress. Vol. I Congress Addresses*. Association Press, 1912.

Mencken, H. L. "Homo Neanderthalensis." *The Baltimore Evening Sun*, June 29, 1925. www.positiveatheism.org/hist/mencko1.htm.

Micheaux, Oscar, dir. *Body and Soul*. Film. Chicago: Facets Video, 1994.

———. *Within Our Gates*. Film. Grapevine Video, 2007.

Molesworth, Charles. *And Bid Him Sing: A Biography of Countée Cullen*. U of Chicago P, 2012.

Moon, Henry Lee. "History of 'The Crisis.'" *Crisis*, vol. 77, no. 9, 1970, November, p. 321.

Moran, Jeffrey P. "Reading Race into the Scopes Trial: African American Elites, Science, and Fundamentalism." *The Journal of American History*, vol. 90, no. 3, December 2003, pp. 891–911.

Moses, Wilson Jeremiah. *Afrotopia: The Roots of African American Popular History*. Cambridge UP, 1998.

———. *Religious Myth*. Pennsylvania State UP, 1998.

Moss, Candida R. *The Myth of Persecution: How Early Christians Invented a Story of Martyrdom*. Harper One, 2013.

Musser, Charles. "To Redream the Dreams of White Playwrights: Reappropriation and Resistance in Oscar Micheaux's *Body and Soul*." *The Yale Journal of Criticism*, vol. 12, no. 2, 1999, pp. 321–56.

Nelsen, Hart M., Raytha L. Yokley, and Anne K. Nelsen, editors. *The Black Church in America*. Basic Books, 1971.

Nelson, Scott Reynolds. *Steel Drivin' Man: John Henry, The Untold Story of an American Legend*. Oxford UP, 2006.

Noll, Mark A. *The Scandal of the Evangelical Mind*. Inter-Varsity, 1994.

North, Michael A. *Dialect of Modernism: Race, Language, and Twentieth-Century Literature*. Oxford UP, 1994.

Nugent, Bruce, and Thomas H. Wirth. *Gay Rebel of the Harlem Renaissance: Selections from the Work of Richard Bruce Nugent*. Duke UP, 2002.

O'Neill, Eugene, dir., *The Emperor Jones*. Film. Image Entertainment, 2003.

O'Neill, Eugene, and Travis Bogard. *Complete Plays, 1913-1943*. Literary Classics of the United States, 1988.

"Percent of Negro and White Men and Women in Church, 1926, 1916, and 1906." *Historical Statistics of Black America, Volume II. Negro Year Book: An Annual Encyclopedia of the Negro, 1937-1938*, edited by Monroe N. Work. Tuskegee Institute, Negro Year Book, 1937, p. 228.

Plant, Deborah. *Every Tub Must Sit on It's Own Bottom: The Philosophy and Politics of Zora Neale Hurston*. U of Illinois P, 1995.

Pochmara, Anna. *The Making of the New Negro: Black Authorship, Masculinity, and Sexuality in the Harlem Renaissance*. Amsterdam UP, 2011.

Poplawski, Paul. *Promptings of Desire: Creativity and The Religious Impulse in The Works of D. H. Lawrence*. Greenwood, 1993.

Posnock, Ross. *Color and Culture: Black Writers and the Making of the Modern Intellectual*. Harvard UP, 1998.

———. "How It Feels to Be a Problem: Du Bois, Fanon, and the 'Impossible Life' of the Black Intellectual." *Critical Inquiry*, vol. 23, no. 2, Winter 1997, pp. 325–49.

Pound, Ezra. "Vorticism." *Fortnightly Review*, vol. 102, 1914, pp. 461-471, http://fortnightlyreview.co.uk/vorticism/.

Powell, Adam Clayton, Sr. *Against the Tide: An Autobiography*. Richard R. Smith, 1938.

Powers, Peter Kerry. "Cullen, Frederick Asbury." *Encyclopedia of the Harlem Renaissance*, vol. 1, edited by Cary Wintz and Paul Finkelman. Routledge, 2004, pp. 271–73.

———. "Gods of Physical Violence, Stopping at Nothing: Masculinity, Religion, And Art in The Work of Zora Neale Hurston." *Religion and American Culture*, vol. 12, no. 2, 2002, pp. 229–47.

———. "Harlem Renaissance." *Encyclopedia of the Great Migration*, vol. 1, edited by Steven A. Reich, Greenwood, 2006, pp. 368–72.

———. *Recalling Religions: Resistance, Memory, and Cultural Revision in Ethnic Women's Literature*. U of Tennessee P, 2001.

———. "Religion." *Encyclopedia of the Harlem Renaissance*, vol. II, edited by Cary Wintz and Paul Finkelman. Routledge, 2004, pp. 1035–39.

———. "Religious Organizations." *Encyclopedia of the Harlem Renaissance*, vol. II, edited by Cary Wintz and Paul Finkelman. Routledge, 2004, 1039–43.

———. "'The Singing Man Who Must Be Reckoned With': Private Desire and Public Responsibility in the Poetry of Countee Cullen." *African American Review*, vol. 34, no. 4, 2000, pp. 661–78.

———. "The Treacherous Body: Isolation, Confession, and Community in James Baldwin." *American Literature: A Journal of Literary History, Criticism, and Bibliography* vol. 77, no. 4, 2005, pp. 787–813.

———. "W.E.B. DuBois." *Encyclopedia of the Great Migration*, vol. I, edited by Steven A. Reich. Greenwood, 2006, pp. 263–66.

Rampersad, Arnold. *I, Too, Sing America: The Life of Langston Hughes, Volume I, 1902–1941*. Oxford UP, 2002.

Ransom, Reverdy C. *Making the Gospel Plain: The Writings of Bishop Reverdy C. Ransom*, edited by Anthony B. Pinn. Trinity Press International, 1999.

———. "The New Negro." Ohio Historical Society. The African American Experience in Ohio, 1850-1920. The Reverdy C. Ransom Collection. Author, Rev. Reverdy C. Ransom. Item Date, 1923. Item Location, National Afro-American Museum and Cultural Center, Call Number 85-6, Medium, Manuscript. URL dbs.ohiohistory.org/africanam/det.cfm?ID=13906.

———. *The Pilgrimage of Harriet Ransom's Son*. Sunday School Union, 1949.

Rath, Richard Cullen. "Echo and Narcissus: The Afrocentric Pragmatism of W.E.B. Du Bois." *The Journal of American History*, vol. 84, no. 2, September 1997, pp. 461–95.

Regester, Charlene B. "Oscar Micheaux on the Cutting Edge: Films Rejected by the New York State Motion Picture Commission." *Popular Culture Association in the South*, vol. 17, no. 2, April 1995, pp. 61–72.

Reimonenq, Alden. "Countee Cullen's Uranian Soul Windows." *Critical Essays: Gay and Lesbian Writers of Color*, edited by Emmanuel S. Nelson. Haworth, 1993, pp. 143–65.

Ross, Marlon B. *Manning the Race: Reforming Black Men in the Jim Crow Era*, New York UP, 2004.

————"Some Glances at the Black Fag: Race, Same-Sex Desire, and Cultural Belonging." *Canadian Review of Comparative Literature/Revue Canadienne de Litterature Comparee*, vol. 21, no. 1–2, 1994, pp. 193–219.

Schuyler, George S. "Black America Begins to Doubt." *American Mercury*, vol. 25, 1932, pp. 423–30.

Schwarz, A. B. Christa. *Gay Voices of the Harlem Renaissance*. Indiana UP, 2003.

Scruggs, Charles. *The Sage in Harlem: H.L. Mencken and the Black Writers of the 1920s*. Johns Hopkins UP, 1984.

Segel, Harold. *Body Ascendant: Modernism and the Physical Imperative*. Johns Hopkins UP, 1998.

Sernett, Milton C., editor. *African American Religious History. A Documentary Witness*. Duke UP, 1999.

————. *Bound for the Promised Land: African American Religion and the Great Migration*. Duke UP, 1997.

Shucard, Alan R. *Countee Cullen*. Twayne, 1984.

Singh, Amritjit, William S. Shiver, and Stanley Brodwin, editors. *The Harlem Renaissance: Revaluations*. Garland, 1989.

Smith, Charles Spencer. *A History of the African Methodist Episcopal Church, Being A Volume Supplemental to A History of the African Methodist Episcopal Church, By Daniel Alexander Payne, D.D., Ll.D., Late One of Its Bishops: Chronicling The Principal Events in The Advance of the African Methodist Episcopal Church from 1856 To 1922*. Book Concern of the A. M. E. Church, 1922. docsouth.unc.edu /church/cssmith/smith.html.

Smylie, James H. "Countee Cullen's 'The Black Christ.'" *Theology Today*, vol. 38, no. 2, July 1981, pp. 160–73.

Sorett, Josef. *Spirit in the Dark: a Religious History of Racial Aesthetics*. Oxford UP, 2016.

Spencer, Jon Michael. "The Black Church and the Harlem Renaissance." *African American Review*, vol. 3, no. 3, Autumn 1996, pp. 453–60.

Spengler, Oswald, and Charles F. Atkinson. *The Decline of the West*. Knopf, 1926.

Stansell, Christine. *American Moderns: Bohemian New York and the Creation of a New Century*. Metropolitan Books, 2000.

Stepto, Robert B. *From Behind the Veil: A Study of Afro-American Narrative*. U of Illinois P, 1991.

Stowe, Harriet Beecher. *Uncle Tom's Cabin*. Oxford UP, 2002.

Summers, Martin A. *Manliness and Its Discontents: The Black Middle Class and the Transformation of Masculinity, 1900-1930*. U of North Carolina P, 2004.

Sundquist, Eric. *To Wake the Nations: Race in the Making of American Literature*. Belknap-Harvard UP, 1993.

Taylor, Clarence. *Black Religious Intellectuals: The Fight for Equality from Jim Crow to the Twenty-First Century*. Routledge, 2002.

Thompson, Mark C. *Black Fascisms: African American Literature and Culture Between the Wars*. U of Virginia P, 2007.

Thurman, Wallace, ed. *Fire!!: A Quarterly Devoted to the Younger Negro Artists*. Fire!! Press, 1926.

Toomer, Jean. *Cane: An Authoritative Text, Backgrounds, Criticism*, edited by Darwin T. Turner. W.W. Norton, 1988.

———. *A Jean Toomer Reader: Selected Unpublished Writings*, edited by Frederik L. Rusch. Oxford UP, 1993.

———. *Jean Toomer: Selected Essays and Literary Criticism*, edited by Robert B. Jones. U of Tennessee P, 1996.

———. *The Wayward and the Seeking: A Collection of Writings by Jean Toomer*, edited by Darwin T. Turner. Howard UP, 1982.

Townsend, Kim. "'Manhood' at Harvard: W.E.B. Du Bois." *Raritan*, vol. 15, no. 4, Spring 1996, pp. 70–82.

Turner, Darwin. *In a Minor Chord*. Southern Illinois UP, 1971.

Tuttleton, James W. "Countee Cullen at 'The Heights'." *The Harlem Renaissance: Revaluations*, edited by Amritjit Singh, William S. Shiver, and Stanley Brodwin. Garland, 1989, pp. 101–38.

Twain, Mark. *Adventures of Huckleberry Finn*. In *The Writings of Mark Twain*, vol. XIII. Harper & Brothers, 1884, 1912. Electronic Text Center, U of Virginia Library. etext.lib.virginia.edu/toc/modeng/public/Twa2Huc.html.

Van der Veer, Peter. "Spirituality in Modern Society." *Social Research: An International Quarterly*, vol. 76, no. 4, 2009, pp. 1097–1120.

Vidor, King, dir. *Hallelujah*. Film. Turner Entertainment, 2006.

Vogel, Shane. *The Scene of Harlem Cabaret: Race, Sexuality, Performance*. U of Chicago P, 2009.

Wagner, Jean. *Black Poets of the United States: From Paul Laurence Dunbar to Langston Hughes*, translated by Kenneth Douglas. U of Illinois P, 1973.

Wagner, Johanna M. "(Be)Longing in Quicksand: Framing Kinship and Desire More Queerly." *College Literature*, vol. 39, no. 3, 2012, pp. 129–59.

Walker, David, and Charles M. Wiltse. *David Walker's Appeal, In Four Articles, Together With a Preamble, to the Coloured Citizens of the World, but in Particular, and Very Expressly, to Those of the United States of America*. Hill and Wang, 1965.

Wallace, Michelle. "The Celluloid Cabin: Satirical Distortions of Uncle Tom in Animated Cartoon Short, 1932-1947." *Studies in Popular Culture*, vol. 23, no. 3, April 2001, pp. 1–10.

Ward, Geoffrey C. *Unforgivable Blackness: The Rise and Fall of Jack Johnson*. Knopf, 2004.

Washington, Booker T. *My Larger Education: Being Chapters from My Experience*. Doubleday, 1911.

———. *Up from Slavery. Three Negro Classics*, edited by John Hope Franklin. Avon, 1965.

West, Cornel. "The Dilemma of the Black Intellectual." *The Journal of Blacks in Higher Education*, vol. 2, 1993, pp. 59–67.

Westphal, Merold, editor. *Postmodern Philosophy and Christian Thought*. Indiana UP, 1999.

Whalan, Mark. *Race, Manhood, and Modernism in America: The Short Story Cycles of Sherwood Anderson and Jean Toomer*. U of Tennessee P, 2007.

———. "'Taking Myself in Hand': Jean Toomer and Physical Culture." *Modernism/modernity*, vol. 10, no. 4, November 2003, pp. 597–615.

Williams, Raymond. *Marxism and Literature*. Oxford UP, 1977.

Williams, William C. *Paterson*, edited by Christopher J. MacGowan. New Directions, 1992.

Woodson, Carter G. "Things of the Spirit." *African American Religious History*, edited by Milton C. Sernett, Duke UP, 2000, pp. 415–22.

Woolf, Virginia. *A Room of One's Own*. Harcourt, Brace, Jovanovich, 1957.

Wright, Richard. "Between Laughter and Tears." *New Masses*, October 5, 1937, pp. 22–25.

———. *Black Boy*. Harper-Perrenial, 1993.

———. "Blueprint for Negro Writing." *Richard Wright Reader*, edited by Ellen Wright and Michel Fabre. Harper & Row, 1978, pp. 97–106.

———. *Uncle Tom's Children*. Harper-Perrenial, 1993.

X, Malcolm, and Alex Haley. *The Autobiography of Malcolm X*. Ballantine Books, 1992.

Young, Joseph. *Black Novelist as White Racist: The Myth of Black Inferiority in the Novels of Oscar Micheaux*. Greenwood, 1989.

INDEX

Du Bois, W. E. B. (cont'd)
    and leadership, 8, 21–26, 41–42, 179;
    and lynching, 90–94; and masculinity,
    8, 25–26; and music, 31–34, 37–42,
    212n7; and racial identity, 27, 38, 41;
    religious beliefs, 3, 5, 13, 16, 22–24,
    42–43; and sexuality 146–47, 161;
    and sociology, 30–31
        —Works: Fiction
        "Jesus Christ in Texas" (Darkwa-
            ter), 92–93; "Of the Coming
            of John" (Souls of Black Folk),
            85–91, 100; "The Second Com-
            ing" (Darkwater), 24
        —Works: Non-fiction
        "Credo" (Darkwater), 23; "Faith
            of the Fathers" (Souls of Black
            Folk), 26–42, 201; "Of the
            Sorrow Songs" (Souls of Black
            Folk), 39–42, "Wings of A
            tlanta" (Souls of Black Folk)
            80–81, 84
        —Works: Poetry
        "Litany of Atlanta" (Souls of Black
            Folk), 23; "Prayers of God"
            (Darkwater), 23

education: and African American culture,
    19, 21, 67, 80–81, 105, 140; and anti-
    intellectualism, 67, 71; and Booker T.
    Washington, 71, 115; and Christian-
    ity, 14, 66–67, 71–74; in fiction and
    film, 85–91, 96–101, 105–12, 123–25,
    131–36; and freedom, 19, 84; and
    leadership, 28; and martyrdom, 92,
    94–95
Eros: and artistic creation, 142–47, 179;
    and Christianity, 152, 168, 178, 182,
    197

fascism, 126–27, 132, 189–90, 216n4
Faulkner, William: depictions of African
    American Christians, 119, 121; depic-
    tions of intellectuals, 68

folk: and artistic creation, 49–50,
    58–59, 76–79; and gender, 52, 212n;
    and modernity, 51, 57; and racial
    authenticity, 14, 27, 45, 101, 163, 194;
    and religion, 41, 46, 52, 62 107–8,
    111–12, 129; theories of, 45, 51, 87
Frank, Waldo, 50, 103, 140
frenzy, 31–34, 37, 41, 87, 129, 202; and
    music, 37

Garrett, David: We Own the Night,
    206–8, 219
Garvey, Marcus, 14, 132, 218
Gates, Henry Louis, 201–2
Griffiths, D.W.: Birth of a Nation, 123, 139

Harlem Renaissance: effectiveness and
    influence of, 52, 82, 96, 201–10;
    interpretations of, 5–7, 17, 20, 157
homosexuality, 146–49, 159–61, 207
Hughes, Langston: and body, 144–46; and
    Christianity, 5, 7, 14, 16, 19, 43, 46, 52–
    63, 95–96, 99, 153, 214n; and educa-
    tion, 79, 96; false conversion, 7, 52–57;
    and folk, 45–57; and gender roles, 135;
    influence, 204; and literary culture, 6,
    17, 47–52, 160; and martyrdom, 94–95,
    100–101; and masculinity, 61; recep-
    tion, 14, 49–50, 61–63, 153, 157, 164;
    and sexuality, 146–47, 152, 159, 179,
    216–217n3; and socialism, 6, 154
        —Works: Autobiography
        The Big Sea, 47–48, 52, 56–62, 96,
            135
        —Works: Drama
        Mulatto, 96–98, 114
        —Works: Fiction
        "Father and Son," 96–101, 111, 128
        —Works: Poetry
        "A Christian Country," 61; "Gods,"
            61; "Goodbye Christ," 1, 59–63,
            96, 153; "I, too Sing America,"
            144; "Prayer for a Winter Night,"
            61; "To Certain Brothers," 61